YOUR QUESTIONS ANSWERED

BY
SHAYKH MUFTI SAIFUL ISLĀM

JKN PUBLICATIONS

First Published in April 2010

ISBN 978-0-9565504-0-8

British Library Cataloguing in Publication Data
A catalogue record for this book is available from the British Library.

Publisher's Note:

Every care and attention has been put into the production of this book. If however, you find any errors it is our own, for which we seek Allāh's 🕮 forgiveness and reader's pardon.

Published by:

JKN Publications
118 Manningham Lane
Bradford
West Yorkshire
BD8 7JF
United Kingdom

t: +44 (0) 1274 308 456 | w: www.jkn.org.uk | e: info@jkn.org.uk

Author: Shaykh Mufti Saiful Islām

Typeset: Mujibur Rahmān

Printed and Bound in the United Kingdom

"In the Name of Allāh, the Most Beneficent,
the Most Merciful"

CONTENTS

4. CHAPTER ON SUNNAH 87

5. CHAPTER ON SALĀH 95

6. CHAPTER ON ZAKĀT 128

7. CHAPTER ON RAMADHĀN & FASTING 135

8. HAJJ & UMRAH 144

9. CHAPTER ON QURBĀNI   158

10. CHAPTER ON DEATH & INHERITANCE   163

12. CHAPTER ON MARRIAGE   219

13. CHAPTER ON DIVORCE   225

14. CHAPTER ON WOMEN   236

15. CHAPTER ON INNOVATION   248

INTRODUCTION

"In the Name of Allāh, the Most Beneficent the Most Merciful"

All praises be to Allāh ﷻ, the Lord of the worlds, the Creator of mankind and everything that is contained within the universe and may peace and salutations be upon His beloved Messenger Muhammad ﷺ.

May Allāh's ﷻ peace, mercy and blessings be upon you my dear brothers, sisters and friends wherever you may be. We praise Allāh ﷻ together and seek His forgiveness and refuge from the evils within ourselves and the mischief of our deeds. May Allāh ﷻ protect our souls, Āmeen!

May the infinite peace and blessings be upon the last of all the Messengers, who was sent as a mercy for mankind, our beloved Prophet Muhammad ﷺ. It is from his ocean of knowledge and radiant light that the Ulamā (Scholars) of the Ummah inherit.

Throughout history, Allāh ﷻ has blessed and guided many of His servants from the time of Sayyidunā Ādam ﷺ, until the present day to show His true path to mankind whether it is through their lofty character, speeches or writings.

Allāh ﷻ states in the Holy Qur'ān:

"Allāh is the Walee (Protector) of those who believe. He extracts them out from (the depths of) darkness to light. And for those who disbelieve, their friends are the rebels. They bring them out from the light to (the depths of) darkness. Those are the dwellers of the Hellfire. Wherein they shall remain forever." (2:257)

The true believers are those whom Allāh ﷻ has chosen to revive and propagate His Deen (Islām) throughout the world.

15

All praises be to Allāh ﷻ, amongst those servants of Allāh ﷻ is my beloved teacher, friend and spiritual mentor Shaykh Mufti Saiful Islām, who at this very young age has embarked upon the same path as those of the pious predecessors.

Jāmiah Khātamun Nabiyeen, commonly known as JKN was established in June 1996 from the residence of my beloved Shaykh, Mufti Saiful Islām. Al-hamdulillāh, through the Infinite Grace, Mercy and Help of Allāh ﷻ JKN has become a prominent institution both in the UK & internationally, through which many brothers and sisters have acquired the true understanding and knowledge of Islām, the teachings of the Holy Qur'ān and the Sunnah of the Holy Prophet Muhammad ﷺ.

Allāh ﷻ has granted my beloved Shaykh the zeal for knowledge in which he has strived and acquired for many years. He is the founder and Principal of our Institute Jāmiah Khātamun Nabiyeen and director of numerous JKN projects and activities. He is also the Editor of the popular family magazine Al Mu'min and he has published many books and literature in the field of Islām. It is due to his great efforts and sacrifices that today we are witnessing and reaping the rewards of his achievements.

As time is passing by and we are drawing closer to the Last Day (Day of Judgement), we are witnessing our Ummah in a state of crisis. Ignorance has prevailed, misguided "so-called scholars" have emerged in great numbers issuing incorrect verdicts (Fatwas) and misleading people, therefore Fitnah (corruption) is spreading at an alarming rate.

Taking all the above matters into consideration and to fulfil the aspirations of many brothers and sisters, my beloved Shaykh, Mufti Saiful Islām, with the Help of Allāh ﷻ has compiled this valuable book, *"Your Questions Answered"* with the spiritual regeneration of the Ummah in mind. Praying to Allāh ﷻ that He makes it a means of removing ignorance and spreading the true and correct teachings of Islām to a wider audience.

This book, which is before you is an evidence of his great work and sacrifice for Deen. I am very grateful to Allāh ﷻ that He has given me the ability to be a part of this great work.

I pray to Allāh ﷻ that He keeps me steadfast in the service of Deen and He keeps me in the pious company of my beloved Shaykh, Mufti Saiful Islām.

This book, titled *"Your Questions Answered"* is an outstanding, very comprehensive, yet simple Fatāwa book compiled by my beloved Shaykh with the hope that it becomes a source of guidance and reaches out to a wider audience i.e. the English speaking Muslims and non-Muslims alike.

Based on Islamic Laws, this book will answer commonly posed questions relating to beliefs, knowledge, Sunnah, pillars of Islām, marriage and divorce as well as other contemporary issues. Alhamdulillāh, this is the first volume of the many to be published in the near future, Inshā-Allāh.

May Allāh ﷻ increase my beloved Shaykh's blessed knowledge and give us all the ability to benefit from it. May Allāh ﷻ accept my beloved Shaykh's efforts and make it a means of his and our salvation in the Hereafter. May Allāh ﷻ give my beloved Shaykh the ability to continue and increase in the service of Deen and make it a means of guidance for the Muslim Ummah of our beloved Prophet Muhammad ﷺ.

I pray to Allāh ﷻ that He protects us all from the evil whispers of Shaytān and from the mischief of the society we live in. I further pray that Allāh ﷻ gives us the ability to carry out the work of Deen with full sincerity only to please Him and that He grants us Jannah.

Finally, I pray with tearful eyes and a weeping heart that Allāh ﷻ showers His Mercy upon the Muslims around the world who are suffering from the oppression of the oppressors.

"They conspire but Allāh ﷻ also plans and indeed Allāh ﷻ is the best of all planners."

I pray that Allāh ﷻ keeps us steadfast upon His Deen and unite the Muslim Ummah, Āmeen!

Mujibur Rahmān
Student of JKN, Bradford, UK
April 2010

BRIEF BIOGRAPHY OF THE AUTHOR

It has been my longing desire to write a biography of my beloved teacher and spiritual mentor, Shaykh Mufti Saiful Islām. At last I have been given the opportunity to fulfil my aspiration. My beloved Shaykh has authored this book *"Your Questions Answered"* therefore I have written a brief account of his life and works to highlight his achievements. I am eternally grateful to Allāh ﷻ for including me in the pious company of my Shaykh, who has been an inspiration in my life and undoubtedly in the life of many others too. This is a brief biography of Shaykh Mufti Saiful Islām and I am hopeful that in the future a comprehensive biography will be made available, Inshā-Allāh.

Birth
Shaykh Mufti Saiful Islām was born on the 17th of Rajab 1394 A.H (6th of August 1974) in the small village of Duhal in the town of Biswanath, district Sylhet, Bangladesh. His father was Muhammad Ali and his grandfather was Soyd Ali. He is the second eldest of four brothers and three sisters. He was initially given the name Shamsul Islām by the elders of his family but later his uncle kept his permanent name as Saiful Islām.

Migration to England
On the 1st of March 1981, Shaykh Mufti Saiful Islām's father decided to take the family to the UK. They settled in the city of Bradford which is situated in the Yorkshire region of England.

Education & Studies
In the year 1987 at the age of 13, Shaykh Mufti Saiful Islām successfully completed his Hifzul-Qur'ān (memorisation of the Holy Qur'ān) at his local Maktab, Tawak'kulia Jāmi Masjid in Bradford, UK. He also studied basic Urdu, Fiqh, Islamic History, Sarf (Etymology) and Nahwa (Syntax).

In 1988, Shaykh Mufti Saiful Islām was admitted in the grand Dārul Uloom in Bury to pursue his knowledge further in the field of Islām. This was when he first met Shaykhul Hadeeth Shaykh Yūsuf Motāla Sāhib.

In 1995 at the age of 20, Shaykh Mufti Saiful Islām graduated from Dārul Uloom Bury as an Ālim (Islamic Scholar).

In his final academic year he studied the main six books of Ahādeeth taught by prominent scholars at Dārul-Uloom, Bury. Saheeh Al-Bukhāri under Shaykhul-Hadeeth Shaykh Islāmul-Haq Sāhib ﷺ, Saheeh Al-Muslim by Shaykh Yūsuf Motāla Sāhib, Abū Dāwood by Shaykh Hāshim Sāhib, Tirmizi by Shaykh Mufti Shabbir Sāhib, Nasai by Shaykh Bilāl Sāhib and Ibn Mājah by Shaykh Abdur Raheem Sāhib. In 1996 he completed his Iftā course and thus granted the title of "Mufti".

Establishment of JKN

In 1996, Shaykh Mufti Saiful Islām went through hardships and sacrifices for establishing Jāmiah Khātamun Nabiyeen (JKN) from his residence. With the Infinite Grace, Mercy and Help of Allāh ﷺ, JKN accelerated to become a nationally and internationally recognised institute of learning.

Responsibilities

As well as the Founder, Principal and Director of JKN, Shaykh Mufti Saiful Islām took up responsibilities in many other departments locally, nationally and internationally. He is the Editor of "Al Mu'min" the famous family magazine.

He currently holds the posts of President of Tawak'kulia Jāmi Masjid; Chair-person of Al-Kawthar Welfare Foundation; Chairperson of Jamiatul Ulamā UK; Vice-Chairperson of Majlis Tahaffuz-e-Khatme-Nabuwwat (Bradford) and Vice-Chairperson of Izhār-e-Haq in Oldham. He is also the patron of Al Mu'min Primary School, Olive Secondary Schools for both boys & girls and Al-Hudā Academy in Oldham.

Shaykh Mufti Saiful Islām is also the Founder & Patron of Jāmiah Zakariyya ﷺ, situated in Biswanath, Sylhet and Jāmiah Al-Kawthar, which is situated in Netrokuna, Mymensingh as well as many other Makātibs in Bangladesh.

Teachings and Works

Shaykh Mufti Saiful Islām has been teaching the Holy Qur'ān and Islamic knowledge since his students years at Dārul Uloom, Bury. Ever since the establishment of JKN he has taught every subject from the basics of Arabic, Fiqh and Tajweed etc. through to Usool, Hadeeth and Tafseer.

His works include many compilations and supervised books such as Pearls of Wisdom, Miracle of the Holy Qur'ān, Stories for Children, Islamic Poems, Clear Proofs of Allāh ﷻ, Who is the Monkey?, The Miracles of the Holy Prophet ﷺ, What's with the Monkey Business?, Ziyārat of Madeenah Munawwarah and Ādābul Muāsharāt, as well as many other literature.

His latest work *"Your Questions Answered"* has been a long term project. During his Iftā at Dārul Uloom, Bury, Shaykh Mufti Saiful Islām was assigned the task to research and answer contemporary Fatāwas as part of the completion of the course. He worked on numerous Fatāwas and eventually completed his Iftā course to become a qualified and authorised Mufti.

On a daily basis, his 24 hour timetable is scheduled around worship, teaching the Holy Qur'ān and Ahādeeth, research and study, helping people and dealing with issues affecting their daily lives, directing and supervising all the projects of JKN and answering questions regarding religious issues based on the Islamic Law put forward by people from all walks of life.

It is my sincere prayer that Allāh ﷻ grants my beloved Shaykh good health and a long life so that he may continue the work of Deen and helping the Muslim Ummah, Āmeen. I also humbly request you to pray to Allāh ﷻ that He preserves and protects my beloved Shaykh and all the righteous scholars of Islām.

Mujibur Rahmān
Student of JKN, Bradford, UK
April 2010

JKN
HISTORY & PROJECTS

History
Jāmiah Khātamun Nabiyeen, commonly known as JKN was established in June 1996 from the residence of Shaykh Mufti Saiful Islām. With the Help of Allāh ﷻ, JKN has accelerated to become a nationally and internationally recognised institute of learning. Some of the projects and activities of JKN which operate under the guidance and instruction of Shaykh Mufti Saiful Islām are mentioned below:

JKN Institute
JKN has over 14 years of experience in teaching classical Islamic Texts to adults from all backgrounds ranging from the most basic texts in Arabic up to some of the most advanced classical texts such as Hidāya (Hanafi Fiqh Book) and the six Authentic Hadeeth Books (i.e. Saheeh al-Bukhāri, Muslim etc).

JKN is one of the first Institutes in the UK that has developed a curriculum, which recognises the needs and caters for the education of adults with families, those in full-time employment and other commitments. At present it is the only traditional institute in the UK that teaches classical Arabic text in Arabic/English to the most advanced levels. JKN has been continually modifying its course design to suit the needs of its students, such as the academic full-time Ālim course, Hifz course, Tajweed and Nāzirah courses for children and the 'New Modular' Islamic Theology Course in English for male and female adults.

Schooling Projects
JKN provides for the secular and Islamic educational needs from primary school up to secondary school including Hifzul-Qur'ān and the full-time Ālim course.

In 2007 Al-Mu'min Primary School was appraised by a Lead Inspector as "a benchmark for all future inspections of Islamic Independent schools, with a good quality of education". The curriculum framework is based upon seven areas of development; social, physical, spiritual, moral, intellectual, emotional and cultural.

Olive Secondary School for (Boys) opened its doors to the local community in 2005 and in 2006 the Girls School commenced, opening the doors of opportunity for girls to acquire both Islamic education, and secular education through the National Curriculum Syllabus.

Olive Secondary School caters for both boys and girls in separate facilities and ensures every child reaches their full potential in all aspects of learning and development in a safe, friendly and comfortable environment.

JKN Publications
Over the past 13 years, JKN Publications has produced many books and numerous Islamic literature on various subjects. The popular publication and also the forefront of JKN is the family magazine "Al-Mu'min".

Al-Mu'min is a widely read magazine with readers worldwide. Currently Al-Mu'min is in its 11th year of publication with subscribers increasing everyday.

Al-Kawthar Welfare Foundation
Al-Kawthar Welfare Foundation (AKWF) is a UK registered charity project in a joint venture with JKN. AKWF was established in February 2005 by some concerned scholars in order to help the poorest and needy Muslims around the world. JKN has taken the lead role in maintaining and overlooking the project work and fund raising.

Primarily, JKN and AKWF have jointly set up a number of Makātibs (elementary schools) for orphans and poor children. AKWF's major projects includes the establishment of Jāmiah Zakariyya ﷺ and Jāmiah Al-Kawthar in Bangladesh.

22

Al-Mu'min Nikāh Service

Considering marriage as an important part of life and with the demand for a match making service that complies with the Islamic Law, JKN has taken up the responsibility of providing this special Nikāh service.

Many of our Muslim brothers and sisters have taken interest in this service and many are reaping the rewards where successful cases have lead to Nikāh performed by Shaykh Mufti Saiful Islām himself.

JKN Fatāwa Department

One of the busiest projects is JKN's Fatāwa Department which provides answers to religious questions based on the Islamic Law on a daily basis. JKN Fatāwa Department has successfully dealt with thousands of questions via the telephone, post, e-mail, personal meetings, interviews etc.

Advice and Counselling

JKN provides a regular advice and counselling service on religious and re-lated social affairs matters through gatherings, written correspondence and telephone. Enquiries are received from people from all walks of life with a variety of subject matters, such as religious, social, national, international, matrimonial and domestic just to name a few.

Spiritual Guidance

JKN runs programmes that cater for the spiritual upliftment of one's Nafs (inner-self) under the guidance of Shaykh Mufti Saiful Islām. The primary motive of a spiritual traveller is to achieve Divine Pleasure which is acquired by total obedience to Allāh's ﷻ commands. These are performing Salāh, performing Hajj, giving Zakāt, fasting and Zikr (remembrance of Allāh ﷻ) and all other obligations.

Guidance for New Muslims

Through the activities and popularity of JKN, many people have embraced Islām taking the Shahādah on the hands of Shaykh Mufti Saiful Islām. JKN provides free advice, guidance, literature and information to new Muslims as well as non-Muslims.

Da'wah Activities
JKN reaches out to brothers and sisters all over the UK. Through JKN books, literature and Al-Mu'min magazine, the true knowledge of Islām is being spread. By the Grace of Allāh ﷻ many people have come back to practicing Islām.

Weekly Tafseer Sessions
JKN organises and facilitates a weekly gathering on the commentary of the Holy Qur'ān delivered in English by qualified and authorised scholars, held at the local Masjid (Tawak'kulia Jāmi Masjid).

Programmes for Brothers & Sisters
JKN has the honour of organising speeches and talks held at Tawak'kulia Jāmi Masjid. Prominent scholars from across the UK are invited to enlighten the gatherings with topics based on Islām.

Weekly and monthly speeches are specially held for women of the local community and beyond. Talks are delivered in English, Urdu and Bangla by qualified female scholars. Scholars from across the UK and abroad offer advice and guidance on topics relating to women.

Al-Mu'min Bookshop
Al-Mu'min bookshop was first opened in 2003, providing a whole range of Islamic books in English, Urdu, Arabic and Bangla. The bookshop also caters for students of knowledge, stocking Dars-e-Kitābs (i.e. classical text books such as al-Hidāya, Saheeh Al-Bukhāri and Tafseer Jalālain etc.)

Al-Mu'min Bookshop is a retailer and wholesaler of Islamic merchandise, with products ranging from audios, CDs, Jilbābs, scarves, Hijābs, Jubbas, Topis, Islamic games, children's books, beautiful fragrances, Islamic frames gifts and much more.

For more information and latest updates on JKN visit our website:

www.jkn.org.uk | info@jkn.org.uk

1. CHAPTER ON IMĀN

BELIEF

Definition of Īmān

Q What does Imān mean?

A Imān literally means to believe and to proclaim it verbally. Technically it means to believe in Allāh ﷻ and the teachings of our Holy Prophet ﷺ.

Existence of Planets

Q Do planets exist according to Islamic belief? If so could you please give some Islamic proof regarding this statement?

A To believe in the existence of other planets is not a fundamental part of Islamic belief. However Allāh ﷻ has created the universe and many things inside it. Although the existence of the other planets in the Solar System is not clearly mentioned in the Holy Qur'ān, we do know that there are so many other things in the universe that exist other than our Earth.

The Holy Prophet's ﷺ Parents

Q When did the Holy Prophet's ﷺ parents pass away?

A The Holy Prophet's ﷺ father, Abdullāh passed away before his birth and his mother, Āminah passed away when he was six years old. The Holy Prophet ﷺ received Prophethood at the age of forty. It is evident from this that his parents were not alive during the period of his Prophethood.

To Dislike and Mock the Beard

Q Many people nowadays dislike keeping the beard and also despise it. Some people even go to the extent of mocking the person who keeps a beard. What does Islām say regarding such people?

A To understand the answer to this question, one should bear in mind a basic principle, that to mock or jeer at any of the distinguishing features of Islām and to degrade or disgrace any of the Sunnah of the Holy Prophet ﷺ is equal to Kufr (disbelief) whereby a person leaves the fold of Islām.

The Holy Prophet ﷺ has affirmed in many Ahādeeth that the beard is a distinguished sign of Islām and was the unanimous practice of all the Prophets عليهم السلام and the Companions رضى of the Holy Prophet ﷺ.

People who regard the beard as disgusting and detestable on the basis of it being a distortion of nature or being unattractive, and prevent others from keeping it, or even mock and jeer at them, should seriously ponder over the condition of their Imān. It is incumbent on them to sincerely repent and also renew their Nikāh (marriage), if they are married.

Shaykh Ashraf Ali Thānwi ﷺ writes in his book Islāhur-Rusoom, "Amongst these customs, the shaving of the beard or trimming it in such a way that it is less than one fist in length, and the lengthening of the moustache has become a fashion of most youth."

In a Hadeeth it is stated that the Holy Prophet ﷺ said, "Lengthen the beard and trim the moustache." (Bukhāri, Muslim)

It should be noted well that the Holy Prophet ﷺ has used the commanding tense in both these actions and the commanding tense in the Arabic language signifies the obligation or incumbency of an action. Hence, we draw a conclusion that these two actions are Wājib (compulsory) and to disregard them is Harām (not allowed). Therefore both the shaving and the trimming of the beard (below one fist length) is Harām.

Furthermore, it has been mentioned in another Hadeeth that the Holy Prophet ﷺ said, "The person who does not trim his moustache is not from amongst us." (Tirmizi, Ahmad and Nasai)

Now that we have established it to be a sinful act, then those people who persist in doing it, or consider the lengthening of the beard as a defect and jeer and ridicule those who keep it, will find it rather difficult to maintain their Imān. It is necessary for such people to sincerely repent, renew their marriages and formulate their lives in accordance with the commands of Allāh ﷻ and His Holy Prophet ﷺ.

Qiyāmah (Day of Judgement)

Q When will Qiyāmah take place?

A No one knows the exact day and time of Qiyāmah. However, only this much is known that on one Friday, Sayyidunā Isrāfeel عليه السلام will be ordered to blow the Soor (bugle), which will signify the commencement of Qiyāmah.

The Holy Qur'ān

Q Once I was talking to an English revert and he asked me a few questions about the Holy Qur'ān. A few days after this incident, I thought about it and tried to answer his questions but have been unsuccessful. Could you please be kind enough to answer my questions? One of the questions he asked was how do we know that the Holy Qur'ān is in its original format?

A Allāh ﷻ states in the Holy Qur'ān, **"Indeed We have revealed the Reminder (Qur'ān) and Indeed We are its Guardians." (15:9)**

Thus, from this verse we realise that Allāh ﷻ has taken the responsibility to preserve and safeguard the Holy Qur'ān. It is also clear that no creation can alter or tamper the authentic book revealed by Allāh ﷻ, when He has become its absolute Guardian. It is a different matter if a certain sect or person alters or tampers with its translation or with his personal copy. But the original text and its correct teachings will remain with the righteous Muslims till the Day of Judgement.

The Holy Qur'ān was memorised at the time of the Holy Prophet ﷺ by his Companions رضى الله عنهم who had extraordinary memories. Whatever portion of the Holy Qur'ān was revealed, it was instantly memorised and also recorded by his noble Companions رضى الله عنهم.

The Holy Qur'ān was then compiled during the era of Sayyidunā Abū Bakr رضى الله عنه under strict conditions and close supervision which has been mentioned in detail in the books of Tafseer (commentary of the Holy Qur'ān). Even today there are millions of Muslims, young and old who preserve the Holy Qur'ān through memory.

Furthermore, one of the main causes of distortion of any divine text is human interference with it after its revelation. Hypothetically speaking, if the Holy Qur'ān did not maintain its original form because of human tampering then there would have been many discrepancies and contradictions in the Holy Qur'ān as Allāh 🕮 states, **"Don't they ponder over the Qur'ān, had it been from anyone besides Allāh then they would have surely found in it many contradictions."** (4:82)

Unfortunately the distortion of the previous revelations was on the account of human interference after the demise of the Prophets 🕮. Therefore, the present day scriptures do not maintain their original format. Contrary to this, the Holy Qur'ān has been protected from human manipulation and has been preserved well, as a result it contains no discrepancies.

There can be no doubt about the authenticity of a book (text) which has been preserved by so many Huffāz (plural of Hāfiz i.e. the one who has memorised the Holy Qur'ān) since the time of its revelation to the present day.

The Holy Qur'ān challenges the whole of mankind to imitate it or produce a text similar to the text and style of its own. This claim of the Holy Qur'ān remains outstanding even today. The Holy Qur'ān is the only religious book on the face of the earth that gives a falsification test. This means that the Holy Qur'ān is openly challenging mankind to disprove its authenticity by producing a comparable Sūrah. No one has succeeded to produce anything like the Holy Qur'ān and nor will they be able to do so in the future. Hence, it is a clear proof that this Qur'ān is the same original Qur'ān as it was revealed to the Holy Prophet 🕮. Furthermore, the authenticity of the Holy Qur'ān has been transmitted to us from the Holy Prophet 🕮 as 'Mutawātir'.

*Mutawātir means anything reported unanimously by such an overwhelming number of people that it is impossible to believe that they could either fabricate or conspire upon a lie and this condition being found upto the last narrators who narrated the Hadeeth or fact. To believe in this kind of narration as true is compulsory upon every Muslim.

Pillars of Islām

Q **What are the pillars of Islām?**

A Islām stands on five pillars which are evident from the Holy Qur'ān and Ahādeeth. The five pillars are as follows:

1. Shahādah (Testimony) - Every Muslim must believe and accept whole-heartedly with sincerity and declare verbally the Kalimah, "There is none worthy of worship but Allāh 🕮 and Muhammad 🕮 is Allāh's 🕮 Messenger."
2. Salāh - Daily five time prayers.
3. Zakāh - Charity given at a fixed rate.
4. Sawm - Fasting in the Holy Month of Ramadhān.
5. To perform Hajj - Visiting the House of Allāh 🕮 during the days of Hajj at least once in a life time.

Angels - A Special Creation of Allāh 🕮

Q **We are told that many angels exist and they are invisible. Can you mention the reason they are created and the tasks they undertake?**

A Angels are a special creation of Allāh 🕮 who have been created out of light. They have been created to carry out the orders of Allāh 🕮. They have been given various duties to perform but because they are not visible to us, we cannot observe the duties they undertake. From the Holy Qur'ān and Ahādeeth we come to know that various angels are in charge of various duties. Amongst them there are four famous angels that are the most superior from all the others.

They are:

1. Sayyidunā Jibreel 🕮 who brought Allāh's 🕮 books, orders and messages to all the Prophets 🕮. He was also sent to help the Prophets 🕮 at times and fight against their enemies.

2. Sayyidunā Meekāeel 🕮 is in charge of food and rain. Other angels work under him who are in charge of clouds, oceans, seas, rivers and the wind. He receives orders from Allāh 🕮 and thereafter orders the other angels under his command.

3. Sayyidunā Izrāeel 🕮 takes away life with the order of Allāh 🕮. He is in charge of death. Numerous angels work under him. Some take away the lives of good people whilst others looking very fearful in appearance take away the lives of sinners and disbelievers.

4. Sayyidunā Isrāfeel 🕮 will blow the Soor (trumpet) on the Day of Judgement. The sound will destroy and kill everything that is on Earth and in the skies. When he blows for the second time (which will be after 40 years) all will come back to life with the order of Allāh 🕮.

Other than these four famous angels there are two angels on our shoulders called the "Kirāman Kātibeen". Their duty is to write the good deeds and the bad deeds. The angel on the right shoulder writes the 'good deeds' whilst the angel on the left shoulder writes the 'bad deeds'.

Munkar and Nakeer are two angels who question a person in the grave when he dies. Allāh 🕮 has assigned some angels who are in charge of Heaven and some of Hell, some for looking after the children, the old, the weak and others whom Allāh 🕮 wishes to protect.

Previous Divine Books

Q How do we know that the Tawrah (Old Testament), Zaboor (Psalms of David) and the Injeel (New Testament) are Divine Books. Is it necessary to have belief in them?

A The Holy Qur'ān affirms the fact that they are Divine Books of Allāh 🕮.

1. Regarding Tawrah, Allāh 🕮 says in the Holy Qur'ān, **"Verily, We have revealed the Tawrah and therein is true guidance and light."** (5:44)

2. Allāh 🕮 mentions in the Holy Qur'ān about the Zaboor, **"We bestowed the Psalms (Zaboor) to Dāwood."** (4:163)

3. Regarding Injeel, Allāh 🕮 says in the Holy Qur'ān, **"We have sent Eesā (Jesus) the son of Maryam (Mary), and bestowed upon him the Injeel (Bible)."** (57:27)

A person who refuses to acknowledge the Tawrah, Zaboor and Injeel as the Books of Allāh 🕮 is a Kāfir (disbeliever) because the Holy Qur'ān testifies regarding them that they are Divine Scriptures. So anyone denying their heavenly descent, disbelieves the Holy Qur'ān, and thus becomes a Kāfir.

We must also remember that these Divine Books have been tampered with by their religious scholars and rulers throughout history. The Tawrah and the Injeel available nowadays are not in their original form due to alterations and distortions.

Our belief should be that whatever Allāh 🕮 has revealed in the original format are the authentic Divine Scriptures of Allāh 🕮, which were free from any mistakes, alterations and distortions.

Belief in Jinns

Q Can you explain in detail regarding the Jinn. Some people do not believe in the Jinns and claim that it is just a myth. Can you explain when did Allāh 🕮 create the Jinn and from what source are the Jinns created from. Please can you quote Quranic verses as evidence?

A To believe in the existence of Jinn is an integral part of Imān because Allāh 🕮 mentions them in the Holy Qur'ān in numerous verses. Jinn is an Arabic word which refers to the invisible creatures that were created from fire.

Allāh 🕮 mentions in the Holy Qur'ān, **"And He created Jinns from fire free of smoke." (55:15)**

In another place Allāh 🕮 says, **"And the Jinn race, We had created them before from the smokeless fire." (15:27)**

In Sūrah al-A'rāf it mentions the following, **"He (Allāh) said, 'What prevented you from prostrating when I commanded you?' Iblees said, 'I am better than he. You created me from fire and him from clay." (7:12)**

32

Again in Sūrah Sād after Allāh ﷻ questioned why he refused to prostrate to Sayyidunā Ādam ﷺ, Iblees answered, **"I am better than he. You created me from fire and you created him from clay."** (38:76)

Regarding the time they were created, it is mentioned that Allāh ﷻ created them well before Sayyidunā Ādam ﷺ was created. This is mentioned in the verse of Sūrah al-Hijr (26:27). However, nothing is clearly mentioned about the duration of time between the creation of the Jinn and mankind.

Hajar Aswad - The Black Stone

Q I've heard that the Hajar Aswad is a stone from the stones of Jannah, is this claim true?

A Yes, Hajar Aswad is a stone from the stones of Jannah, which is embedded in the eastern corner of the Ka'bah.

In the beginning when it descended from Jannah, it was whiter than milk but the sins of the children of Ādam ﷺ have turned it black.

The Holy Prophet ﷺ said, "By Allāh ﷻ, Allāh ﷻ will resurrect it (i.e. Hajar Aswad) on the Day of Judgement. It will have two eyes with which it will see and a tongue with which it will speak. It will bear witness for those who have made Istilām of it with honesty and sincerity."

Note: Istilām is to place both hands on the Hajar Aswad and to kiss it gently between the two palms.

It is stated in another Hadeeth, "Qiyāmah shall not come as long as the Hajar Aswad and the Maqām-e-Ibrāheem are not uplifted from this world."

Iblees - Jinn or Angel?

Q Is Iblees a Jinn or an angel?

A The Holy Qur'ān states, **"He was one of the Jinn."** Hence he is a member of the Jinn species. He is the chief of all the Jinn.

Reincarnation

Q **Where does the Rooh (soul) go after a person's death? Does Islām accept the belief of re-incarnation?**

A Allāh 🕮 says in the Holy Qur'ān, **"Say the soul is by the command of my Sustainer and you have been given little knowledge pertaining to it." (17:85)**

From this verse it is clear that a very small amount of knowledge has been given to mankind regarding the soul. The verse mentions that the Rooh is by the direct command of Allāh 🕮. Unlike matter, the soul does not come into existence through procreation, but comes into existence by the direct command of 'Be' from Allāh 🕮. Therefore the soul must not be regarded in the same light as matter.

Illiyyoon is the place where the souls of the people of Paradise are kept. It is the record room where the names of the inhabitants of Paradise are recorded and their files kept. It is situated above the seventh Heaven.

Sijjeen is the place where the souls of the people of Hell are kept. It is also the record room in which the names of the inhabitants of Hell are written. The angels (Kirāman Kātibeen), who are appointed to write the deeds of every soul, deposit the Book in that Record Office (Sijjeen) after their death. After the termination of their lives, on the file of every person they make a sign whereby it is immediately known that the individual is a dweller of Hell. Sijjeen is situated beneath the seventh Earth. Once the soul leaves the body, it remains there until this world comes to an end. It does not transfer into any other body.

Islām does not accept the belief of reincarnation wherein it is believed that the soul is transferred into the body of some other creature repeatedly depending on how it spent its life. Islām teaches us that this world is Dārul Amal (place of deeds) and once a soul has left this abode it takes its place in another abode, Dārul Jazā (the place of retribution).

For those who believe in the theory of reincarnation, let them answer the following question.

If a soul is placed in different creatures as a result of its evil or good deeds, then when the soul came into existence, on what basis was it placed in the first creature or being?

Light or Human

Q Is the Holy Prophet ﷺ 'Noor' (light) or 'Bashar' (human)?

A Allāh ﷻ has informed us through the Holy Qur'ān that the Holy Prophet ﷺ is from amongst the human beings. Allāh ﷻ states, **"Say, (O Muhammad); I am only a human like you. It has been inspired to me that your God is One God (Allāh)."** (18:110)

In another verse, Allāh ﷻ says, **"Say, (O Muhammad); Glorified (and Exalted) be my Lord (Allāh) (above that evil they [the polytheists] associate with Him) I am but a human (sent as a) Messenger?"** (17:93)

Shaykh Yūsuf Ludhyānwi ﵀ states in his book **'Differences in the Ummah and the Straight Path'**, "My belief regarding the Holy Prophet ﷺ is that not only is he amongst the human kind but he is the highest and the most noble of all humans."

Not only is he the son of Sayyidunā Ādam ﵇ but the chief and leader of all the children of Sayyidunā Ādam ﵇. The Holy Prophet ﷺ is reported to have said the following regarding himself, "I will be the leader of Ādam's ﵇ progeny on the Day of Judgement."

Therefore it is not only the Holy Prophet's ﷺ honour to be a human, but him being from mankind is a fact that inspires envy even amongst the angels. Since the Holy Prophet ﷺ is the noblest of man 'Bashar', in the field of Divine Guidance, his teachings are a luminous light 'Noor'. This is the 'Noor' that makes man recognise his Creator and it is a 'Noor' that will illuminate and remain until the Day of Judgement. Thus my belief regarding the Holy Prophet ﷺ is that he is 'Bashar' as well as a source of 'Noor'.

To accept one point and reject the other is a grave error. 'Bashar' and 'man' mean the same thing. By rejecting the quality of Bashar from the Holy Prophet ﷺ, one expels the Holy Prophet ﷺ from being amongst mankind.

On many occasions, Allāh ﷻ in the Holy Qur'ān clearly proclaims the Prophets as having come from amongst the species of man. Although the Holy Qur'ān has referred to the Holy Prophet ﷺ as Noor and Bashar, he has been referred to as Bashar more often than Noor. It is the unanimous belief of the Ahlus-Sunnah Wal-Jamā'at that Allāh ﷻ has only chosen Prophets from amongst mankind.

The famous book on the beliefs of the Ahlus-Sunnah Wal-Jamā'at 'Sharah Aqā'id Nasafi' defines a Rasool (Messenger) in the following words, "A Prophet is a man whom Allāh ﷻ has chosen to propagate His message and laws."

In another famous Hanafi Fiqh book 'Fatāwa Ālamgeeri' it mentions, "The one who says, 'I do not know whether the Holy Prophet ﷺ is a man or Jinn', is not a Muslim."

Hence we learn that no person of sound reason can reject or negate the fact that the Holy Prophet ﷺ is 'Bashar' (human).

How absurd can we be to put Allāh ﷻ and His creation on one and the same level? People of earlier generations corrupted their religion with such excesses and exaggeration.

The Holy Prophet ﷺ also feared the inevitable occurrence of such excesses and exaggeration in his Ummah.

He therefore forewarned us against such exaggeration in the following words, "Do not praise me excessively as the People of the Book have praised Sayyidunā Eesā ﷺ. They have made him god and the son of god, I am Allāh's ﷻ servant and His Messenger. Regard me only as the servant of Allāh ﷻ and the Messenger of Allāh ﷻ." (Bukhāri)

In the light of the above Hadeeth, it can be quite clearly concluded that the Holy Prophet ﷺ is the best of all creation. No creation can surpass his high and noble qualities and character. However, he is human and not Allāh ﷻ. These are the teachings of Islām and upon them are our beliefs.

Mukhtār-e-Kul (Omnipotent)

Q Has the Holy Prophet 🌸 got overall power over the creation?

A Shaykh Yūsuf Ludhyānwi 🌸 writes in his famous book **'The Differences in the Ummah and the Straight Path'**, "The fatal consequences of ascribing the exclusive qualities of Allāh 🕌 unto the Holy Prophet 🌸 is the belief that the Holy Prophet 🌸 shares certain powers with Allāh 🕌. Hence, we have people holding the erroneous view that Allāh 🕌 has granted the Holy Prophet 🌸 complete power over His creation."

Thus, they belief that the Holy Prophet 🌸 is Mukhtār-e-Kul. However, according to the Holy Qur'ān, Hadeeth and the belief of the Ahlus-Sunnah Wal-Jamā'at, there is no room for such beliefs in Islām. Allāh 🕌 has not given any such overall control or power to any of His creation.

Islām teaches us that only Allāh 🕌 has full control and power over everything and nobody shares this attribute with Him.

Life, death, health and illness are all in Allāh's 🕌 power. Therefore, from Sayyidunā Ādam 🌸 to our beloved Prophet 🌸, all the Prophets used to supplicate to Allāh 🕌 alone and regarded only Allāh 🕌 as the Provider of good and bad, profit and loss, life and death, health and sickness. This was also the case with all the pious servants of Allāh 🕌.

No Prophet or saint has even claimed to possess power or control over any portion of Allāh's 🕌 creation. The Holy Prophet's 🌸 belief in regard to this attribute of Allāh 🕌 can be judged by the following Hadeeth. Sayyidunā Abdullāh Ibn Abbās 🌸 reports that he was once riding behind the Holy Prophet 🌸. The Holy Prophet 🌸 told him, "O Child! Protect the rights of Allāh 🕌 and Allāh 🕌 will protect you. Protect Allāh's 🕌 rights and you will find Allāh 🕌 with you; whenever you ask for anything, ask from Allāh 🕌. When you are in need of help, turn towards Allāh 🕌 and be assured that if everybody gets together to do any good to you, they would not be able to benefit you, but to that extent which Allāh 🕌 has ordained for you and if everybody gets together to harm you, they will be unable to inflict harm but that which Allāh 🕌 has ordained for you." (Mishkāt)

In explaining this Hadeeth, Mulla Ali Qāri ﷺ writes, "Ask Allāh ﷻ means ask Allāh ﷻ alone for only He owns everything, whatever we have is all from Allāh ﷻ."

He is most Generous and He is Independent, we should therefore only hope for His blessings and only ask Him.

We should rely on Him alone and we should not ask from anybody but Allāh ﷻ, for none but He has the power to give.

He has power over everything. In the explanation of the word 'everybody' used in the Hadeeth, he writes, "Without doubt the whole Ummah, meaning, all the creation, Prophet or non-Prophet, pious or non-pious, if the whole creation gets together to harm you they will not be able to harm you..." (Mishkāt)

Shaykh Abdul Qādir Jilāni ﷺ says, "Most certainly the entire creation is powerless and incapable. They do not have the power to destroy nor do they have any ownership. They do not have wealth nor do they possess property. Besides Allāh ﷻ they have no Deity, no Giver, no Protector, and no Giver of life or death." This is the belief of the pious people and the Ahlus-Sunnah Wal-Jamā'at.

Whatever miracles were experienced by the Prophets عليهم السلام or whatever supernatural act is experienced by any pious person is a direct blessing of Allāh ﷻ conferred on them, and it is only the Power of Allāh ﷻ, i.e. a manifestation thereof. It is called a 'Mu'jiza' or 'Karāmat'. Allāh ﷻ states, **"And no Prophet is able to bring forth any sign except with the permission of Allāh."** (40:78)

To attribute the quality of control over the universe to a person merely because he carried out a few miracles is most surprising. The People of the Book fell prey to this same concept when certain miracles were performed through the hands of Sayyidunā Eesā عليه السلام. They fell prey to the belief of trinity and attributed Sayyidunā Eesā عليه السلام with qualities of divinity. The Holy Qur'ān invites man to the Oneness of Allāh ﷻ. The main task of the Prophets was to invite man to the realisation of the Divine Oneness of Allāh ﷻ.

38

The Oneness of Allāh ﷻ has been explained very clearly in the Holy Qur'ān with substantiated proofs. The Holy Qur'ān questions man, **"Who is the controller of the universe? Who gives sustenance? Who has the power over life, death, illness and health?"**

Ascribing partners to Allāh ﷻ in His attributes would in fact be a negation, and an attempt to render void almost one third of the Holy Qur'ān.

Surely if others are made partners with Allāh ﷻ in these attributes, a third of the Holy Qur'ān will be left void.

All the Prophets and pious saints have regarded themselves completely under the control of Allāh's ﷻ Will. Thus attributing the qualities of Mukhtār-e -Kul to anybody is also against the teachings of the Prophets and the pious servants of Allāh ﷻ.

Hāzir Nāzir (Omnipresent)

Q **Is the Holy Prophet ﷺ 'Hāzir Nāzir' (Omnipresent)?**

A Shaykh Yūsuf Ludhyānwi ﷻ writes, "It is necessary to understand the term 'Hāzir Nāzir'…

…This is an Arabic term which means 'present and seeing' and when used together it qualifies a being whose presence encompasses the entire universe and he sees and has complete knowledge of everything in this universe.

Our belief is that only Allāh ﷻ is 'Hāzir Nāzir' and this is an exclusive attribute of Allāh ﷻ.

We are all aware that the Holy Prophet ﷺ is resting in his Holy Grave in Madeenah Munawwarah and all the Muslims travel to Madeenah for the 'Ziyārat' of the Holy Prophet's ﷺ grave. Thus to believe that the Holy Prophet ﷺ is present at all places and is seeing everything is contrary to sound reason as well as contrary to the Islamic beliefs.

'Hāzir Nāzir' is the attribute of Allāh ﷻ only and no creation shares this attribute with Him.

It is also a false belief to say that after the departure of the Holy Prophet 𝕾, his soul has been given the power to present itself whenever it wishes. Even if this false belief was true, it would not qualify the Holy Prophet 𝕾 as being 'Hāzir Nāzir'.

Even a citizen of a country has the right to go to any part of his country; this does not make him 'Hāzir Nāzir'. To be given the right to go wherever one wishes does not make one present everywhere. On the other hand to say the Holy Prophet 𝕾 is present at a certain place is an independent claim for which there should be proof.

Since there is no substantial proof from the Holy Qur'ān and Ahādeeth, to hold such a belief is not permissible. Some people go to the extent of attributing the qualities of 'Hāzir Nāzir' to the saints - I am surprised at the claim of these people. How casually they associate the exclusive attributes of Allāh 𝕸 to His creation.

The scholars of the Ahlus-Sunnah Wal-Jamā'at do not tolerate these false beliefs. Thus Fatāwa Bazāzia says, "Our scholars have stated that whomsoever says, 'The souls of the pious are present and that they know everything' is a disbeliever."

Blessed Shadow of the Holy Prophet 𝕾

Q Did the Holy Prophet 𝕾 have a shadow?

A Before answering this question one must firmly understand that all the miracles the Holy Prophet 𝕾 showed throughout his noble life, have all been preserved and established through authentic narrations. In order to assert that the Holy Prophet 𝕾 did such and such a miracle one must primarily present an established and authentic proof, only then will it be accepted otherwise it will be rejected. As far as this question is concerned the most authentic view of the Ahlus-Sunnah Wal-Jamā'at is that the Holy Prophet 𝕾 did have a shadow. Sayyidah Zainab 𝕸, the wife of the Holy Prophet 𝕾 relates that one afternoon she suddenly saw the shadow of the Holy Prophet 𝕾. (Shamā'il Kubrā)

However there is an extremely weak Hadeeth that Imām Jalāl-ud-Deen Suyūti ❀ relates in his book on the authority of Sayyidunā Zakwān ❁ that the Holy Prophet's ❀ shadow was not seen in the sun (during the day) and neither in the moon (during the night). In other words, he did not have a shadow. However, Mufti Muhammad Shafee Sāhib ❀ comments that this Hadeeth is not acceptable due to the following reasons:

a) The narrator Abdur Rahmān Ibn Qais Zafrāni, mentioned in the beginning of the chain of narration, has been criticised as being an imposter and highly unreliable.

b) This Hadeeth is Mursal (the student of the Sahābi ❁ states the Holy Prophet ❀ said, exempting the Sahābi ❁ from the chain) which many great scholars of Hadeeth do not accept.

c) Whenever the Holy Prophet ❀ travelled during the day on an expedition then a huge gathering of the Sahābah ❁ would also accompany him on every occasion. If the Holy Prophet ❀ was free from having a shadow miraculously then a huge party of the Sahābah ❁ would surely narrate this because they witnessed before their eyes and recorded every minute Sunnah and miracle of the Holy Prophet ❀ (and this was also the case with the other miracles). This would then attain the level of Tawātur (undisputable fact). On the contrary, there is not a single Hadeeth to be found in the entire collection of the six highly regarded Hadeeth books regarding this miracle.

(Jawāhirul Fiqh vol. 3 pg. 20)

Due to the above mentioned reasons, the Hadeeth (mentioned by Imām Jalāl-ud-Deen Suyūti ❀) will be regarded as very weak. Therefore, we conclude that the Holy Prophet ❀ did have a shadow.

Splitting of the Chest of the Holy Prophet ❀

Q I have read that the Holy Prophet's ❀ chest was split open and washed by Sayyidunā Jibreel عليه السلام with Zam Zam water when he was young, is this authentic?

A What you have read is completely true and authentic. One of the specialities of the Holy Prophet ﷺ is that on various occasions, the Holy Prophet's ﷺ blessed chest was split open, and his heart was washed and filled with faith and wisdom. Hence it was 'immunised' against devilish influences and evil whispers.

This phenomenon is referred to as 'Shaqqus-Sadr'. Shaqqus-Sadr, as the narrations indicate, occurred four times during the Holy Prophet's ﷺ lifetime.

The First Occasion
The first occasion was during early childhood, when the Holy Prophet ﷺ was living at the home of his foster mother Haleemah Sadiyah. One day whilst the Holy Prophet ﷺ was playing outside, Sayyidunā Jibreel عليه السلام appeared and after making the Holy Prophet ﷺ lie down, he split open his blessed chest and removed the heart. He split open the heart and removed a blood-clot from it. He then washed the Holy Prophet's ﷺ heart in Zam Zam water which he had brought with him in a gold utensil. Thereafter he replaced the heart and stitched up the Holy Prophet's ﷺ blessed chest.

The other children who were with the Holy Prophet ﷺ at that time, rushed to his foster mother Haleemah Sadiyah and informed her that somebody was killing the Holy Prophet ﷺ.

She immediately hurried out, and when she saw the Holy Prophet ﷺ, he looked frightened and pale. After narrating this story, Sayyidunā Anas رضى الله عنه stated that the stitches of that 'operation' were clearly seen.

The Second Occasion
Shaqqus-Sadr occurred for the second time when the Holy Prophet ﷺ was approximately ten years old. This Hadeeth has been reported by Sayyidunāh Abū Hurairah رضى الله عنه, and it is recorded in Saheeh Ibn Hibbān.

The Third Occasion
The third occasion of Shaqq-us-Sadr was at the time when the Holy Prophet ﷺ received Prophethood. The incident is recorded in the Musnad of Abū Dāwood at-Tayālisi.

The Fourth Occasion
This occurred prior to the miraculous journey of Mi'rāj. According to the Hadeeth reported by Sayyidunā Mālik Ibn Sa'sa'ah ﷺ, the Holy Prophet ﷺ narrated that one night, whilst he was resting in the Hateem area of the sacred Ka'bah, two angels appeared.

The procedure of this incident is almost identical to the procedure mentioned under the first occasion of Shaqqus-Sadr. (Mishkāt)

Note: The phenomenon of Shaqqus-Sadr surely defies all reason and logic, but it has been reported through numerous chains, which makes it compulsory to have faith upon it.

The Purpose of Shaqqus-Sadr
On the first occasion, a blood clot was removed from the Holy Prophet's ﷺ heart. This in actual fact was symbolic as being the source of sin and vice, from which the Holy Prophet ﷺ was divinely purified. The heart was washed as well, so as to remove any traces of the blood-clot.

The second time this occurred was for the sake of purifying the Holy Prophet's ﷺ heart from the natural tendencies of getting involved in play and amusements, which usually begins at around that age. The third time this phenomenon occurred was to prepare the Holy Prophet ﷺ to receive the pure speech of Allāh ﷻ, and to contain the vast knowledge of the recognition of Allāh ﷻ.

The fourth occasion was for the sake of preparing the Holy Prophet ﷺ for his journey into the unseen, and for the direct communion with Allāh ﷻ.

Note: The Shaqqus-Sadr was an occurrence that was special to the Holy Prophet ﷺ, other Prophets ﷺ did not share this privilege. The Muhaddithoon (scholars of Hadeeth) and historians differ regarding the number of times this phenomenon occurred. Shaykh Suhaylee ﷺ for instance views that it occurred twice only, whilst Hāfiz Ibn Hajar ﷺ says that it occurred thrice.

Imām Mahdi

Q Is Imām Mahdi already born?

A I do not know, only Allāh 🕮 knows.

The Use of Words 'We' and 'He' by Allāh 🕮

Q In Sūrah Yāseen it says the following, "We have not taught the Prophet poetry, nor is it suitable for him."...."Does not man see that We have created him from Nutfah (semen). Yet behold he (stands forth) as an open opponent. And he puts forth for Us a parable, and forgets his own creation. He says, 'Who will give life to these bones after they are rotten and have become dust?' Say, 'He will give life to them Who created them for the first time! And He is the All Knower of every creation!'"..."Verily, His Command, when He intends a thing, is only that He says to it, 'Be!' and it is!" (36:69, 77-79, 82)

I believe in Allāh's 🕮 words but why does He refer to 'We', 'Us', 'He' when it is Allāh 🕮 Himself speaking to the whole of mankind via Sayyidunā Jibreel 🕮 and Holy Prophet 🕮. Could you please answer my question as soon as possible as I would like to tell another brother the answer to this puzzle?

A In the Arabic language, plural is used for two purposes:
1. For its original use, i.e. the multiple of singular.
2. To express respect (royal plural).

It is only natural and customary for Allāh 🕮 to use the pronouns of the plural terms in many verses of the Holy Qur'ān. We believe He is the One and Only God, He has no partners nor children, but He uses the plural term to show and express His respect, dignity and pride, and without any doubt He alone is worthy of all respect, dignity and pride.

The Holy Prophet 🕮 narrates a Hadeeth Qudsi that Allāh 🕮 states, **"Pride is my upper garment and dignity is my lower garment. Whoever attempts to snatch them from Me, I shall throw him in the Fire of Hell."** The Holy Prophet 🕮 also said, **"In comparison to Allāh 🕮, there is none who loves being praised so much."**

44

We understand from the two narrations that only Allāh ﷻ is worthy of worship. He is our Lord, the Glorious, the Creator, the Sustainer and only He is worthy of all Praises. This is why He uses the pronoun 'We' for respect.

It is necessary to be aware that we should not be confused, nor should we create questions in our mind that if Allāh ﷻ is One, then why does He say, "We have done this, We have created this etc." Thus the word 'We' point towards the belief of the Trinity.

The answer is very clear from what I have mentioned that He uses the plural pronoun solely to express respect, highness and dignity.

Also the same Holy Qur'ān which uses 'We' rejects any partnership to Allāh ﷻ by saying, **"Surely those disbelieve who say Allāh is the third of three."** The Holy Qur'ān declares the Oneness of Allah ﷻ by proclaiming, **"Say! He is Allāh, the One, Allāh, the Eternally Independent He begets not nor was He begotten and there is none equal to Him."** (Sūrah al-Ikhlās)

The Holy Qur'ān has the finest articulate and eloquent Arabic. Thus Allāh ﷻ also uses We, Us, He to enhance the eloquence and the beauty of the Arabic language. (Mukhtasarul-Ma'āni)

Definition of Ghaib (The Unseen)

Q What does Ghaib mean?

A Ghaib literally means 'the unseen.' In Islamic terms it refers to all those things that are unseen by mankind. However believing in them is essential, such as Jannah, Jahannam, angels etc. It is compulsory upon a Muslim to believe that no one has the knowledge of the unseen except Allāh ﷻ.

Vision of Allāh ﷻ

Q Will we be able to see Allāh ﷻ in Jannah? Please can you provide some evidence from the Holy Qur'ān and Ahādeeth.

A According to Ahlus-Sunnah Wal-Jamā'at, the people of Jannah will be able to see Allāh ﷻ. In fact, the greatest blessing in Jannah will be the actual vision of Allāh ﷻ by the people of Jannah. Allāh ﷻ states, **"The Day when faces will be radiant looking at their Lord."** **(75:22-23)** This verse clearly refers to the vision of Allāh ﷻ.

It is narrated by Sayyidunā Suhayb Roomi ؓ that the Holy Prophet ﷺ said, "When the righteous people will enter Jannah, Allāh ﷻ will enquire from them, 'Do you desire that We grant you one more favour?' (i.e. bestow upon you a blessing in addition to what you already have received). They will reply, 'You have illuminated our faces and saved us from Jahan-nam and granted us Jannah. What more can we ask for?' The veil will then be lifted and they will be able to see Allāh ﷻ. This blessing will surpass all other blessings that had been bestowed on them."

Thereafter, the Holy Prophet ﷺ recited the following verse from the Holy Qur'ān, **"For those who do good deeds shall be the best place and even more."** **(10:26)** In this verse, al-Husnā (best place) refers to Jannah and Ziyādah (even more) refers to having the honour of seeing Allāh ﷻ Himself.

It is reported in Bukhāri and Muslim that the Holy Prophet ﷺ has said, "You will see your Lord clearly." Sayyidunā Jareer Ibn Abdullāh ؓ narrates, "One night we were sitting with the Holy Prophet ﷺ when he looked up at the moon. It was the fourteenth night of the month and the full moon was shining in the sky. The Holy Prophet ﷺ then turned towards us and said, 'Surely you will see Allāh ﷻ as you are seeing the moon. You will not need to make special efforts to see Him, nor will there be any other difficulty."

(Bukhāri, Muslim)

Allāh ﷻ mentions regarding the disbelievers, **"Nay, but surely on that Day they will be veiled from their Lord (and prevented from seeing Him."** **(83:15)** This verse indicates towards this fact that the believers will not be veiled from their Lord but they will be able to see Allāh ﷻ Inshā-Allāh.

Allāh ﷻ Knows Best

2. CHAPTER ON
PURITY

Exposing the Satr (Private Parts)

Q If a person exposes his Satr (the parts of the body which are necessary to cover) after performing Wudhu (ablution) in front of someone or in solitude, does it break his Wudhu?

A It will not break the Wudhu in both circumstances, but it is a grave sin to expose one's Satr in front of someone else.

Pubic Hair

Q What is the maximum period that pubic hair could be left on the body?

A Unwanted hair should preferably be removed once a week. If this is not possible then every second week. Care should be taken that it is not left for more than 40 days. Beyond 40 days, the neglector will be sinful.

Finger and Toe Nails

Q Is there any sequence to be followed when cutting the finger and toe nails?

A Cutting the fingernails should begin at the Shahādat finger (index finger of the right hand). The nails of the next three fingers (of the right hand) should be cut next, in order. Thereafter, continue with the small finger of the left hand and complete the remaining three fingers and thumb, in sequence. Lastly, cut the nail of the right thumb.

Cutting the toe nails should begin at the small toe of the right foot and end at the small toe of the left foot, in order.

Note: The above sequence is desirable, not compulsory.

Fluid Flowing from the Eyes

Q Does the fluid that flows out of the eye whilst yawning, break the Wudhu?

A The liquid that comes out of the eye whilst yawning does not break the Wudhu.

Vomit

Q Does vomiting break Wudhu?

A If the vomit is less than a mouthful then it will not break the Wudhu. However, if the vomit is a mouthful (i.e. the quantity which prevents the person from speaking when in the mouth) or more, whether the mouthful is of blood, food or water, the Wudhu will be broken. But if only phlegm comes out, the Wudhu is not broken. (Durrul Mukhtār)

Vomit of a Baby

Q Is the vomit of a baby pure or impure with regards to clothes for Salāh?

A If it is a mouthful or more, then the vomit and the clothes soiled by the vomit will become impure otherwise not.

Masah (passing wet hands) on Leather Socks

Q What is the ruling regarding Masah on leather socks? Can you explain in detail the method of Masah and the compulsory acts.

A It is from the acts of Sunnah for males and females to make Masah on leather socks.

The Farāidh (compulsory) acts of Masah are:
1. The Masah has to be made on the upper section of the leather socks and not on the sole of the socks.
2. To pass wet fingers of the hand from the toes to the ankles.

The method of Masah is as follows:
1. Wet at least three (i.e. the index, middle and ring) fingers of both hands with clean water. (If more than three fingers are used it is permissible. However, if less than three fingers are used, Masah will not be done).

2. Then place these three wet fingers on the leather socks and pass them from the toes stretching towards the ankles and also the area above it, thus forming wet lines on both the leather socks.

Dripping of Urine

Q I have a severe problem of retaining my Wudhu due to the constant dripping of urine. How shall I perform my Salāh?

A A person who is unable to retain or renew his Wudhu due to continuous dripping of urine, bleeding, flowing of pus, passing of wind etc. and he remains in this condition for the complete duration of a Fardh Salāh time, then such a person is referred to as Ma'zoor. A person will remain a Ma'zoor as long as that illness continues for the duration of one complete Fardh Salāh time from the first time the illness began. If it continues thereafter for the following Fardh Salāh or the illness occurs even once during the next Salāh time then the person will continue to remain a Ma'zoor.

The ruling is that a Ma'zoor should perform his Wudhu at the beginning time of every Fardh Salāh. The Wudhu of this Salāh will remain intact irrespective of the continuous illness which a person is suffering until the time of that Fardh Salāh ends. Thereafter the Ma'zoor's Wudhu will break upon the expiry time of a Fardh Salāh. However, if any other acts which break the Wudhu occur during the Salāh time other than the actual illness, then it will break the Wudhu of a Ma'zoor.

He will no longer be regarded a Ma'zoor if the illness does not occur at least once from the beginning to the end time of a particular Fardh Salāh.

Method of Using the Miswāk

Q What is the correct method of using a Miswāk?

A The Miswāk or Siwāk is a kind of toothbrush made of fibrous wood about a hand span long. The correct method of using the Miswāk is to hold it with the right hand, the thumb at one end and the little finger below the other end. The remaining fingers should remain on the upper portion of the Miswāk and held with the fist. First brush the upper teeth on the right side length wise and then on the left side.

In the same manner, brush the lower teeth beginning with the right side. After using it once, dry it by squeezing it after removing it from the mouth. Then wet it again with water and brush the teeth a second time. Repeat a third time in the same way. Finally wash the Miswāk and place it upright against a wall etc. Do not place it on the ground directly.

Doubt About Wudhu

Q What is the ruling if one forgets if he has Wudhu or not?

A If one remembers having performed Wudhu but does not remember whether he broke it or not then the Wudhu is considered valid and he may perform Salāh on that basis. But it is better to renew the Wudhu.

(Durrul Mukhtār)

Noticing Blood After Wudhu

Q I was blowing my nose when I noticed blood on my handkerchief. Does that affect my Wudhu in any way?

A If dry blood comes out of the nose while blowing it, then the Wudhu is not broken. Wudhu will only break if the blood is in a fluid state.

Performing Wudhu Due to Doubt

Q Before starting my Salāh, a sudden doubt came into my mind regarding whether I had Wudhu or not. In this situation, shall I ignore the doubt and perform my Salāh or shall I perform a fresh Wudhu?

A A doubt will not break the Wudhu. If one remembers that Wudhu was performed but cannot remember if the Wudhu was broken, then in such a case of doubt the Wudhu will be considered valid. (Durrul Mukhtār)

Wetting the Head Due to Injury or Illness

Q My brother suffered a head injury due to which he is unable to pour water over his head. Is his Ghusl (bath) valid without wetting the head?

A If due to some sickness, illness or injury, it is harmful to pour water over the head; then one should do Masah over the head. If Masah is harmful for the head then wash the entire body excluding the head. However upon recovery, it is compulsory to wash the head. There is no need to renew the Ghusl.

Fluid Flowing from the Ears

Q I often have ear-aches which causes the flowing of fluid from the ears. I don't remember having a sore or pimple in my ear. What is the ruling regarding my Wudhu?

A Fluid flowing from a painful ear will break the Wudhu even if there is no sore or pimple in the ear.

Alcohol Touching the Body

Q Is Ghusl necessary prior to performing Salāh if alcohol or any other Harām substance touches the body?

A No, Ghusl is not necessary. Only that portion of the body or clothes which is impure should be washed by water thrice.

We should remember that dealing with alcohol is Harām. How disrespectful it is to deal with alcohol (whether it is buying, selling or drinking) and then proceeding to the Masjid to stand before Allāh ﷻ.

Wudhu After Ghusl

Q Is it necessary to perform Wudhu after having taken a bath?

A No, it is not necessary.

Vomiting Phlegm

Q If someone vomits but only phlegm comes out from ones mouth, does it affect the Wudhu?

A Wudhu does not break if only phlegm comes out of the mouth.

Wudhu Breaks whilst Performing Wudhu

Q During Wudhu, if the Wudhu breaks due to passing wind or bleeding, then what should one do?

A Whilst performing Wudhu or Tayammum if any breakers of Wudhu occur i.e. passing wind or blood comes out then the Wudhu should be re-started or at least the Fardh (compulsory) parts should be washed again.

(Munyatul-Musalli)

Blood Flowing from the Gums

Q I felt blood come out of my gums which I accidentally swallowed. Does this in anyway affect my Wudhu?

A If blood comes out of the gums and it is swallowed but its quantity cannot be determined, then it would be preferable to make fresh Wudhu. If any blood is noticed in the saliva but it is very small in quantity and the colour of the saliva is white or yellowish then the Wudhu is intact but if it is red in colour then the Wudhu is broken.

Nail Polish and Wudhu

Q Is it compulsory to remove nail polish or lip stick when performing Wudhu or Ghusl?

A It is compulsory to remove nail polish, lipstick or any other substance which does not allow water to penetrate through to the skin before performing Wudhu or Fardh Ghusl. Otherwise the Wudhu and Ghusl will not be valid.

Emission of Milk

Q Does the emission of milk from a woman's breasts break the Wudhu?

A Emission of milk from a woman's breasts does not break the Wudhu.

Changing the Nappy of a Baby

Q It is commonly believed that by changing the nappy of a baby the Wudhu breaks. Is this correct?

A Changing the nappies of a baby or an ill adult does not break Wudhu.

Touching the Private Parts

Q If someone touches his private parts, will that break his Wudhu? Is there any difference if it is touched over a cloth or not?

A Touching ones private parts does not break the Wudhu. There is no difference if it is touched over a cloth or with bare hands. In both circumstances the Wudhu will remain intact (unbroken). (Durrul Mukhtār)

Cutting the Nails after Wudhu

Q If after performing Wudhu, nails are cut or dead skin of a wound is scratched, will the Wudhu remain valid?

A The Wudhu will remain valid and it will not be necessary to re-wash those parts again.

Saliva of a Dog

Q If a dog touches a person, should he wash all his clothing?

A Only the saliva of a dog is Najis (impure). The dry body of a dog is not impure. If the dog's mouth touches the body or the clothes, then only the affected parts should be washed. It is not compulsory to wash the whole body nor the whole garment. If any part of the dog's dry body touches someone, nothing is needed to be washed. If the dog's body is moist, the parts touched by the moist body should be washed.

Removing Earrings for Wudhu

Q Should a woman remove her earrings for Wudhu? Is it necessary to wet the earlobes?

A No, it is not necessary to wet the earlobes in Wudhu. Masah (wiping) is sufficient.

Masah on Ordinary Socks

Q Why is it not permissible to do Masah on ordinary socks (i.e. nylon, cotton)?

A It is not permissible to do Masah on ordinary socks because it is contrary to the commandment of the Holy Qur'ān. Allāh ﷻ says, **"O you who believe! When you intend to offer Salāh, wash your faces and hands up to the elbows, wipe (by passing wet hands over) your heads, and (wash) your feet up to the ankles." (5:6)**

All the Ahādeeth which show the permissibility of doing Masah on ordinary socks are weak and there are no Saheeh Hadeeth to prove permissibility. This is confirmed by authentic and reliable scholars. As there is no Saheeh Hadeeth, it is not permissible to perform Masah on ordinary socks nor to prove its permissibility by such weak Ahādeeth.

When the purpose of Masah on socks is to keep water out, how could Masah be permissible on ordinary socks, since doing so allows the water to reach the feet.

Masah on Kuffain (Leather Socks)

Q Why is it permissible to do Masah on Khuffain (leather socks) when this is also contradictory to the commandment of the Holy Qur'ān ?

A The Ahādeeth which proves the permissibility of doing Masah on Khuffain are all Saheeh (authentic). Furthermore, its permissibility is a consensus of the four great Imāms (Jurists of the Ummah) as well as the Muslim Ummah. The Ahādeeth of performing Masah upon leather socks are in such abundance (approximately 70-80) that they attain the level of Tawātur whereby according to the scholars of Hadeeth a status parallel to the Holy Qur'ān is attained. In other words it holds the same ruling as that of the Holy Qur'ān.

Note: There are so many Ahādeeth on this subject that according to Imām Abū Haneefah 🕮 and Imām Mālik 🕮 to acknowledge the permissibility of performing Masah on Kuffain is a sign of the people of Ahlus-Sunnah Wal-Jamā'at. Imām Abū Haneefah 🕮 is reported to have said, "I was not convinced (of the permissibility of performing Masah on Kuffain) until the Ahādeeth reached me in such vast numbers like the bright morning light."

Masah on Cotton or Cloth Socks

Q Is it permissible to do Masah on any particular type of cotton or cloth socks?

A Yes, according to the four Imāms it is permissible to do Masah on those socks (cloth, cotton etc.) that fulfil the following conditions:
1. The socks are so thick that if water was sprinkled on top of them it does not reach the feet.
2. The socks would stay on without tying them to the foreleg.
3. The socks are such that it is suitable to walk continuously in them without shoes on, and without them tearing (for at least 1 mile).

The permissibility of performing Masah on the above mentioned socks is not on the basis that they are ordinary socks, but rather if they fulfil the aforementioned criteria they would be classed in the same category of Khuffain (leather socks). Thus it would be permissible to perform Masah on such socks.

There are also two other types of socks on which Masah is permissible:

1. Those cotton or cloth socks which are covered top to bottom in leather.
2. Those cotton or cloth socks which have their soles covered in leather.

From the aforementioned points it is clear that it is not permissible to perform Masah on ordinary socks. This is the view held by the four Imāms and the majority of scholars.

Talking whilst having a Bath

Q Is it permissible to speak whilst having a bath?

A It is Makrooh (undesirable) to talk unnecessarily whilst ha
with the Satr uncovered.

Hadath (Impurity)

Q What is Hadath?

A Hadath literally means impurity. Hadath is of two types, Hadath Akbar and Hadath Asgar. Hadath Akbar is that impurity which makes Ghusl compulsory. Hadath Asgar is that impurity which makes Wudhu compulsory.

Age of Maturity

Q When is a child considered a Bāligh (mature)?

A According to the Shari'ah, when a child attains puberty he/she is said to have become Bāligh.

A boy is said to be Bāligh (mature) if he experiences any of the following:
1. He has a wet dream and semen is discharged.
2. He is able to make a woman pregnant.

A girl is said to be Bāligh (mature) if she experiences any the following:
1. She experiences a monthly period - Haidh (menstruation).
2. She has a dream (and she ejaculates).
3. She becomes pregnant.

If the above signs are not evident but he/she reaches the age of 14 years and 7 months then he/she will be regarded as having reached the age of puberty. On reaching the age of puberty all the principles of Islām such as Salāh, fasting becomes Fardh (obligatory). If he/she disobeys or neglects any of these, then he/she becomes a sinner.

Haidh (Menstruation)

Q What is the ruling regarding a woman who bleeds for more than seven days when her Haidh habit is seven days?

A If a woman with a seven days Haidh habit bleeds for more than seven days, then she must be observant.

There are two scenarios:

1. If it stops on the tenth day or prior to that (for instance on the eighth or ninth day) then she should have a bath immediately when her bleeding ends and perform her Salāh just before the Mustahab time expires. It will then be considered that she now has a new (longer) period of menstruation and Qadha for the Salāh missed is not necessary. She will now continue to observe this new (longer) period and no longer the seven days.

2. However if the bleeding continues from her seven day period beyond ten days; for instance it continues up to the twelfth day, then the seven days will remain her Haidh period and the remaining five days will be Istihādah. On the tenth day she is required to have a bath and begin to perform her Salāh. Furthermore, she must also perform Qadha Salāh for the last three days. She must therefore have a proper record of all the bleedings and ensure that she does not neglect Salāh under such circumstances. Her period will still remain as seven days in this case.

Nifās (Post-Natal Bleeding)

Q What is the ruling regarding a woman who had Nifās previously and on the second occasion the bleeding pattern is different to the previous one?

A A woman who already had Nifās previously and on the second occasion the bleeding pattern is different to her former habit i.e. she bled for twenty five days the first time and the second time she bled for less or more, e.g. thirty five days, then all this is regarded as Nifās. If on the second occasion of the childbirth, she bled for more than forty days, then whatever extra days she bled beyond her habit is Istihādah e.g. the first time she bled for twenty five days and the second time she bled for more than forty days, then after the fortieth day she should take a bath and begin performing Salāh while the fifteen days, which are more than her habit of twenty five days are regarded as Istihādah. She must perform Qadha Salāh for these fifteen days.

Her bathing upon the completion of the forty days will make her clean and whenever the bleeding stops after the forty days period, it will not be necessary for her to take a bath because this is Istihādah. Only Wudhu will suffice.

Note: The general impression is that Nifās is for forty days whereas this is only the maximum period. Due to this misunderstanding, Salāh etc. are unfortunately neglected. Bleeding can stop prior to forty days.

There is no minimum period for Nifās, nor is there a maximum period for Istihādah.

Allāh ﷻ Knows Best

3. Chapter on
Knowledge

Evil Dreams

Q Sometimes I see such evil dreams which cause me extreme anxiety, e.g. having sexual relations with a Mahram relative. Please advise me.

A A person is not liable for dreams. No matter how bad and evil a dream may appear, one will not be questioned for it by Allāh 靈. One has no control over dreams. Furthermore, sometimes an extremely bad dream can have a beautiful interpretation. One should therefore not become unduly disturbed when one sees such dreams. However, if one ponders over such matters during one's time of wakefulness, then it is quite possible that the bad dream could be the result of such thoughts which then reflect in the dreams. If one is in the habit of such thoughts, one should repent and refrain from them.

Khātamun Nabiyeen

Q What is the meaning of Khātamun Nabiyeen?

A In the Holy Qur'ān, Allāh 靈 has referred to our Holy Prophet 靈 as Khātamun Nabiyeen in Sūrah al-Ahzāb (33:40) which implies to the seal of the Prophets i.e. no Prophet is to come after him. If anyone claims Prophethood after the Holy Prophet 靈, then such a person is an imposter and a disbeliever.

Following a Particular Imām

Q How are Masā'il (rulings) derived from the Holy Qur'ān and Ahādeeth? What methods are used if the Mas'alah cannot be clearly understood from the Holy Qur'ān and Ahādeeth? What is the importance of Taqleed (following a Muslim jurist) in the Shari'ah? Why are we limited to the schools of the four Imāms?

A The original source of guidance is the Holy Qur'ān but generally it is the fundamental principles and Masā'il which are stated in the Holy Qur'ān.

It was the duty of the Holy Prophet 靈 to explain in detail these Masā'il.

Allāh ﷻ says, **"And We have revealed to you the Reminder (Qur'ān) so you may explain to mankind of what has been revealed to them and so that they may contemplate." (16:44)**

Example No. 1

It is stated in the Holy Qur'ān, **"Establish Salāh."** How to perform Salāh is not mentioned at all. The method of performing Salāh, the different types, and their respective rulings are all related to us by the Holy Prophet ﷺ through Ahādeeth. For instance, the number of Rak'āts in each Salāh, in which one is only Sūrah al-Fātihah recited and in which one an additional Sūrah is recited. Furthermore, which are the ones in which Qir'āt is recited quietly and in which ones Qir'āt is recited loudly. It is impossible to ascertain all this information from the Holy Qur'ān only. Support from the Sunnah is required.

Example No. 2

It is stated in the Holy Qur'ān, **"Pay Zakāh."** The Holy Qur'ān has not mentioned anything regarding this.

All the details on how the Zakāh is calculated on silver, gold, goats, cows, camels etc. have been mentioned in the Ahādeeth.

Example No. 3

It is stated in the Holy Qur'ān, **"And pilgrimage to the house is a duty upon mankind for Allāh ﷻ for those who can." (3:97)**

The details on how Tawāf should be done and how many rounds there are in one Tawāf, the Masā'il of Arafah, Minā, Muzdalifah and Ramee etc. have all been explained by the Holy Prophet ﷺ.

To understand the Holy Qur'ān, it is important to acquire the knowledge of Ahādeeth. It is impossible to understand the Holy Qur'ān whilst neglecting the Ahādeeth. The Ummah has been commanded to derive guidance from the Holy Qur'ān under the explained instructions of the Holy Prophet ﷺ.

In this respect, the obedience of the Holy Prophet ﷺ means the obedience of Allāh ﷻ. **"He who obeys the Prophet has indeed obeyed Allāh ﷻ."**
(4:80)

Therefore it is mentioned in the Ahādeeth, "Perform Salāh in the manner that you have seen me perform." (Bukhāri)

The Holy Prophet 🌸 did not say, pray the way you understand from the Holy Qur'ān.

Different Types of Ahādeeth

Those statements that were made verbally by the Holy Prophet 🌸 himself, are called 'Hadeeth-e-Qawli', and what the Holy Prophet 🌸 practically demonstrated are known as 'Hadeeth-e-Fe'li'. Sometimes certain actions were done in front of the Holy Prophet 🌸 or were brought to his attention but he did not affirm nor reject them, instead he preferred to remain silent. This is taken as their confirmation. This is called 'Taqreer'. These three types of Ahādeeth are a source of guidance for the entire Ummah.

Qiyās (Analogical Deduction)

Qiyās is the application (Illat), also referred to as pretext or prime factor, that is found in the Holy Qur'ān, Sunnah or Ijmā (consensus) to a modern day contemporary issue. This is essentially required when the ruling of a particular contemporary issue is not clearly understood and nor to be found categorically in the Qur'ān, Sunnah nor Ijmā. Thus, as a last resort Qiyās will be used in order to determine the ruling of a contemporary matter by carefully analysing which prime factor from the Qur'ān, Sunnah or Ijmā is similar to the current issue.

There were certain questions that the Holy Prophet 🌸 was asked, he would reply to them and to further facilitate the questioner's understanding he would sometimes give a logical reason by posing a logical question to the questioner knowing that the answer would become apparent to the questioner.

Example: A Sahābi 🌸 once inquired that since Hajj was due upon my mother (who had passed away), would it be sufficient if I were to perform it on her behalf? The Holy Prophet 🌸 replied in the affirmative. Then he posed a (logical) question to the questioner that suppose if your mother took a loan from somebody and you paid it off (on her behalf), would it be acceptable or not? He replied that yes it would be acceptable.

The Holy Prophet 饗 then said that paying off the loan of Allāh 饗 is more likely to be accepted. (Bukhāri)

In the Shari'ah this is known as Qiyās, Ijtihād, Istinbāt and I'tibār. Teachings of this nature are supported by the Holy Prophet 饗. Its conditions and details can be found in the books of Usool (rules of Islamic jurisprudence).

The Holy Prophet 饗 sent Sayyidunā Mu'āz Ibn Jabal 饗 as a judge to Yemen. Whilst he was going, the Holy Prophet 饗 walked alongside him and gave him a lot of counselling until the Holy Prophet 饗 came to a point to bid him farewell. During the advice, the Holy Prophet 饗 asked him, "According to which law will you make your judgements?" He replied, "According to the Holy Qur'ān." The Holy Prophet 饗 then inquired, "What if you do not find it in the Holy Qur'ān?" He answered, "Then according to the Sunnah of Rasūlullāh 饗." Then he asked, "What will you do if you do not find it in the Sunnah either?" He replied, "I will do Ijtihād." The Holy Prophet 饗 expressed great happiness upon this reply and was in full support of this decision and he thanked Allāh 饗 for this selection. (Abū Dāwood)

Ijtihād

When a Mas'alah cannot be clearly found in the Holy Qur'ān and the Ahādeeth, then a Mujtahid (jurist) will thoroughly analyse through analogy and evidences to determine its ruling. This is known as Ijtihād and Qiyās, as understood from the aforementioned. If this is agreed upon unanimously, it is called Ijmā (consensus). This is why the Ulamā of Usool (experts in the field of juristic principles) have written that Qiyās does not establish the decree, but it just makes it evident.

A ruling that exists in the Holy Qur'ān or Ahādeeth, but is not quite apparent for a layman to understand, a Mujtahid having done Qiyās on its analogies or by analysing evidently, implicitly or by way of necessity, would make that ruling apparent. Imām Bukhāri 饗 has compiled a specific chapter regarding this.

Taqleed

Whoever does not have the capability of Ijtihād, following a Mujtahid becomes compulsory for him. This is known as Taqleed.

The greatest benefit of Taqleed is that it enables one's Deen to be systematic and easy to practice. Moreover, by doing Taqleed there is less probability for the desires to intervene in a person's Deen. Deprived of Taqleed a person will begin to pick and choose in Deen those things which are in conformity with his desires unlike for a Muqallid (a person who practices Taqleed) there would be no scope for him to pick and choose.

This is why Sayyidunā Mu'āz ؓ was sent as a judge, so that the Masā'il and rulings he derived from the Holy Qur'ān, Ahādeeth and Ijtihād would be implemented. Following these three would in fact mean obeying the Holy Prophet ﷺ.

It has been narrated from Sayyidunā Abū Hurairah ؓ that the Holy Prophet ﷺ said, "Whoever obeyed me has indeed obeyed Allāh ﷻ and whoever disobeyed me has indeed disobeyed Allāh ﷻ, and whoever obeyed the Ameer (leader) has indeed obeyed me and whoever disobeyed the Ameer has indeed disobeyed me." (Bukhāri)

The Categories of Masā'il
There are two types of Masā'il. Firstly, those that have been mentioned in the Nas (Holy Qur'ān or Ahādeeth). Secondly, those which have not been mentioned in the Holy Qur'ān or Ahādeeth.

The first category will further divide into two forms; the first form is that the Nas will either have a ruling in the positive or in the negative only. The second form is, that there are two types of Nas regarding the same Mas'alah. In some we find a ruling in the positive and in others in the negative. For example, from some we find out about the Āmeen-bil-Jahr (saying Āmeen loudly) and from some we find about Āmeen-bis-Sir (saying Āmeen softly). Some inform us about Raf'ul-Yadāyn (raising the hands), whilst others tell us about Tark'ur-Raf'ul-Yadāyn (not raising the hands).

There are also another two groups of Masā'il. The first one is when historic evidence or other circumstances indicate that one Nas has preference over the other. The second type is, when it is not known which Nas has been given preference over the other and nor is it known which came first and which came later.

In total there are four types of Masā'il:

First
That type of Nas which is so clear that it only renders one interpretation giving no scope for any other interpretation, no Qiyās or Ijtihād will be done, neither would Taqleed be permissible if it opposes the Nas. Instead the Nas will be acted upon. All of the four Imāms are unanimous in this category because there can be no scope for differences. For instance the fundamental articles of belief, the prohibition of interest and alcohol etc.

Second
Those Masā'il which have two types of Nas and it is also known which came first and which came second. Generally, the first one will be abrogated, while the second one will be applicable. There is no need for Qiyās, Ijtihād or Taqleed in this type either.

For instance Allāh ﷻ states in the Holy Qur'ān, **"And upon those who have the strength (to fast) is Fidya (compensation)." (2:184)**

However, in another place Allāh ﷻ states, **"So those of you that witness the month (of Ramadhān) must fast." (2:185)**

In the early days of Islām when the Ramadhān fasts were newly prescribed, then initially a person was given the option to either fast or give Fidyah irrespective of whether he or she was rich or poor. The former verse indicates towards this option. Subsequently, this concession was then abrogated (Mansūkh) by the latter verse so, that now until the Day of Judgement, whoever has the strength to fast in the month of Ramadhān has to fast. The second verse clearly shows this obligation. In this case both the abrogated (Mansūkh i.e. the former verse) and the abrogator (Nāsikh i.e. the latter verse) are known.

Third
Those Masā'il where there are two types of Nas and it is not known which comes first and which comes second. For instance, the issue of Rafʿul-Yadāyn (raising the hands during Salāh besides the Takbeer-e-Tahreemah) and Tark Rafʿul-Yadāyn (not raising the hands on other occasions besides Takbeer-e-Tahreemah).

Fourth
Those Masā'il regarding which there is no Nas at all.

In the last two categories a layman will be in one of the two situations. Either a person is acting upon it or he is not acting upon it and wandering aimlessly. Well, there is no permission for the latter. Allāh 🕮 says, **"Does man think that he will be left in vain?" (75:36)**

This is not the case, a person is obliged to obey Allāh's 🕮 commands in every aspect. Well, what is he then going to act upon? In the third type, which Nas does he apply? If he acts upon one, the other is omitted. He cannot appoint a Nas on his own behalf. He does not have the knowledge regarding which Nas came first and which came second, so that he can abrogate the first and act upon the second. In the fourth type, there is no categorical Nas at all. So without knowledge what is he going to act upon?

Allāh 🕮 says in the Holy Qur'ān, **"Do not pursue what you have no knowledge about." (17:36)** This leaves no alternative but to do Ijtihād. It is necessary in the third type because one of the Nas has to be appointed to be acted upon, and in the fourth type because the ruling has to be found.

It is also quite obvious that not everybody has the capability and qualification to do Ijtihād and Istinbāt (deduction of laws). This verse of the Holy Qur'ān makes this clear as well. Allāh 🕮 says, **"If they had referred it to the Messenger and to those who have authority amongst them, the proper investigators would have known it from them (direct)." (4:83)**

Anybody can claim to make a decision, regardless of it being right or wrong, but only he will be called a Mustanbit and Mujtahid, who possesses the qualifications of Istinbāt (extensive analysis and deduction) in accordance to the Sharī'ah. If he cannot, then he will be known as a Muqallid (follower).

Hence it is important for a Mujtahid to apply Ijtihād in the third and forth type of Masā'il and as for the Muqallid, it is important for him to do Taqleed. Even if the Mujtahid makes an error, the Mujtahid will not be deprived of reward because his Ijtihād was according to the Sharī'ah. If his Ijtihād is correct then he will be entitled to a double reward.

A doubt might arise as to why Taqleed is restricted to the four Imāms, i.e. Imām Abū Haneefah, Imām Mālik, Imām Shāfi'ee and Imām Ahmad 🌸 only, despite there being many Mujtahidoon amongst the Sahābah 🌸, Tābi'een and the Tabi'-Tābi'een? What is the harm in doing Taqleed of anybody else, especially those Sahābah 🌸 whose virtues have been mentioned in the Holy Qur'ān and in many Ahādeeth. The answer to this is that indeed the Sahābah 🌸 have a higher status than the four Imāms.

The reason for doing Taqleed of the four Imāms is not because they are thought to be greater than the Sahābah 🌸, rather when doing Taqleed it is important to acknowledge the Masā'il in which Taqleed is done. There are three fundamental conditions for doing Taqleed of a particular Imām:

a)   That their entire Fiqh and Madhab has been preserved from the chapter of purity to inheritence. This is essential so that a person or a scholar can refer to this Imām at all times regarding any aspect of life.

b)   The science of deriving laws and Usools have also been preserved in order for a contemporary scholar to derive new laws of contemporary issues that emerge based upon the Usools set by the Imām that are extracted from the Holy Qur'ān and Sunnah.

c)   The Imām has left behind students and scholars to propagate and teach his Fiqh.

Today, there are vast amounts of details and explanations available about the Masā'il, compiled and collected in the schools of the four Imāms, from the chapter of Tahārah (purity) to Kitābul-Farā'idh (chapter on inheritance), including Ibādah, dealings etc. In short, vast numbers of Masā'il in all the fields and spheres have been collected. This type of detailed and compiled Madhab (school) cannot be found from the Sahābah 🌸, Tābi'een or the Tabi'-Tābi'een. So if one was to do Taqleed of anybody apart from the four Imāms, then how would he do it? This is why Taqleed of the four Imāms alone has been chosen by the scholars.

Allāh 🌸 bestowed upon the four Imāms the knowledge of the Holy Qur'ān and Ahādeeth in depth and the complete skills of Istinbāt (deduction of laws). They also had access to the Ahādeeth of the Holy Prophet 🌸 which were spread throughout the world by the Sahābah 🌸.

It is possible that there will be narrations that one of them knew about but the other did not, but it would be rare to find narrations that none of them knew about.

Shāh Waliullāh Muhaddith Dehlawi ❀ has written about the spreading and circulation of Ahādeeth and about Madeenah, being the headquarters of knowledge. He writes, "These four Imāms are such that their knowledge collectively encompassed the whole world and those four Imāms are Imām Abū Haneefah, Imām Mālik, Imām Shāfi'ee and Imām Ahmad ❀."

Definition of Taqleed

Q What is the definition of Taqleed? Will a person still remain a Hanafi if he acts upon Imām Abū Yūsuf's ❀ or Imām Zufar's ❀ view. Also will he still remain a Hanafi if he acts upon the opinion of Imām Shāfi'ee ❀ or Imām Mālik ❀ at the time of need?

A Definition: Taqleed means to follow and accept an opinion and a legal verdict of a particular Mujtahid without demanding proof and evidence from him who has attained the highest calibre and proficiency in the four sources i.e. the Holy Qur'ān, Hadeeth, Ijmā and Qiyās, and mastering all of the necessary requirements in order to achieve that status of proficiency along with meeting the spiritual requirements. This is known as Taqleed.

When it is said that 'without demanding proof' it does not mean that it is impermissible to demand proof nor does it mean that the Imām will have no evidence at all. But relatively it implies to the accepting of the statement with the conviction that his legal opinion has been derived from the four sources of Shari'ah i.e. the Holy Qur'ān, Hadeeth, Ijmā and Qiyās. Therefore there is no need to ask for proof due to his expertise. For a non-Mujtahid to follow a Mujtahid, trusting him that he has the proof and evidence for it and he does not ask him for the evidence, is also known as Taqleed.

It is through the principles of Imām Abū Haneefah ❀ which his students have described in detail and from which other Masā'il are derived, whether these Masā'il are directly from Imām Sāhib ❀ or not, that a person who adopts them will still remain a 'Hanafi'.

The views of Imām Sāhib's students are in actual fact Imām Sahib's views, regardless of whether they are directly or indirectly from Imām Sahib. Therefore, acting upon them on special occasions does not expel an individual from Hanafiyyah, (he still remains a Hanafi). Imām Shāmi ﷺ has stated this in his Fatwa book, "Rasmul Mufti".

Sometimes, because of the variations in occurrences and incidents, the ruling changed in a way that the scholars of the later era understood that if Imām Sāhib ﷺ was still alive today, he would have made this new revised ruling in that particular Mas'alah. Therefore, they decided upon that ruling, regardless of whether that was the view of Imām Shāfi'ee ﷺ or an opinion of any other Imām.

These types of changes, like the excellence of Nafl Hajj and Sadaqah etc. can be found in the time of Imām Sāhib ﷺ himself. Hence, they do not relate to any changes in Hanafiyyah.

Importance of Taqleed

Q **Why is it important to do Taqleed (follow) of only one Imām? What harm is there in following one Imām for one Mas'alah, then another Imām for another Mas'alah, the way it was in the time of the Sahābah ﷺ and the Tābi'een? They were not dependant on one individual in following the whole Madhab (school of thought).**

A During the era of the Sahābah ﷺ, virtue and prosperity had the upper hand and generally there was no part in Deen for fulfilling personal desires.

That is why when someone inquired about a Mas'alah, he asked with a good intention and he would act upon it as well, regardless of whether it coincided with his desires or not.

In later times this was not the case. Instead, people started having the urge to ask one Mas'alah from a certain Ālim (scholar) and if the answer was against their desires, they would walk off to another Ālim in search of ease. Still not content with this, they were stricken with a growing concern about how they would find a way out in every Mas'alah which would satisfy them. It is apparent that this cannot be the motive for the search of truth.

Sometimes this can cause a lot of damage to a person's Imān. For example, a person made Wudhu and then touched his wife, somebody following the Madhab of Imām Shāfi'ee 🌸 says to him, "Repeat your Wudhu because touching your wife breaks your Wudhu." He replies, "I do Taqleed of Imām Abū Haneefah 🌸 and Wudhu does not break in his opinion on this situation." Then this person vomits. Somebody following the Madhab of Imām Abū Haneefah 🌸 says to him, "Repeat your Wudhu because vomiting breaks the Wudhu in the opinion of Imām Abū Haneefah 🌸." He replies, "I am following the Madhab of Imām Shāfi'ee 🌸 and in his view, Wudhu does not break by vomiting." Now, this person's Salāh is not valid in accordance with the Madhab of Imām Abū Haneefah 🌸 or Imām Shāfi'ee 🌸. This is known as Talfeeq which is void and not permissible by unanimous decision. Following in this manner is in actual fact doing Taqleed of neither of the Imāms. Instead it is fulfilling personal desires which is forbidden in the Shari'ah. It leads a person astray and away from the path of Allāh 🌸. Allāh 🌸 says in the Holy Qur'ān, **"And do not follow your personal desires, for they will lead you astray from the path of Allāh." (38:26)**

This is why it is important to do Taqleed of only one particular Imām. The Holy Qur'ān has associated obedience with repentance, **"And follow the path of him who turns to Me." (31:15)**

On this basis, any individual who had a strong presumption about Imām Abū Haneefah 🌸 that he was repentant, correct and that his Ijtihād was in accordance with the Holy Qur'ān and Ahādeeth, chose to do his Taqleed. Anybody who had the same thought regarding Imām Shāfi'ee 🌸, Imām Mālik 🌸 or Imām Ahmad 🌸 started doing their Taqleed. Now, it is incorrect to leave one's own Imām whenever a person desires and start following a different Imām. Because without the permission of the Shari'ah it becomes Talfeeq and fulfilment of personal desires which ultimately leads a person astray.

Hence, Shaykh Muhammad Husain Sāhib 🌸 has written in his compilation Ishā'atus-Sunnah, after opposing Taqleed for a very long period of time and then becoming affected with a bitter experience for not doing Taqleed, he writes, "We discovered after 25 years of experience that those people who abstain from the Mujtahids and Taqleed, they end up saying farewell to Islām. Some either leave Islām while others end up without any Madhab at all. Rebellion and disobedience of the Shari'ah is a grave result of this freedom."

This is why those learned scholars that had a deep insight of the Holy Qur'ān and countless treasures of the Ahādeeth of the Holy Prophet ﷺ and the Sahābah ☀, whose hearts were enriched with fear of Allāh ﷻ and whose lives were enlightened with the light of the Sunnah of the Holy Prophet ﷺ still chose to adopt Taqleed despite having these qualities and virtues themselves. Moreover, it is also well known that the profound scholars of the six prominent Hadeeth collections i.e. Imām Bukhāri ☀, Imām Muslim ☀, Imām Tirmizi ☀ etc also practiced Taqleed. For example, Imām Abū Dāwood ☀ was a Hanbali and according to some a Shāfi'ee whilst Imām Muslim ☀, Imām Nasai ☀, Imām Tirmizi ☀ and Imām Ibn Mājah ☀ followed the Shāfi'ee school of thought.

Regarding Imām Bukhāri ☀ there are different opinions; according to some he was a Mujtahid whilst other scholars class him to be a Shāfi'ee follower. With the exemption of Imām Bukhāri ☀ all of the scholars are unanimous that the aforementioned five Muhaddithoon (scholars of Hadeeth) would adhere to a particular Imām.

Moreover, besides the above mentioned eminent Muhaddithoon, there were many other prominent scholars in the past who adhered to a particular Imām. These are as follows:

1. From amongst the Hanafi school of thought:

a) Imām Yaqūb Ibn Ibrāheem famously known as Imām Abū Yūsuf ☀, a renowned Faqih (jurist), a scholar of Hadeeth and a senior student of Imām Abū Haneefah ☀. He was granted the title "Qādhi-ul-Qudhāt" (judge of judges). Demise 182 A.H.

b) Imām Muhammad Ibn Hasan ash-Shaybāni ☀, also a renowned Faqih and a seniour student of Imām Abū Haneefah ☀. Demise 189 A.H.

c) Muhammad Ibn Abdullāh al-Muthannah ☀, who was from the progeny of a noble Sahābi Sayyidunā Anas Ibn Mālik ☀. He was a Qādhi (judge) and amongst the teachers of Imām Bukhāri ☀, Imām Ahmad Ibn Hanbal ☀ and others. Demise 215 A.H.

d) Imām Ahmad Ibn Muhammad Abū Ja'far at-Tahāwi ⚜. An authority in the field of Hadeeth and also a Faqih. He is the author of the Hadeeth collection Sharhul Ma'āni al-Āthār. Demise 321 A.H.

e) Mahmūd Ibn Ahmad al-Badr al-Ainee ⚜, famously known as Allāma al-Ainee ⚜, a Muhaddith (an expert in Hadeeth) and the author of Umdatul Qāri which is a volumnous commentary of Saheeh al-Bukhāri. Demise 855 A.H.

f) Ali Ibn Sultān Muhammad al-Qāri al-Harawi ⚜, famously known as Mulla Ali Qāri ⚜, a great Muhaddith and the author of Mirqātul Mafātih which is a famous commentary of Mishkātul Masābih. Demise 1014 A.H.

2. From amongst the Māliki school of thought:

a) Muhammad Ibn Abdus-Salām, Ibn Suhnun, Abū Abdullāh al-Qairawāni ⚜, a very high ranking scholar of Hadeeth. Demise 256 A.H.

b) Hāfiz Ibn Abdul Barr ⚜, a great scholar of Hadeeth. Demise 463 A.H.

c) Ismāeel Ibn Ishāq, Abū Ishāq, al-Qādhi al-Juhdāmi ⚜, a contemporary of Imam Bukhāri ⚜. Demise 282 A.H.

d) Aslam Ibn Abdul Azeez Ibn Hishām, Chief Justice of Andalusia and also an expert in Hadeeth. Demise 319 A.H.

3. From amongst the Shāfi'ee school of thought:

a) Abū Bakr, Ahmad Ibn al-Husain ⚜ known as Imām Baihaqi ⚜, the author of the volumnous Sunnan al-Baihaqi. Demise 458 A.H.

b) Abdullāh Ibn Muhammad, Abū Bakr Ibn Abū Shaibah ⚜, a famous teacher of Imām Bukhāri, Muslim, Abū Dāwood and Ibn Mājah. Demise 235 A.H.

c) Ahmad Ibn Ali, known as Hāfiz Ibn Hajar al-Asqalāni ⚜, the author of Fathul Bāri a famous commentary of Saheeh al-Bukhāri. Demise 852 A.H.

d) Ismāeel Ibn Umar Imād-ud-Deen famously known as Ibn Katheer 🏵, an authority in the field of Tafseer, Hadeeth and Islamic History. He is the author of Tafseer Ibn Katheer (commentary of the Holy Qur'ān), al-Bidayā wan-Nihāya (a volumnous collection of Islamic History) and many more. Demise 774 A.H.

e) Muhi-ud-Deen Abū Zakariyyā, Yahya Ibn Sharaf an-Nawāwi, famously known as Imām Nawāwi 🏵, a profound scholar in Hadeeth and a famous commentator of Saheeh al-Muslim. Demise 676 A.H.

f) Imām Tabarāni 🏵 the author of Tabarāni. Demise 360 A.H.

4. Followers of the Hanbali school of thought:

a) Ahmad Ibn Abdul Haleem, Abul Abbās Ibn Taimiyyah 🏵, an expert in Hadeeth. Demise 728 A.H.

b) Hāfiz Ibn Qayyim al-Jawziyyah 🏵, an expert in various field and an author of many books. Demise 751 A.H.

c) Abdur Rahmān Ibn Ahmad, known as Ibn Rajab 🏵, one of the commentators of Saheeh al-Bukhāri and also Sunan Tirmizi. Demise 795 A.H.

d) Ahmad Ibn Ja'far, Abū Bakr al-Qāti, a teacher of many famous Muhaddithoon such as Dārul Qutni and others. Also one of the narrators of Musnad Ahmad. Demise 368 A.H.

These eminent scholars that have been mentioned are just a fraction, otherwise there are countless scholars up to this day that adhere to one of the Imāms. As we have cited above it is apparent that it would not be an exaggeration if it was said that these Ulamā reached such a status only through following the Holy Prophet 🏵 and doing Taqleed of the pious servants of Deen and the great Mujtahidoon.

Shaykh Sarfrāz Sāhib 🌼 states, "O readers! This is an ocean that has no shore. Take a look into the books on biographies, the books on the categories of Muhaddithoon, the Fuqahā, the Historians, the Mufassiroon (the commentators of the Holy Qur'ān) and the grammatarians and observe. You will certainly find that at least 98% of all of them were Muqallidoon i.e. followed an Imām.

Meaning of Fatwa

Q **Nowadays we hear very often in the media the word Fatwa given by certain Muslim clerics. What does it mean?**

A Fatwa literally means to answer a question irrespective of whether such a question relates to an Islamic issue or not. Technically it means to issue a legal verdict by a qualified Mufti in response to a question relating to a matter of Islām.

We must remember that it is not permissible to issue a Fatwa unless a person has studied Fiqh (jurisprudence - the science of Islamic Law) in depth under the supervision and guidance of competent and qualified experts in the field. Our pious predecessors used to exercise great caution in matters of Fatwa. Imām Ahmad Ibn Hanbal 🌼 used to frequently say, "I don't know." Imām Mālik 🌼 is reported to have said that the Mufti must be conscious of accountability to Allāh 🌼 before responding to any question. According to Sayyidunā Abdullāh Ibn Mas'ood 🌼 and Sayyidunā Abdullāh Ibn Abbās 🌼, a person who answers every question is mad. Unfortunately there are many people who claim to have the authority of issuing Fatwa (legal verdict) without proper training and without having acquired the necessary expertise, thereby causing confusion and misunderstanding amongst the masses.

Meaning of Ijmā

Q **What does the word Ijmā mean. Has this got any basis in the Shari'ah?**

A The word Ijmā refers to the consensus of opinion of the Companions 🌼 and their successors on a particular matter of Shari'ah or a legal rule. It is not permissible to hold a contrary view when a matter has been unanimously agreed upon through Ijmā.

The evidence of Ijmā as a source of Islamic Law has been derived from both the Holy Qur'ān and Hadeeth. Allāh ﷻ says, **"Whoever follows a path other than the path of the Muslims, We shall assign to him what he has chosen and shall cause him to enter the Fire and it is an evil abode." (4:115)** The reference to the path of the Muslims in this verse is a reference to Ijmā. The Holy Prophet ﷺ said, "My nation will not unite upon error." (Mishkāt)

Interpretation of Dreams

Q I saw a dream which made me very scared and I narrated it to my friend. He lacked the knowledge regarding the interpretation but even then he gave the interpretation. Is it permissible to give an interpretation if you are not talented in the field of dreams?

A The Holy Prophet ﷺ said, "Ru'yā (the dream of a believer) is a portion from the forty six portions of Prophethood." (Bukhāri)

That is why an unqualified person is not allowed to give the Ta'beer (interpretation) of dreams. Imām Ibn Sīreen ﷺ who was a leading authority in this field during his time has listed in his book 'Dreams & Interpretations' the necessary requirements for a person to become a qualified interpreter.

The following qualifications are:

1. He must have adequate knowledge of the commentary of the Holy Qur'ān.
2. He must be a Hāfiz of Ahādeeth or at least have adequate knowledge of the Ahādeeth of the Holy Prophet ﷺ.
3. He must be well versed in the Arabic language.
4. He must be familiar with the roots of words so that he knows where they are derived from.
5. He must be familiar with the nature and status of people.
6. He must be familiar with the basic principles of interpretation.
7. He must be a righteous person and implement Islām in his day to day life.
8. He must be a person with sound morality.
9. He must be honest in speech and conduct.

It is essential to have the above qualities because when giving the Ta'beer (meaning) of a dream, the aspect of time is taken into account and at other times, the meaning is given directly from the Holy Qur'ān or Hadeeth and again, at other times, the usage and wording is taken into account. Sometimes instead of taking into consideration the one who sees the dream, the Muabbir (interpreter) will take into account someone who resembles him in personality or name. Sometimes an interpretation is given by a name only or by the meaning of a word only or by its contrasting meaning. Again at other times the root meaning of a word is taken into account, or the lesser or greater meaning of a word is taken into account.

It is necessary that the Muabbir (interpreter) understands fully and properly every detail of a dream seen by any person. He should be able to weigh it on the scale of the rules of interpretation. If the numerous facts emerging from a dream are such that they correspond with each other logically then such a dream will be deemed as a genuine and authentic dream. But if the facts emerging from such a dream are such that they do not correspond with each other, then the interpreter should reflect on the apparent meaning of the words.

Whichever ruling is nearest to the rules of interpretation should be adopted. If a dream is of a complicated nature that it cannot be weighed on the scale of the rules of interpretation then such a dream will be deemed as meaningless.

Who are the Ahlus-Sunnah Wal-Jamā'at

Q Who are the real Ahlus-Sunnah Wal-Jamā'at? Nowadays every sect is claiming to be amongst the Ahlus-Sunnah Wal-Jamā'at. What does the Ahādeeth say regarding this matter? How will I know that I am in the right group? Please explain in detail.

A Ahlus-Sunnah Wal-Jamā'at (the followers of the Sunnah and the group of Sahābah ﷺ) are the Ahle-Haq (the truthful and the authentic people) and the ones who conform to the Sunnah of the Holy Prophet ﷺ and the guided Sahābah ﷺ.

This has been clearly mentioned in one Hadeeth, "My Ummah (nation) will be divided into seventy-three sects. Every sect will be in the Fire of Hell except one." The Sahābah ☙ asked, "O, Rasūlullāh ☙, which is that sect?" The Holy Prophet ☙ replied, "That sect which follows the path on which I and my Companions are." (Tirmizi)

The statement made, "Every sect will be in the Fire of Hell except one" implies that they will be thrown into Hell on account of their evil beliefs. Subsequently, those whose beliefs did not transgress to Kufr (disbelief) will, after serving the punishment on the account of their sins, come out of Hell and be admitted into Paradise.

Sayyidunā Abdullāh Ibn Umar ☙ in a long Hadeeth mentions ten signs of Ahlus-Sunnah Wal-Jamā'at. He says, "Anyone who has in him the following ten signs, he is of the Ahlus-Sunnah Wal-Jamā'at."

1.   He performs the five times Salāh with the congregation.
2.   He does not speak ill of any of the Sahābah ☙.
3.   He does not draw his sword against a (upright) Muslim ruler.
4.   He does not doubt in his own Imān (belief) and he calls himself a believer and a Muslim.
5.   He has belief in fate, that good and bad is from Allāh ☙.
6.   He does not dispute about the religion of Allāh ☙ (i.e. he does not argue nor object against it).
7.   He does not accuse anyone of Kufr (disbelief) on the account of sin.
8.   He does not omit the funeral prayer of anyone who is a Muslim.
9.   He accepts the permissibility of wiping over leather socks whilst on a journey and at home.
10.   He considers it proper to perform Salāh behind an Imām, pious or sinful. (Bahrur-Rāiq)

Hence those people who conform to the ten signs will Inshā-Allāh be classified as Ahlus-Sunnah Wal-Jamā'at. May Allāh ☙ bestow the correct guidance and understanding upon everyone.

May He make us all true Ahlus-Sunnah Wal-Jamā'at. Āmeen!

Islām and Evolution

Q Can you explain what Evolution is and how wrong Charles Darwin's theory is regarding man? What does the Holy Qur'ān say about the beginning of life?

A The Evolution theory discusses the origin of life on Earth based on a doctrine that all living species evolved from one another i.e. man evolved from apes etc. This theory has been attributed to a well-known Evolutionist, Charles Darwin. To commemorate this great discovery for the Materialists, you can now find him on a £10 note. When this theory was propounded to many Scientists, they refuted it.

Here is a brief explanation of his theory. He proposed that at the beginning there was no life, and suddenly due to great lengths of time and chance the correct conditions were found for life to initiate by itself.

He further theorised that once life had started, then by mutation and natural selection, the simple one-celled creature (amoeba) evolved over a long period of time (millions of years) into all the creatures around us. The theory has been refuted scientifically and by the only true religion, Islām.

I will begin by primarily explaining through logic and science and thereafter conclude with the highest knowledge (Allāh's ﷻ Word).

To this day, no scientist anywhere in the world has been able to start life in a laboratory, even though they have access to the technology, chemicals and knowledge of all mankind from now back to the dawn of science. In fact the starting blocks of life, amino acids, cannot be produced in the laboratory without isolating them and putting them under very specific conditions. If left "cooking" with everything else, they return to the base elements. To elaborate further, the chances of an average protein molecule being arranged in the correct quantity and sequence, in addition to the chance of all the amino acids it contains to be left-handed and being combined with only peptide bonds is one in 10^{950}. That means one chance in a number one with 950 zeros after it. Mathematically proved to be impossible.

However, let's give the believers in evolution the benefit of doubt and say that life came into existence spontaneously.

The next phase of the theory is that one species evolved into another species by mutation. This means that for some reason one creature mutated and that this mutation was beneficial. This mutation was such that the original species had now become a different species altogether.

Let me explain by example: Imagine a fish-type species living in the water which swims about looking for food. Then, a normal pair of male and female fish have a baby fish. However, this baby fish is a mutant and has long legs!

This proves to be an advantage because when food is scarce in the water, the baby fish would walk on to the beach and look for food. It survives, meets another mutant, gives birth to more fish-leg creatures and gradually they evolve to become land creatures, distinctively different from their forefathers i.e. a new species.

There's also a problem with this part of the theory. All the mutations observed in the world have proved to be detrimental and no advantage has been observed, in fact quite the opposite. Research carried out on the fruit fly has produced all sorts of mutants.

Legs growing out of the head, the abdomen, eyes on the abdomen, two pairs of wings, the list is endless. No mutant gave an advantage over its normal parent. Few lived as long as their normal relatives. They had problems moving, eating and in all other activities. When the mutant fruit fly had offspring, then not surprisingly they were normal fruit flies, not mutants.

Let's look back at our land fish. Our land fish needs to mutate several times in order to survive on land because it isn't possible with only legs. It must develop balance and a sense of awareness; its body must be able to cope with the pressure or lack of pressure on the land; it must develop a means of breathing and all the required anatomy; something to protect its eyes; its skin will need to be able to adapt to a dry environment; its digestion system will need to develop as its food has changed and there are many more. All of these mutations have to occur at the same time.

If any one of them is missing, the land fish will not survive. It seems contrary to common sense that all of these mutations occurred after such a long time when, for a period nothing happened and then all of them happened after that, at the same time! There are many other reasons why the evolution theory is flawed, e.g. lack of intermediate species, anomalies (irregularities) and lack of knowledge at the time when the theory was put forward, which is available now, are to name a few; however, that would require a book.

So after all this, why do the Materialists still believe in evolution if it has so many flaws? I will answer that by posing a question. What would they believe in, instead?

Now presenting it in another perspective, if life didn't start by itself then it must have been created. They would then have to acknowledge and accept a Greater Being, a Creator, but the Materialists have everything to lose if they accept that fact.

If evolution is not the means by which we have come about, then how did humans inhabit the world? What was our beginning? Where have we come from? Are we a product of chance or have we a purpose? Did a one-celled being evolve into an ape-like creature and man evolved from him or was man as he is now, from the beginning?

Let us look at the Holy Qur'ān. There are many verses in the Holy Qur'ān, which gives answers to all these questions. However, as before it would require a book to include them. One particular verse which is quoted below, summarises the origin of man and his potential state.

Allāh 🕮 the Creator of the Universe and everything it contains, the One who possesses Infinite Knowledge, in fact who else would know about the origin of man if not the Creator who was there at the time and created man with His Hands. Allāh 🕮 the Almighty says, **"Indeed We created mankind from dried (sounding) clay of altered mud. The Jinn, We created before from a smokeless flame of fire. (Remember) when Your Lord said to the Angels, 'I am going to create a man (Ādam) from dried (sounding) clay of altered mud. So when I have fashioned him completely and breathed into him the soul that I have created for him, then fall down prostrating yourselves to him'."** (Surah al-Hijr 15:26-29)

Makhraj of the Letter Dhād

Q What is the Makhraj (place of pronunciation) of the letter Dhād? Many people pronounce it as a Dhāl. What is the correct way?

A The letter Dhād is pronounced from the back edge of the tongue, upturned, when touching the roots of the molars and the premolars.

There are three ways of pronouncing the Dhād:
1. From the right side.
2. From the left side.
3. From both sides at the same time.

But it is commonly easier to pronounce the Dhād from the left side. The letter Dhād is known as Harfe-Hāfiyah because it is pronounced from the upturned sides of the tongue. The letter Dhād has the Sifat (quality) of Istitālat. Istitālat is that quality which when pronounced, the voice of the letter will remain from the beginning of the Makhraj till the end. This quality is found only in the letter Dhād. The correct way of pronouncing the letters can only be known fully by learning from an experienced and well-versed Qāri. Practical display is essential for these matters.

Branches of Knowledge: The Essential Knowledge for a Mufassir (Commentator)

Q I have come across commentaries of the Holy Qur'ān which are contradictory to the commentaries of our pious predecessors. Many even have translations of verses which are clearly wrong. Such modernists have completely ignored the status of the Holy Qur'ān and have commentated on the Holy Qur'ān according to their own personal opinions. Can you mention in detail the branches of knowledge which are essential pre-requisites for a commentator?

A Specialist scholars have emphasised that anyone wanting to achieve the status of a commentator of the Holy Qur'ān should be well versed in fifteen subjects. These are briefly given below and will show that it is not possible for everybody to understand the underlying significance and real meanings of the Holy Qur'ān or to draw their own conclusions and to commentate.

1. <u>Lughāt</u> - i.e. the philosophy of language, which helps in understanding the appropriate meanings of words. Imām Mujāhid ﷺ says, "One who believes in Allāh ﷻ and the Day of Judgement should not open his lips in respect of the Holy Qur'ān, unless he is thoroughly fluent with the meaning of the Arabic language. Quite often an Arabic word has several meanings. A person may know only one or two of them, though in a given context the actual meaning may be quite different."

2. <u>Nahw</u> - i.e. syntax, a branch of grammar, which helps in understanding the relationship of one sentence with another and also of I'rāb (vowel sounds) of the letters of a particular word. A change in I'rāb often renders a change in the meaning.

3. <u>Sarf</u> - i.e. etymology, another branch of grammar, which helps in knowing the root words and conjugations. The meaning of a word changes with the change in the root and with a change in its conjugation.

Shaykh Ibn Fāris ﷺ says, "One who loses the knowledge of etymology loses a great deal." Shaykh Zamakhshari ﷺ mentions that a certain person sat to translate the verse, **"The Day when We shall call together all human beings with their leader." (17:71)**

He ignorantly mistranslated it thus, "The Day when We shall call together all human beings with their mothers." He misunderstood that the singular Arabic word 'Imām' (i.e. leader which is mentioned in the verse) to be the plural of the Arabic word 'Umm' (mother). If he had been familiar with etymology, he would have known that the plural of 'Umm' is not 'Imām'.

4. <u>Ishtiqāq</u> - i.e. derivatives. It is necessary to have the knowledge of derivatives and their root words, because if a word has been derived from two different root words, it will have two different meanings, e.g. the word 'Maseeh' is derivable from 'Masah' which means to touch over, to move wet hands over, and also from 'Masāhah' which means measurement.

5. <u>Ilmul-Ma'āni</u> - i.e. knowledge of semantics, because phrase constructions are understood from their meanings.

6. Ilmul-Bayān - i.e. knowledge of figurative speech, like similes and meta-phors, due to which expressions or shades of meaning or similes and meta-phors become known.

7. Ilmul-Badee - i.e. knowledge of rhetoric, the knowledge which reveals the beauty of language and its implications.

Note: The last three are the branches of Ilmul Balāghah (knowledge of oratory), and are considered very important subjects, which a commentator should master, because the Holy Qur'ān is a perfect miracle and its amazing constructions can only be understood after mastering these subjects.

8. Ilmul-Qirā'ah - i.e. knowledge of the art of pronunciation, because differ-ent methods of recitation sometimes convey different meanings, and some-times one meaning is to be preferred over the other.

9. Ilmul-Aqā'id - i.e. knowledge of the fundamentals of faith. This is neces-sary to explain certain analogies. The literal meaning of a certain verse refer-ring to Allāh 🌟 may not be correct. For example, the analogy in the verse, **"The Hand of Allāh is over their hands," (48:10)** will have to be explained because Allāh 🌟 has no physical hands.

10. Usoolul-Fiqh - i.e. principles of Islamic Jurisprudence. These are neces-sary for reasoning out and finding arguments in support of statements.

11. Asbābun-Nuzool - i.e. the event which caused the revelation. The mean-ings of a verse will be better understood if we know how and when it had been revealed. Sometimes the true meaning of a verse is understood only if we know the circumstances in which the verse had been revealed.

12. An-Nāsikh wal-Mansūkh - i.e. knowledge of commandments that have subsequently been abrogated or changed so that abrogated commandments may be distinguished from those that are applicable.

13. Ilmul-Fiqh - i.e. knowledge of Islamic Jurisprudence, because it is only through this knowledge that we arrive at a complete understanding of gen-eral principles.

14. <u>Hadeeth</u> - Knowledge of such Ahādeeth that are a commentary on certain verses of the Holy Qur'ān and to be acquainted with the Seerah (biography) of the Holy Prophet 🕌.

15. The last but most important is the Wahabi (bestowed) Ilm, or the gifted understanding, bestowed by Allāh 🕌 upon His selected ones, as it is referred to in the Hadeeth, "Whosoever acts upon what he knows, Allāh 🕌 bestows upon him the knowledge of things not known to him."

It is this special understanding that was implied in the reply of Sayyidunā Ali 🕌 when he was once asked by the people if he had received from the Holy Prophet 🕌 any special knowledge or instructions which were not received by others. Sayyidunā Ali 🕌 replied, "I swear by Him Who made Paradise and created life that I possess nothing special, except the clear understanding which Allāh 🕌 bestows upon a person in regards to the Holy Qur'ān."

Shaykh Ibn Abid Dunyā 🕌 states that the knowledge of the Holy Qur'ān and that which can be derived out of it are as vast as a boundless ocean.

The branches of knowledge described above are the tools, i.e. essential prerequisites for a commentator.

A commentary written by a person who is not thoroughly acquainted with these branches of knowledge will be based on his personal opinion, which is prohibited. The Sahābah 🕌 already had Arabic language as their mother-tongue, and they reached the depth of the rest of the knowledge by means of their illuminating contact that they had with the Holy Popohet 🕌.

Imām Jalāl-ud-Deen Suyūti 🕌 states that those who think that it is beyond the capacity of a man to acquire Wahabi-Ilm (gifted understanding) are not right.

To get this knowledge from Allāh 🕌 one should adopt the means e.g. acting upon the knowledge that one has acquired and disinclination towards the world.

It is stated in 'Keemiyā-e-Sa'ādat' that three people are not blessed with complete understanding of the Holy Qur'ān.

Firstly, one who is not well versed in Arabic. Secondly, one who persists in committing a major sin or indulges in an act of religious innovation, because these actions darken his heart, which in turn prevent him from understanding the Holy Qur'ān. Thirdly, one who is a rationalist, even in the matter of faith, and feels embarrassed when he reads a verse of the Holy Qur'ān which he is not able to fully rationalise.

Allāh ﷻ Knows Best

4. CHAPTER ON

SUNNAH

The Turban

Q Did the Holy Prophet ﷺ wear the turban? Please answer in detail.

A Concerning the turban, Shaykh Muhammad Zakariyya ﷺ has written the following in his commentary of 'Shamāil Tirmizi', 'Khasāil-e-Nabawi', "The tying of the turban is a 'Sunnate-Mustamirrah' (constantly adhered practice of the Holy Prophet ﷺ)."

The Holy Prophet ﷺ has enjoined the tying of the turban. It has been reported, "Tie the turban. It will increase you in patience."

It is also reported that somebody enquired from Sayyidunā Abdullāh Ibn Umar ﷺ whether the tying of the turban was Sunnah or not. He replied in the affirmative.

True love demands that you do everything as your beloved would like to see it. In fact a true devotee of the Holy Prophet ﷺ would be prepared to give his life for the practical preservation of even one minute Sunnah. Such is the overwhelming thirst for emulation present in a true follower that it does not matter to him whether the Sunnah is a constant act or occasional, whether the Sunnah is connected to Ibādah (the manner in which the Holy Prophet ﷺ carried out the various acts of worship) or whether the Sunnah pertains to his habit or lifestyle (the manner of his speech, manner of walking, eating, dressing etc.) As long as it can be determined that our Holy Prophet ﷺ did it, then a true Āshiq-e-Rasool (lover of the Holy Prophet ﷺ) will go to any length to implement it in his life.

The turban is one such Sunnah which every Muslim should adhere to whether he is a scholar or not, whether he is literate or illiterate. It is a misunderstanding by many people that the turban should be tied by the Ulamā only.

There are numerous Ahādeeth which emphasise upon the tying of the turban by the Holy Prophet ﷺ.

1. Sayyidunā Amr Ibn Umayya Damri ﷺ reports, "I saw the Holy Prophet ﷺ making Masah of his Kuffain (leather socks) and turban." (Bukhāri)

2. Sayyidunā Mugheerah Ibn Shu'bah ﷺ reports that the Holy Prophet ﷺ performed Wudhu and made Masah of the front portion of his head as well as of his turban and leather socks. (Muslim)

Note: It is the opinion of most of the Fuqahā (jurists) that Masah of only the turban is not permissible and not sufficient for absolving oneself from the compulsory act of Masah of the head in Wudhu. However one should cover a quarter of the head in Masah and then pass the hand over the turban then it will suffice. Hadeeth No. 2 establishes that this is what the Holy Prophet ﷺ did.

3. Sayyidunā Huraith ﷺ reports that the Holy Prophet ﷺ addressed the people while wearing a black turban. (Muslim, Ibn Abi Shaibah)

In another narration it is reported, "I saw the Holy Prophet ﷺ wearing a black turban." (Tirmizi, Ibn Mājah)

4. Sayyidunā Jābir ﷺ reports that on the occasion of the Conquest of Makkah, the Holy Prophet ﷺ entered Makkah while wearing a black turban.
(Muslim, Tirmizi, Ibn Mājah)

5. It is also reported that the Holy Prophet ﷺ said, "Wear the turban as it is a sign of Islām."

One should note that all these narrations are of the Sahih (absolutely authentic) category.

The Kurta (Long Shirt)

Q Did the Holy Prophet ﷺ wear the Kurta? If he did, can you tell me what the length of his sleeves were and how long the Kurta was? I've observed many people wearing the Jubba (Kurta) below the ankles. Is this correct?

A The Holy Prophet ﷺ preferred the Kurta over all other types of clothing. Sayyidah Umme Salamah ﷺ narrates that the Holy Prophet ﷺ preferred the Kurta over all types of clothing. (Tirmizi, Abū Dāwood, Nasai, Ibn Mājah)

The scholars have attributed the following qualities to the Kurta:

1. It conceals the body better than other forms of clothing such as the Chādar (a loose sheet that used to be worn) and Lungi etc.

2. It does not cost very much and is light in weight that it carries no burden on the wearer.

3. There is humility in its nature.

Shaykh Muhammad Zakariyya ﷺ says in Khasāil-e-Nabawi, "The Kurta is a wonderful concealer of the Satr (that part of the body for which concealment is obligatory) whilst fulfilling the natural demand of beauty and elegance that we have in our choice of dress."

Regarding the length, Sayyidunā Abdullāh Ibn Abbās ﷺ reports that lengthwise the Kurta of the Holy Prophet ﷺ would be above his ankles whilst the sleeves would reach up to his fingers. It is therefore prohibited to wear any clothes, whether it be the Jubba, lungi, trousers etc. below the ankles.

It is reported by Sayyidunā Abdullāh Ibn Umar ﷺ that if Isbāl (allowing clothing to be excessively long which is prohibited) occurs with the Lungi, Kurta or turban, then on the Day of Judgement, Allāh ﷻ will not look towards that individual who wore excessively long clothes (that flows beneath the ankles) due to pride.

Shu'ba ﷺ reports that he met Muhārib Ibn Dinār ﷺ, whilst the latter was riding a horse on his way to the court for a case. I asked him about this particular Hadeeth. He replied that he heard Sayyidunā Abdullāh Ibn Umar ﷺ saying that the Holy Prophet ﷺ said, "He who wears excessively long clothes (which flow below the ankles) due to pride, Allāh ﷻ will not look towards him (with mercy) on the Day of Judgement."

Shu'ba ﷺ says that he asked Muhārib ﷺ whether Sayyidunā Abdullāh Ibn Umar ﷺ had mentioned only the Lungi (i.e. does this only apply to the Lungi?) Muhārib ﷺ replied that the ruling was general and applies to all types of clothing i.e. Kurta, Lungi, turban, trousers and Jubbas etc. (Bukhāri)

Some people are of the habit of objecting to this ruling by claiming that they wear their clothing below the ankles but this is not done out of pride. The implication is that they consider themselves exempt from this warning. Such people should consider the following Hadeeth of the Holy Prophet ﷺ, "Guard against lengthening your clothes (below the ankles) for such lengthening itself is an act of pride." (Abū Dāwood)

It is thus understood that wearing the clothes below the ankles will be viewed as an act of pride in the eyes of Allāh ﷻ whether motivated by such intentions or not. Yet people are unaware of this and explain their wrong actions with feeble and weak excuses.

Length of the Kurta

Q **What is the Sunnah length of the Kurta?**

A The Kurta should be below the knees and well above the ankles. It should be about midway between the knees and the ankles. The below ankle-length worn by many people nowadays is not permissible.

Shaving the Head

Q **Many people hold the view that shaving the head is a Sunnah practice. They quote the practice of Sayyidunā Ali ﷺ who habitually shaved his head. What is the correct view?**

A Allowing the hair to grow long on the entire head is Sunnah. However, shaving or cutting the hair is Mubāh (permitted).

The shaving of the head on occasions other than Hajj and Umrah is not established from the practice of the Holy Prophet ﷺ. However, there is no established Hadeeth where the Holy Prophet ﷺ prohibited men from shaving the head. Similar was the habit of the Sahābah ﷺ except for Sayyidunā Ali ﷺ who habitually shaved his head.

Sayyidunā Ali ﷺ on grounds of precaution in matters of Ghusl used to remove his hair completely. He himself narrates that the Holy Prophet ﷺ said, "Impurity (Janābat) exists beneath every strand of hair." (Mishkāt)

Complying with the mentioned Hadeeth he states, "The one who overlooks an area equivalent to a single strand whilst performing Ghusl-Janābat (bathing after ritual impurity) will be dealt like this and like that in Hell." (A reference to strict punishment). Upon narrating this, he states, "Owing to the declaration of such threatening phrases, I chose to create enmity with my head (i.e. remove all my hair)."

It is reported in Mawāhib, "To the best of my knowledge, shaving the head is not an established practice of the Holy Prophet ﷺ except on the occasion of Umrah and Hajj. Hence, allowing the hair to grow is Sunnah. Not to keep hair is also Mubāh (permissible) without rejecting the established Sunnah."

Certain scholars support the view that both Halq (shaving of the head) and Tark (allowing hair to grow) are Sunnah practices. But the first view is more authentic.

Accepting Invitations

Q **What is the ruling regarding accepting invitations? Many a times incidents take place which are contrary to the Shari'ah. What should one do on these occasions?**

A To accept an invitation is a Sunnah of the Holy Prophet ﷺ. Sayyidunā Anas ⚬ reports that once a tailor prepared food and invited the Holy Prophet ﷺ. Sayyidunā Anas ⚬ says that he accompanied the Holy Prophet ﷺ. In another Hadeeth, Sayyidunā Abū Moosā al-Ash'ari ⚬ relates that the Holy Prophet ﷺ said, "Free the slaves, accept the invitations of those who invite you and visit the sick." (Bukhāri)

Sayyidunā Abdullāh Ibn Umar ⚬ relates a similar Hadeeth that the Holy Prophet ﷺ said, "Accept the invitation when you are invited." (Muslim)

Furthermore, in one Hadeeth the Holy Prophet ﷺ admonishes a person who does not accept invitations. Sayyidunā Abū Hurairah ⚬ narrates that the Holy Prophet ﷺ said, "Whoever does not accept an invitation has disobeyed Allāh ﷻ and His Messenger ﷺ." (Bukhāri)

But we have to remember that these Ahādeeth apply only when the invitation conforms to the Sunnah and it is based on sincerity. When the objective is to show off or boast, or expecting to receive something in return or the arrangements contradict the Sunnah, or only the wealthy are invited, then it would be permissible, and in certain cases compulsory to decline the invitation. For this precise reason, Islām has discouraged from attending such invitations where the laws of Islām will be violated.

Imām Nawāwi ﷺ writes that if the following things occur, a person will be discouraged from attending:

1.   A person doubts if the food is Halāl.
2.   Only wealthy people are invited.
3.   Evil people will be present in the gathering.
4.   The invitation is given for show.
5.   It is an occasion where evil will take place.
6.   Alcohol will be served.
7.   People will be sitting on silky cloths.
8.   Gold or silver utensils will be used.

Nowadays, generally most invitations contain at least one of the above evils. Hence we should be more precautious in accepting invitations.

Drawing Lots

Q The Holy Prophet ﷺ drew lots before he went on any journey. Can you quote any Hadeeth regarding this matter?

A It is reported on the authority of Sayyidah Ā'ishah ﷺ that when the Holy Prophet ﷺ intended to go on a journey, he used to draw lots amongst his wives. Whosoever's name came out, used to accompany the Holy Prophet ﷺ in that journey. (Bukhāri, Muslim)

Virtues of Shaking Hands

Q What is the virtue of shaking hands and when should it be done?

A Imām Abu Dāwood ﷺ has mentioned a Hadeeth in his Sunan in which the Holy Prophet ﷺ mentions, "When two Muslims meet each other and shake hands, their (minor) sins are forgiven before they depart."

(Abū Dāwood)

It is Sunnah to shake hands when a Muslim greets another Muslim with Salām. Sayyidunā Abū Dharr ﷺ reports that the Holy Prophet ﷺ shook his hands every time they met. (Abū Dāwood)

According to a Hadeeth of Tirmizi, the Musāfahah is a completion of Salām. Therefore, Salām should be said before shaking hands. Many a times people make Musāfahah without doing Salām. This is contrary to the noble practice of the Holy Prophet ﷺ. Shaykh Ashraf Ali Thānwi ﷺ says, "It is permissible to shake hands upon arrival and upon departure."

Allāh ﷻ Knows Best

5. CHAPTER ON

SALĀH

Salāh whilst the T.V is On

Q A person is watching the T.V whilst another person is performing his Salāh. The person who is watching, puts the volume completely down and the person who is performing the Salāh is in front of the T.V (his back is facing the T.V). Will his Salāh be accepted or not?

A The person's Salāh will be correct. However the person who is at the time watching the T.V will be sinful for disrespecting the Salāh and the recitation of the Holy Qur'ān.

Salāh Wearing Tight Clothes

Q If a person performs Salāh with tight trousers which reveals the shape of the body, is the Salāh valid?

A Although the Salāh is valid, it is Makrooh (disliked) and sinful to perform Salāh in this shameless way. It is not permissible to display the shape of the Satr with such tight-fitting garments.

Second Jamā'at (congregation) after the First has Finished

Q A group of people reached the Masjid at such a time when the Jamā'at (congregational) Salāh had already finished. What should the group of people do? Should they perform Salāh in congregation or individually and should the Adhān and Iqāmat be given?

A In the mentioned situation, the group of people should perform the Salāh individually without Adhān and Iqāmat. It is Makrooh to perform a second congregation in the same place where the previous congregation was held.

It is written in Mabsooth of Imām Sarakhsi ✿: "If a group of people reach the Masjid at such a time when the Salāh has been performed then it is Makrooh for them to perform the Salāh in congregation with Adhān and Iqāmat, but instead they should perform it separately without Adhān and Iqāmat." (Mabsooth, Chapter of Adhān)

Raising Hands for Du'ā after Adhān

Q Is it Sunnah to recite the Du'ā with the hands raised after the Adhān has been called out? In my Masjid some people raise their hands and read the Du'ā whilst others read the Du'ā without raising them. What is the correct way?

A To raise the hands when reciting the Du'ā after Adhān is not evident from any Hadeeth itself. Nevertheless, the raising of the hands for supplication itself is proven from numerous Ahādeeth. Therefore the lifting of the hands for the supplication will not be against the Sunnah. But keeping in mind that it is not evident from the Ahādeeth to raise the hands at this particular moment, it will be more virtuous not to raise the hands. It is also not appropriate to argue and cause disunity amongst each other for these kind of matters.

Nafl (Optional) Salāh in the Sitting Posture

Q Many people perform the two Rak'āts of Nafl after the Witr in a sitting posture. They claim that the Holy Prophet 🌸 performed them sitting down. What was the Holy Prophet's 🌸 practice?

A It is superior and more virtuous to perform the two Nafl Rak'āts after the Witr standing. The Holy Prophet 🌸 stated that there is only half the reward for performing the Nafl Salāh sitting. Both these methods are proven from the practice of the Holy Prophet 🌸 but he used to attain the full reward even when he performed the Nawāfil (optional prayers) in a sitting position.

This was specific for him only because in this, it was a practical lesson for the followers that standing was not obligatory for the Nawāfil. It was amongst the duties of the Holy Prophet 🌸 to educate the Ummah through practical demonstrations as well as through statements. Hence, performing the Nafl in a sitting posture infact was discharging one of the duties (of educating), the reward of which is greater than of Nafl Salāh.

Takbeer of Salāh

Q When should the Takbeer of Salāh start and when should it end? I refer here to the Takbeers of Ruku and Sajdah. Many Imāms either make it so short that it is hard to differentiate between the different postures, whilst many continue the Takbeer long after they've gone into Ruku or Sajdah. What is the correct method?

A The Sunnah method of reciting the Takbeers of Ruku and Sajdah is to commence while bending for Ruku and finishing with it and similarly the Takbeer of Sajdah should commence while going into Sajdah and terminated with it (i.e. on reaching the ground). To recite the Takbeer in the position of Ruku and Sajdah is against the Sunnah.

There are two incorrect things in this situation. Firstly, for wasting the prescribed time of Takbeer and secondly for reciting it late, because this is the time of reciting the Tasbeeh of Ruku and Sajdah and not for reciting the Takbeer. (Munyatul-Musalli)

Duration between Fardh and Sunnah Salāh

Q For what duration can a person delay in performing his Sunnah Salāh after his Fardh?

A A person can recite different Du'ās and Tasbeehāt after his Fardh before commencing his Sunnate-Muakkadah. This is proven by different Ahādeeth. It is reported by Sayyidunā Mugheerah Ibn Shubah ⁕ that the Holy Prophet ⁕ recited the following Du'ā after his Fardh Salāh, (translation): "There is no one worthy of worship except Allāh ⁕. He is alone. He has no partner. For Him is the kingdom and for Him is all praise. He gives and takes lives. In His hand is all good and He is all powerful, O Allāh ⁕ none can prevent that which You bestow and none can bestow that which You prevent and the wealth of the rich cannot help them (from Your anger) for wealth is from You." (Bukhāri, Muslim)

It is reported in Saheeh al-Muslim, "Whoever recites regularly 33 times Sub-hān-Allāh, 33 times Alhamdulillāh and 34 times Allāhu-Akbar after every Fardh Salāh will never be unsuccessful."

In one Hadeeth, it is mentioned that all his sins will be forgiven, even though they may be as numerous as the waves of the ocean.

The Tasbeehs were specially taught to Sayyidah Fātimah 🌸 by the Holy Prophet ﷺ. They are thus known as the Tasbeehāt-e-Fātimee.

It is reported by Sayyidunā Ali ؓ that he heard the Holy Prophet ﷺ whilst he was on the pulpit saying, "The person who recites Āyatul-Kursi after each Salāh, there is no barrier between him and Paradise except death."

It is stated in Durrul-Mukhtār, "There is no harm in delaying the Sunnah by engaging in Du'ā."

Nevertheless, it is undesirable to prolong the Du'ās and Tasbeehāt after that Fardh Salāh which is followed by Sunnah Salāh i.e. Zuhr, Maghrib and Ishā. Shaykh Ashraf Ali Thānwi ؓ states: "Those Fardh Salāh where Sunnats and Nawāfil are to be performed after i.e. Zuhr, Maghrib and Ishā then one must not engage in a prolonged Du'ā immediately after the Fardh Salāh but rather make a concise Du'ā and thereafter perform the Sunnats and Nawāfil as they are more virtuous than Du'ā. Whereas after Fajr and Asr it will not be Makrooh (disliked) to do a lengthy Du'ā." (Beheshti Zewar)

Tahajjud in Congregation

Q Is it permissible to perform Tahajjud in congregation?

A Tahajjud Salāh should be performed individually. To perform it in congregation is Makrooh. If however, sometimes two, three men gather without calling each other and perform it in congregation, then it is not Makrooh.

It is an unanimous verdict that it is not Makrooh to perform it when there are only two people beside the Imām. There is a difference of opinion if there are three, however the gathering of four is Makrooh. (Shāmi)

It is written in Majmuah Fatāwa Sadiyyah, "To perform Tahajjud Salāh by calling people is Makrooh and without calling, if by chance, one, two or three individuals follow the Imām, then it is not Makrooh."

It is mentioned in Fatāwa Rasheediyah, "The congregation for optional Salāh except those particular ones that are proven from the Ahādeeth is Makrooh."

It is written in the books of Fiqh that if there is calling and summoning, which means the gathering of four men to be followers in Salāh then it is Makrooh. However, congregation for the Salāh at the time of solar eclipse, Tarāweeh Salāh and Salāh for rain (Istisqā) is correct, for the rest it is Makrooh. (Fatāwa Rasheediyah)

In another place it is written: "A congregation for voluntary prayers (Nawāfil) whether it is Tahajjud or some other Salāh, (except Tarāweeh Salāh, Salāh at the time of a solar eclipse and Salāh for rain) is Makrooh according to Imām Abū Haneefah ﷺ, if there are four followers in Salāh, regardless of whether they gather voluntarily or on calling. There is difference of opinion regarding three and there is no Karāhat (dislike) for two."

(Fatāwa Rasheediyah)

Nevertheless, the Tahajjud Salāh in the month of Ramadhān according to certain Ulamā is exempt from this ruling.

Differences between Males and Females in Salāh

Q **Can you please explain the main differences between the Salāh of a male and a female.**

A The Fuqahā have explained the differences between the Salāh of a male and a female in almost all of the books of Fiqh. Some of them are:

1. A male will lift his hands in line with the ears when saying the Takbeer-e-Tahreemah. A female will lift her hands up to the shoulders.

2. A male will place his hands below the navel and a female will place her hands on the chest.

3. A male will clutch the left wrist with the thumb and the small finger and leave the remaining three fingers straight. A female will merely place the right palm on the back of the left palm.

4. A male will perform Ruku in such a way that the head, back and posterior (buttocks) are in a straight line. A female will only bend so much that her hands can reach her knees.

5. A male will keep the fingers apart when placing them on the knees in Ruku. A female will join the fingers.

6. A male will separate his lower abdomen from the thighs and the forearms from the armpits in Sajdah. A female will keep the lower abdomen attached to the thighs and armpits.

7. A male will raise the elbows from the ground whilst in Sajdah. A female will keep the elbows on the ground.

8. A male will make Sajdah with the toes flush on the ground facing the Qiblah. A female will not do likewise. Her feet will remain in place as they were in the sitting posture.

9. A male will sit with the right foot vertical and the left foot horizontal. A female will sit on the posterior with both feet protruding (coming out) from the right side.

Folding the Hands Below the Navel

Q I have observed many people performing Salāh. Some keep the hands below the navel whilst others keep them above the navel and below the chest. Yet others have their hands kept on the sides. What should I do in this situation? Can you explain the differences?

A These differences are due to the different schools of thought. According to Imām Abū Haneefah ﷺ, the Sunnah method is to place one hand upon the other below the navel.

This is proven from a Hadeeth narrated by Sayyidunā Abū Juhaifah ﷺ that Sayyidunā Ali ﷺ said, 'The Sunnah method is to place one palm upon the other below the navel." (Abū Dāwood)

Hence, a person following the Hanafi Fiqh should place the palm of his right hand on the back portion of the left hand, clutching the wrist with the thumb and the small finger of the right hand, as well as keeping the remaining three fingers straight on the left hand. This method is applicable to males only. A female should place her right palm on the back of the left without clutching the wrist (like males) as well as placing her hands on her chest.

A person following the Hanbali Madhab (school of thought) can keep his hands above or below the navel. A person following the Māliki Madhab will keep his hands on the sides. According to Imām Shāfi'ee 🕮 the hands will be kept above the navel on the chest. This is substantiated by a Hadeeth reported by Sayyidunā Wā'il Ibn Hujr 🕮 who states, "I performed Salāh with the Holy Prophet 🕮. He placed his right hand upon the left on the chest." (Ibn Khuzaimah)

According to the unanimous verdict of the scholars all the Madhabs (schools of thought) are correct.

Times of Each Salāh

Q Can you explain to me the beginning and ending time of each Salāh? I have just started performing my five times Salāh and I will be very happy if you could explain each Salāh time clearly.

A It is best for you to follow your local Masjid timetable. It usually has the starting and ending time written on them. Nevertheless, the times are mentioned below:

Fajr - It commences at Subah Sādiq (true dawn) and finishes until just prior to sunrise. Subah Sādiq commences when a whitish light that spreads horizontally, appears on the eastern horizon.

Zuhr - It commences after Zawāl (i.e. when the sun begins to decline from its zenith). It ends when the shadow of an object becomes twice the size of the object in addition to the shadow of the object cast at Zawāl.

Asr - It commences when the shadow of an object becomes twice its size in addition to the shadow cast at Zawāl, and finishes at sunset.

Maghrib - It begins after sunset and ends when the whitish light on the western horizon disappears.

Ishā - It begins when the whitish light on the western horizon disappears and ends before Subah Sādiq.

Fajr Salāh at Sunrise

Q Can I perform my Fajr Salāh when the sun is rising?

A It is prohibited to perform any type of Salāh including Fajr during the three times which are mentioned below:

Sunrise - From the moment the tip of the sun is visible until the sun has fully risen (i.e. all of the sun is visible).

Zawāl - At midday when the sun is at its zenith (highest point).

Sunset - From the moment the bottom tip of the sun touches the horizon till the sun has disappeared from sight.

Note: It is Makrooh to perform Janāzah Salāh or perform Sajdah Tilāwat during the above times.

Reciting the Holy Qur'ān without Moving the Lips

Q I have observed many brothers performing their Salāh in such a way that they do not move their lips when reciting the Holy Qur'ān. Is such a Salāh valid?

A The Salāh will not be valid by merely running the thoughts of the words and phrases of the Holy Qur'ān in one's mind (i.e. reading in one's mind). It is compulsory to recite the words by moving the tongue and lips. Also the recitation of the Holy Qur'ān must be done with correct pronunciation and Tajweed. This is impossible without moving the lips and tongue.

(Fatāwa Hindiyyah)

103

Sajdah Tilāwat

Q What is the method of Sajdah Tilāwat, and is it compulsory to make Sajdah?

A There are fourteen verses of Sajdah in the Holy Qur'ān where it is Wājib to perform Sajdah after reciting or listening to any one of them. There are two Fardh for the validity of Sajdah Tilāwat without which the Sajdah will be invalid; Takbeer (without raising the hands) and the Sajdah. Its pre-requisites (conditions) are similar to those of normal Salāh e.g facing the Qiblah, Wudhu, clean place etc. The method of Sajdah Tilāwat is to face the Qiblah and make the intention. Then whilst saying the Takbeer go into Sajdah without lifting the hands to the ears. Recite the Tasbeeh in Sajdah and thereafter stand up by saying the Takbeer.

Salāh on Board an Aeroplane

Q What is the ruling regarding performing Salāh on board an aeroplane? Should a person repeat his Salāh after landing?

A A person should perform his Salāh on board an aeroplane. There is no need to repeat the Salāh performed in the air especially when a person is able to stand, perform Ruku and Sajdah properly and face the Qiblah. If the plane changes direction during the Salāh, it will still be valid.

The Salāh of the Hanafi Madhab in the Light of Ahādeeth

Q I met a brother who claims that those people who are following the Hanafi Madhab are not performing the Salāh correctly. He claims that in Salāh the hands should be positioned on the chest and not beneath the navel. Bismillāh and Āmeen should be recited loudly. Sūrah al-Fātihah should be recited by the Muqtadi behind the Imām, and we should raise the hands at the times when we go to Ruku and Sajdah. Are his claims correct? Are there any Hadeeth to prove the authenticity of the Salāh according to the Hanafi Madhab? Can you please quote the Ahādeeth to clarify this important issue.

A At the present time, some individuals have emerged who claim that the Hanafi Madhab is wrong in matters pertaining to Salāh. They are in fact wrong themselves for making such assertions. Alhamdulillāh, the Salāh according to the Hanafi Madhab is completely in accordance with the Ahādeeth of the Holy Prophet 鷺. Regarding the position of the hands in Qiyām (the standing posture), Sayyidunā Ali 鷺 states, "To place one palm over the other, beneath the navel is from the Sunnah of Salāh."

(Abū Dāwood)

Regarding reciting Bismillāh silently, Sayyidunā Anas 鷺 narrates, "I performed Salāh behind the Holy Prophet 鷺, Abū Bakr, Umar and Uthmān 鷺 and I did not hear any of them reciting Bismillāh loudly." (Muslim)

Regarding the saying of Āmeen softly, Sayyidunā Wā'il Ibn Hujr 鷺 narrates that he performed Salāh behind the Holy Prophet 鷺 who when reaching ⟪Ghyril maghdhoobi alayhim waladh-dhwālleen⟫ said Āmeen, keeping his voice subdued. (Ahmad)

Regarding the recitation of Sūrah al-Fātihah behind the Imām, Sayyidunā Abū Hurairah 鷺 narrates that the Holy Prophet 鷺 said, "The Imām has been appointed to be followed. Thus when he says the Takbeer, you also say it, when he recites, remain silent and when he says 'Sami-Allāhu liman hami-dah', say 'Rabbanā lakal hamd'. (Nasai)

Friday Khutbah (Sermon) in English

Q Is it permissible to deliver the Jumu'ah Khutbah in English. In many Masājid, Imāms have commenced the Khutbah in the English language. They argue that the Jumu'ah Khutbah is a lecture, hence it can be given in English or in the language which the people understand. What is the Islamic verdict on this mater?

A The argument that the Jumu'ah Khutbah is a mere 'lecture', therefore it can be given in English or in the language which the people understand, is not correct. In reality, the Friday Khutbah is a form of Dhikrullah (remembrance of Allāh 鷺), and it is absolutely necessary that the Ibādah of Dhikr is carried out in the language of the Holy Qur'ān.

Allāh 🕮 states in the Holy Qur'ān, **"O you who believe! When you are called to Salāh on Friday, hasten towards the Dhikr (i.e. Friday Salāh and Khutbah) of Allāh."** (62:09)

This verse was revealed regarding the Jumu'ah Salāh and the Jumu'ah Khutbah. The term used by Allāh 🕮 in the verse to describe the Jumu'ah Salāh and the Khutbah is Dhikr. All the commentators of the Holy Qur'ān are unanimous in their opinion that the Jumu'ah Khutbah is a form of Dhikr, a Fardh Dhikr.

Sayyidunā Abū Hurairah 🕮 narrates (which is an extract from a long Hadeeth) that the Holy Prophet 🕮 said that when the Imām emerges (i.e. to deliver the Khutbah) then the Angels are present listening to the Dhikr.

(Bukhāri and Muslim)

When this fact is established that the Friday Khutbah is a compulsory Ibādah like the Fardh Salāh, then we should come to the Islamic verdict, "There is no doubt in the fact that the Khutbah in a language other than Arabic is contrary to the Sunnah transmitted from the Holy Prophet 🕮 and the Sahābah 🕮, hence it (the non-Arabic Khutbah) is strictly forbidden."

(Umdatur-Riāyah)

If the Friday Khutbah was a mere 'lecture' then there would have been no need for the stipulation of the many conditions and factors which pertain to the Khutbah of Jumu'ah.

Majlisul Ulamā of South Africa have prepared an excellent booklet entitled, 'The Position of the Friday Khutbah in Islām' in which they have stated 25 such differences between the Friday Khutbah and other lectures.

The Language of the Jumu'ah Khutbah

Q Until now I have been listening to the Jumu'ah Khutbah in Arabic. But recently in few Masājid they have commenced the Khutbah in the English language which the majority of the audience can understand. They claim that the audience cannot understand the Khutbah in Arabic, hence there is no benefit.

A The Khutbah of Jumuah is not essentially a lecture meant for the people. Rather, it is a part of the Salāh of Jumu'ah. It is evident that the number of Rak'āt in Zuhr Salāh is four. On the day of Jumu'ah, two Rak'āt have been substituted by the Khutbah, which basically is a form of Dhikr (remembrance of Allāh 🌣) and it is by this name that it has been referred to in the Holy Qur'ān.

Allāh 🌣 says, **"O you who believe! When you are called to Salāh on Friday, hasten towards the remembrance (i.e. Friday Salāh and Khutbah) of Allāh." (62:09)**

Therefore, being a part of Dhikr, it can only be performed entirely in Arabic, and just as the Salāh of Jumuah cannot be performed in English or any other language, the Khutbah cannot be delivered in any language other than Arabic.

If we refer back to history and observe the victories of the Sahābah 🌣, we discover that the Sahābah 🌣 travelled to different parts of the world to preach Islām. However, they never used a local language whilst offering the Khutbah of Jumuah. They relatively used the local language in normal lectures and sermons but not in the prescribed Khutbah of Friday. This helps the Muslims in at least being in verbal contact with Arabic, the language of the Holy Qur'ān and Sunnah.

To Remain Seated at the Beginning of Tarāweeh

Q When the Tarāweeh Salāh begins, some people remain seated at the back. As the Imām goes into Ruku, they quickly join the Salāh. How is that?

A Doing this is Makrooh and disliked because this clearly displays laziness in performing Salāh and is also the habit of the hypocrites.

Passing Across the Children's Row

Q I arrived for Salāh late and the rows were already formed. Is it permissible for me to pass the children's row to join the adults row?

A It is permissible to pass across the children's row in order to fill up a vacant space in the front row.

Space between the Feet

Q What is the least amount of space which should be kept between the two feet?

A The Fuqahā (jurists) have stated that there should be at least four fingers space between the two feet. The toes should be pointing straight ahead towards the Qiblah. It is against the Sunnah to angle the feet towards the right hand side or left hand side.

Yawning in Salāh

Q How can one restrain his yawning in Salāh? I am usually yawning in nearly every Salāh.

A The urge to yawn can be suppressed by pressing the teeth upon the lower lip. If it cannot be suppressed in this manner, then one should place the right hand over the mouth whilst one is in the standing posture. In other postures, one should place the left hand over the mouth. Another effective method is to create the thought and say to oneself that the Holy Prophet ﷺ never yawned.

The author of Qudoori (a famous Fiqh Kitāb) has written that he used this method and he succeeded. Imām Shāmi ﷺ also had the same successful result. We should adopt these methods to restrain ourselves from yawning because yawning is from Shaytān.

Congregational Salāh with One's Wife

Q On missing the Jamā'at in the Masjid, will it be permissible to perform Salāh in congregation with one's wife at home?

A Yes, it will be permissible, but the woman (wife) should not stand beside the Imām (husband), instead she should stand behind him. (Shāmi)

Reciting the same Sūrah in both Rak'āts

Q What is the ruling if one recites the same Sūrah in both of the Rak'āts?

A It is Makrooh Tanzeehi (undesirable) to recite (without any valid reason) the same Sūrah in both the Rak'āts of Fardh Salāh. But it is permissible (will not be Makrooh) to recite the same Sūrah in both Rak'āts of Nafl Salāh.

Reciting Bismillāh before the Sūrah

Q After reciting Sūrah Al-Fātihah, should one recite Bismillāh before commencing the recitation of another Sūrah?

A It is Mustahab to recite the complete Tasmiyah ⟨Bismillāhir-Rahmānir-Raheem⟩ softly before commencing the recitation of another Sūrah. (Shāmi)

Reciting Sūrah Al-Fātihah in Place of Tashahhud

Q If a person mistakenly recites Sūrah al-Fātihah in the place of At-Tāhiyyātu (Tashahhud) or Tashahhud in the place of Sūrah al-Fātihah then will his Salāh be valid?

A In both circumstances, Sajdah Sahw (remedial prostration) will be compulsory otherwise the Salāh will be invalid.

Leaving One Sūrah Gap

Q I recited Sūrah al-Feel in the first Rak'at of my Salāh and in the second Rak'at, I recited Sūrah al-Mā'oon. Does this have any affect on my Salāh?

A To intentionally omit only one Sūrah in Fardh Salāh between two Sūrahs as mentioned is Makrooh (undesirable). There is a scope of permissibility of doing this in Nawāfil (optional Salāh). (Shāmi, Fatāwa Raheemiyah)

Witr and Sunnats whilst Travelling

Q What is the ruling regarding the Witr Salāh and the Sunnat-e-Muakkadah whilst travelling. Do we have to perform them?

A It is not permissible to perform any Wājib, Sunnat-e-Muakkadah or Sunnat Ghair Muakkadah Salāh as Qasr (in an abridged manner i.e. instead of four Rak'āts to perform two Rak'āts).

Since the three Rak'āts of Witr are Wājib, it is not permissible to omit them even whilst travelling. However, the emphasis on Sunnat-e-Muakkadah Salāh does not apply whilst on a journey and a Musāfir (traveller) will be excused for not performing them. However, if one is not in a hurry and the journey is not too stressful or if there is no fear of losing one's companion or transport then it is best to perform the Sunnat-e-Muakkadah of Fajr Salāh and Maghrib Salāh because these have been greatly emphasised in the Ahādeeth.

If a Musāfir performs any of the Sunnah Salāh, they will cease to be Sunnah and will become Nafl (optional).

Adhān and Iqāmat whilst Travelling

Q Whilst on a journey, is it necessary to perform Adhān and Iqāmat or can they be omitted?

A Whilst on a journey, it is Mustahab for the traveller to call out Adhān and Iqāmat to perform Salāh in congregation. If they only call out the Iqāmat, then it will also suffice. It will be Makrooh for them to perform Salāh in Jamā'at without both the Adhān and Iqāmat unless they are at a place where the Adhān is called out regularly or they fear that the calling of Adhān will lead to some problems or them being mocked at.

Woman Leading Men in Salāh

Q Can a woman lead men in Jumuah Salāh? What does Islām say regarding this matter? Did this kind of incident ever occur at the time of the Holy Prophet ﷺ? Please can you answer in full detail according to the four schools of thought in the light of the Holy Qur'ān and Ahādeeth.

A All the Fuqahā (jurists) are unanimous that a woman cannot lead men in Salāh. If any man performs his Salāh behind a female Imām, his Salāh would be invalid. The Holy Prophet ﷺ said, "When the time for Salāh approaches, then a man amongst you must call out the Adhān and then a man who is the eldest amongst you should lead the Salāh." (Bukhāri)

Below are the opinions of each of the four schools of thought:
1. Hanafi Madhab: "It is not permissible for men to follow a woman in Salāh." (Hidāya)

2. Shāfi'ee Madhab: "A male following a woman in Salāh is incorrect."
(Minhāj)

3. Māliki Madhab: "Salāh will therefore not be correct behind a woman (Imām)." (Bulghatus-Sālik)

4. Hanbali Madhab: "It is not correct in the opinion of the general Fuqahā for a man to follow a woman (in Salāh)." (Al-Mughni Ibn Qudāmah)

Woman Leading Men in Salāh

Q Why can't a woman lead men in Salāh?

A 1. Nothing has been narrated regarding its permissibility from the Holy Prophet ﷺ or the Sahābah ؓ or the Tābi'een ؓ. Had it been permissible, it would have definitely been recorded in the books of Ahādeeth and Fiqh.

2. On the contrary, the Holy Prophet ﷺ had commanded the women to stand at the rear of the congregation (if they do attend the congregational Salāh). The reason being is that women have been commanded to observe Hijāb. If men have to follow a woman Imām in Salāh, they would have to stand behind her. This is in total conflict with the rules of Hijāb.
(Bidāyatul Mujtahid)

3. The Holy Prophet ﷺ said, "A woman should not lead a man in Salāh."
(Ibn Mājah)

Woman Leading a Purely Female Congregation

Q What if a woman leads a purely female congregation? What does Islām say in this particular matter?

A The four schools of thought demonstrate different teachings in light of this subject.

The Hanafi School of Thought
It is however Makrooh Tahreemi for women to form their own congregation. However, if a woman leads the Salāh of a purely female congregation, then the Salāh will be correct (Hidāyah). This is because it is narrated that Sayyidah Umme Salamah ﷺ and Sayyidah Ā'ishah ﷺ used to lead the women in Salāh. (Musannaf Ibn Abi Shaybah)

The Māliki School of Thought
A woman in no circumstance can be the Imām even if the congregation be entirely females. The Salāh of even a woman behind a female Imām is invalid. (Bulghatus-Sālik)

The Shāfi'ee School of Thought
A woman can be the Imām of a purely female congregation. In fact it is Mustahab for them to form their own congregation. (Al-Mughni)

The Hanbali School of Thought
The Salāh of a woman behind a woman is permissible. There is however difference of opinion regarding women forming their own congregation (behind a female Imām). (Al-Mughni)

It is narrated from Sayyidunā Ali ﷺ, "A woman cannot be an Imām," and from Nāfi ﷺ, "I do not know that a woman can lead the women in Salāh." Hanafi scholars also explain that when a woman does lead a purely female congregation, she has one of two options:

1. She stands in front of the first row (just as a male Imām would do). This is however Makrooh because it is contrary to the spirit of Hijāb.

2. She could stand in the middle of the first row (as Sayyidah Ā'ishah 🌸 and Sayyidah Umme Salamah 🌸 did).

This is however also Makrooh because it is Wājib (necessary) in a congregational Salāh that the Imām stands a little in front of the first row.

(Fathul-Qadeer)

Hanafi jurists therefore explain the Hadeeth of Sayyidah Ā'ishah 🌸 and Sayyidah Umme Salamah 🌸 as Mansūkh (abrogated).

Although Shaykh Kamāl Ibn Humām 🌸 has, after discussing the possibility of abrogation, concluded that purely female congregations are Makrooh-e-Tahreemi. The Fatwa (preferred verdict) is also on Tahreem (prohibition). A purely female congregation is Makrooh-e-Tahreemi, even in Tarāweeh.

(Durrul-Mukhtār)

Tarāweeh Salāh 8 or 20?

Q **How many Rak'āts are there in Tarāweeh? Is there any evidence for it from the Holy Prophet 🌸? Some people argue that there are only eight Rak'āts in the Tarāweeh Salāh and there is no evidence of 20 Rak'āts. Can you explain in detail the correct amount of Rak'āts in the light of the Holy Qur'ān and Ahādeeth.**

A Approximately for twelve hundred and fifty years there was very little controversy regarding this issue. It was only at the beginning of the 20th century that some people began to insist that the number of Rak'āts in Tarāweeh Salāh is eight. It was the consensus of the Sahābahs 🌸 and the Tābi'een 🌸 and those that followed them until today that there are twenty Rak'āts of Tarāweeh. Tarāweeh Salāh is Sunnat-e-Muak'kadah for both men and women. There is evidence from the Hadeeth of the Holy Prophet 🌸 and his Sahābah 🌸. The Tābi'een 🌸 (successors of the Sahābah 🌸) and the leading religious scholars like Imām Abū Haneefah, Imām Shāfi'ee and Imām Ahmad Ibn Hanbal 🌸 held the view that there are twenty Rak'āts in Tarāweeh. Imām Mālik 🌸, too, has also considered it to have twenty Rak'āts in one of his statements. The four Imāms did not adopt less than twenty Rak'āts of Tarāweeh. This is an unanimous verdict and the whole Ummah have acted accordingly till this day.

Twenty Rak'āts are offered in the Masjid ul-Harām in Makkah and the Masjid un-Nabawi in Madeenah. The Hadeeth that is often quoted which mentions eight Rak'āts in fact pertains to Tahajjud, not Tarāweeh. Both these are different Salāh.

Evidence of Twenty Rak'āts

Sayyidunā Abdullāh Ibn Abbās ؓ reported that the Holy Prophet ﷺ used to offer twenty Rak'āts (Tarāweeh) and Witr in (the month of) Ramadhān.

(Musannaf Ibn Abi Shaybah)

Note: Although some scholars have classed this narration as weak however this can still stand as evidence due to the following reasons:

a) This Hadeeth has been supported by the consensus of the Sahābah ؓ and the scholars of the past.

b) It is important to note that the amount of Rak'āts stipulated by Sayyidunā Umar ؓ could not have been done of his own accord. The number of Rak'āts for any Salāh cannot be determined by any person unless it has been established from the Holy Prophet ﷺ. Moreover, after establishing twenty Rak'āts, none of the Sahābah ؓ objected to his decision, thus this practice continued from generation to generation until now. Therefore Sayyidunā Umar ؓ must have acquired this stipulated number of Rak'āts from the Holy Prophet ﷺ.

Yazeed Ibn Roomān ؓ relates that at the time of Sayyidunā Umar ؓ people offered twenty Rak'āts (Tarāweeh) and three Rak'āts Witr. Abū Bakr Ibn Abi Shaybah ؓ writes in his Musannaf that Yahyā Ibn Saeed ؓ reported that Sayyidunā Umar ؓ directed a man to lead the people in twenty Rak'āts (Tarāweeh).

Abdul Aziz Ibn Rāfi'ee ؓ reported that Sayyidunā Ubay Ibn K'ab ؓ used to lead people in Madeenah during Ramadhān through twenty Rak'āts (Tarāweeh) and three Rak'āts Witr. (Musannaf Ibn Abi Shaybah)

Sayyidunā Ali ؓ invited the Qurrā (reciters of the Holy Qur'ān) in Ramadhān and directed one of them that he should lead the men in twenty Rak'āts Tarāweeh. The narrator said that Sayyidunā Ali ؓ himself led the Witr Salāh.

(As-Sunanul-Kubrā)

Ibn Qudāmah ﷺ has spoken on this subject in detail in his book Al-Mughni. He has stated that twenty Rak'āts make up Tarāweeh and this Salāh is Sunnat-e-Muak'kadah. They were first performed by the Holy Prophet ﷺ. He led the congregation for two or three days. When he found a great enthusiasm among the Sahābah ﷺ, he feared that it might be made Fardh (obligatory) for the Ummah, so he gave up its congregational form and the Sahābah ﷺ began to offer it individually till the time of Sayyidunā Umar ﷺ. He concluded that with the death of the Holy Prophet ﷺ there was no likelihood of it being made Fardh, so it should be performed in a congregational form once again. Finally, he decided accordingly and appointed Sayyidunā Ubay Ibn K'ab ﷺ as the Imām for Tarāweeh Salāh and none of the Sahābah ﷺ objected to his decision. Rather, they took part in it eagerly. It is known from authentic reports that he instructed Sayyidunā Ubay Ibn Ka'b ﷺ to perform twenty Rak'āts in his time and the Sahābah ﷺ agreed upon that and this consensus is by itself an evidence in Shari'ah. Therefore, there is no doubt whatsoever about the true path and to forsake it, is to go astray.

As there are some people that insist Tarāweeh is eight Rak'āts, hence it is necessary to analyse their evidence, so that we can come to a proper conclusion regarding this matter as to whether the Tarāweeh is eight or twenty Rak'āts.

The advocates of Tarāweeh to be eight Rak'āts quote the famous Hadeeth of Sayyidah Ā'ishah ﷺ which is as follows:

Abū Salma ﷺ once inquired from Sayyidah Ā'ishah ﷺ regarding the Salāh of the Holy Prophet ﷺ during the month of Ramadhān. She explained, "The Holy Prophet ﷺ would not perform more than eleven Rak'āts neither in Ramadhān and nor out of it; he would perform four Rak'āts and do not ask of its beauty and length, thereafter another four and (again) do not ask of its beauty and length after which he would perform three (Witr)." Sayyidah Ā'ishah ﷺ continued, "I asked O Messenger of Allāh ﷺ, do you sleep before you pray Witr?" The Holy Prophet ﷺ replied, "O Ā'ishah, my eyes sleep but my heart does not." (Bukhāri)

Although this Hadeeth is rigorously authentic and is probably most widely used to establish eight Ra'kāts Tarāweeh, there are a number of reasons why this Hadeeth is insufficient to stand as evidence:

a) The Salāh that Sayyidah Ā'ishah 👐 was referring to is actually the Tahajjud Salāh. She stated that the Holy Prophet 👐 would not perform more than eight Rak'āts throughout the year regardless of the month. This is apparent in her statement in the above Hadeeth "The Holy Prophet 👐 would not perform more than eleven Rak'āts <u>neither in Ramadhān and nor out of it.</u>" It is obvious that she could not mean the Tarāweeh Salāh. Firstly, because Tarāweeh is never performed outside of Ramadhān and secondly, Tarāweeh and Tahajjud are two separate Salāh.

b) Although this Hadeeth is unanimously authentic, many of the compilers of Hadeeth like Imām Muslim, Nasai, Abū Dāwood, Tirmizi, Ibn Mājah, Ibn Khuzaima and Imām Mālik 👐 have not included this Hadeeth under the chapter of Tarāweeh but instead have included it under the chapter of Tahajjud or Witr.

c) Moreover, if hypothetically this is meant as Tarāweeh Salāh, then why didn't Sayyidah Ā'ishah 👐 object against the decision of Sayyidunā Umar 👐 of establishing twenty Rak'āts? This is self-evident that Tarāweeh is twenty Rak'āts.

d) Furthermore, some scholars have stated that there is no authentic narration regarding the exact number of Rak'āts performed by the Holy Prophet 👐. Shaykhul Islām Ibn Taymiyah 👐 states: "Whoever assumes that there is a fixed number of Rak'āts reported from the Holy Prophet 👐 concerning Tarāweeh and does not accept greater nor lesser has erred."
(Majmu'al-Fatāwa)

Imām Suyūti 👐 states: "The scholars have differed on the number of Rak'āts (in Tarāweeh), had it been established through the Holy Prophet 👐 they would not have differed regarding it." (Al-Masābih)

Imām Shawkāni 👐 states: "What has been understood from this Hadeeth in this chapter is the validity of the nightly prayer of Ramadhān. However, to confine the Salāh known as Tarāweeh to a stipulated number of Rak'āts is not understood from Sunnah." (Naylul-Awtār)

The aforementioned statements of some eminent scholars are evident that there is no authentic narration stating that the Holy Prophet ﷺ performed a stipulated number of Rak'āts. However, there are a few reports that are weak in narration, for instance a narration reported by Sayyidunā Abdullāh Ibn Abbās ؓ that the Holy Prophet ﷺ performed twenty Rak'āts. This can be taken as evidence as this narration has been supported by the Ijmā (consensus) of the Sahabāh ؓ. The main reason why there is no authentic narration regarding this matter is because (as mentioned previously) there are reports that the Holy Prophet ﷺ would at times perform the Tarāweeh Salāh in congregation and at times instruct his noble Companions ؓ to pray them at home lest the Ummah begins to consider them obligatory. As the Companions ؓ did not observe the Holy Prophet ﷺ performing them at home hence, there is no precise report of the fixed number of Rak'āts for Tarāweeh. It was then Sayyidunā Umar ؓ who congregated everyone together behind Sayyidunā Ubay Ibn Ka'b ؓ and fixed twenty Rak'āts after seeing people dispersed; some performing collectively and some individually. What is important here is that after congregating everyone, none of the Companions objected against Sayyidunā Umar ؓ and neither did Sayyidah Ā'ishah ؓ. This explanation is sufficient to prove that the Hadeeth of Sayyidah Ā'ishah ؓ does not imply Tarāweeh but instead Tahajjud.

Neglecting Tarāweeh Salāh

Q When the entire Holy Qur'ān is recited in Tarāweeh Salāh, some people stop performing the Tarāweeh Salāh for the remaining days of Ramādhan. Is that correct?

A There are two different points to note here which are both Sunnah. One is to recite the entire Holy Qur'ān in Tarāweeh and the other is to perform Tarāweeh Salāh every night of the month.

Tarāweeh Salāh is Sunnat-e-Muakkadah. It begins with the sighting of the moon of Ramādhan and ends with the sighting of the moon for Eid-ul-Fitr. Hence, if the Holy Qur'ān is completed in a few nights, the Tarāweeh Salāh should continue to be performed daily for the rest of Ramādhan. Even though one Sunnah has been discharged, the other remains an obligation for the rest of the month, which we should perform with the congregation as long as Ramādhan remains.

Leading Tarāweeh Salāh

Q Many Huffāz (those who have memorised the Holy Qur'ān) who either are clean shaven or have a trimmed beard lead the Tarāweeh Salāh in Ramadhān. Is it correct to appoint such individuals for the Tarāweeh? Is performing the Salāh behind them correct or not?

A The Hāfiz who shaves or trims his beard has infact committed a sin and in the light of Islām is a Fāsiq (sinner). For him to lead the Tarāweeh Salāh is not correct and to follow him in the Salāh is Makrooh-e-Tahreemi (near forbidden). Those people who permit such Huffāz to lead the Tarāweeh Salāh are also sinful. However, the Tarāweeh Salāh performed behind them will be classed as valid and there will be no need to repeat the Salāh.

Sajdah Sahw (Remedial Prostration)

Q If Durood Shareef is recited by mistake after Tashahhud in the first Qaidah (sitting), should Sajdah Sahw be made?

A It is necessary to make Sajdah Sahw for this error.

Prayer Mat Open at all Times

Q Can a prayer mat stay open at all times?

A Yes, a prayer mat can stay open at all times. It is commonly understood that if the prayer mat is left open then the Shaytān reads on it. This belief is absolutely false and has no evidence from the Holy Qur'ān and Sunnah to support it.

Direction of Qiblah

Q If a person is travelling in a moving vehicle e.g. train, plane etc. How should the Qiblah be determined for Salāh?

A Ask the passengers or the staff. If there is no one to assist, estimate to the best of ones ability and go by the decision of your own heart.

Following a Shāfi'ee Imām in Witr Salāh

Q Is it permissible for a Hanafi (follower of Imām Abū Haneefah ※) to follow a Shāfi'ee Imām in Witr Salāh? The Shāfi'ee Imām performs first two Rak'āts which are concluded with Salām. Thereafter one Rak'āt is performed separately.

A The Hanafi's Witr behind a Shāfi'ee Imām is not valid. Not because the Imām is a Shāfi'ee or it is wrong. We greatly honour and respect Imām Shāfi'ee ※, but on account of two other factors:

Firstly, the three Rak'āts in the Shāfi'ee Madhab are performed separately as explained in the question. To perform one Rak'at separately is not valid in the Hanafi Madhab. Secondly, the Witr Salāh according to the Shāfi'ee Madhab is Sunnat which falls in the Nafl category while according to the Hanafi Madhab it is Wājib. A Wājib Salāh cannot be performed behind an Imām who is performing Nafl Salāh.

These differences are due to the different methodology of deduction of juristic laws from the Holy Qur'ān and Sunnah by the Imāms and how they interpreted them.

Takbeer-e-Tahreemah

Q When raising the hands for Takbeer-e-Tahreemah, how should they be held?

A The thumbs should be held in line with the ear lobes and the palms and the fingers should face towards the Qiblah.

Sayyidunā Mālik Ibn Huwairith ※ relates that when the Holy Prophet ※ would do Takbeer (for Salāh), he would raise his hands until they were parallel to his ears. In another narration it is related that both of them were parallel to his earlobes. (Muslim)

Standing Erect after Ruku

Q Is it Sunnah or Wājib to stand erect after the Ruku?

A The Qawmah (standing erect after Ruku) is Wājib.

Tashahhud

Q In Tashahhud, should the fingers bend over the knees or remain on the thighs?

A The fingers should not bend over whilst gripping the knees during the sitting position. They should be held straight pointing to the Qiblah slightly above the knees.

To Remain Standing During Adhān

Q While the Muaddhin is calling out the Adhān, some people who enter, remain standing in the Masjid for the remaining duration of the Adhān. Is there any significance in this practice?

A There is no significance in this practice. It is not Masnoon (Sunnah) to remain standing while the Adhān is being called out.

Female's Salāh Lead by a Ghair Mahram (Strange Man)

Q Is a female allowed to perform her Salāh behind a Ghair Mahram (in the same room or place) or in the presence of a Ghair Mahram?

A A woman's Salāh will be accepted, but it is disliked to perform Salāh in the presence of a Ghair Mahram without a valid reason.

It will be Makrooh (disliked) for a man to lead the Salāh when there is no other male Mahram or any other female relative of hers present in the house. But we should remember that it is compulsory for a woman to observe Hijāb from her Ghair Mahram relatives. A woman should not perform her Salāh individually behind a Ghair Mahram where no Mahram can see her.

Salāh Inside the Mihrāb (Arch)

Q I recently performed my Salāh in one Masjid where the Imām was leading the Salāh from inside the Mihrāb. Does this have any effect on his or our Salāh?

A It is Makrooh (undesirable) for the Imām to stand inside the Mihrāb by himself. In the books of jurisprudence, it is clearly mentioned: "It is Makrooh for the Imām to stand in the Mihrāb or on an elevated place or land (one arm length high) by himself."

But if there is a valid excuse e.g. lack of space or if someone else also stands with him inside the Mihrāb, then it will be permissible for the Imām to lead the Salāh from inside the Mihrāb. Also if the feet of the Imām are outside the Mihrāb, then it will be correct for him to lead the Salāh without any Karāhat (dislike).

Verses of Sajdah

Q Please mention the places in the Holy Qur'ān where Sajdah Tilāwat is Wājib?

A There are fourteen places of Sajdah in the Holy Qur'ān. They are as follows:

1. Sūrah 7	Al-A'rāf	Verse 206
2. Sūrah 13	Ar-R'ad	Verse 15
3. Sūrah 16	An-Nahl	Verses 49 and 50
4. Sūrah 17	Banee Isrāeel	Verse 109
5. Sūrah 19	Maryam	Verse 58
6. Sūrah 22	Al-Hajj	Verse 18
7. Sūrah 25	Al-Furqān	Verse 60
8. Sūrah 27	An-Naml	Verses 25 and 26
9. Sūrah 32	As-Sajdah	Verse 15
10. Sūrah 38	Sād	Verses 24 and 25
11. Sūrah 41	Hā Meem Sajdah	Verses 37 and 38
12. Sūrah 53	An-Najm	Verses 62
13. Sūrah 84	Al-Inshiqāq	Verse 21
14. Sūrah 96	Al-Alaq	Verse 19

Listening to the Holy Qur'ān on CD or Tape

Q Do I have to perform Sajdah when listening to a recorded recitation on a CD or tape player?

A It is not Wājib to perform Sajdah Tilāwat when listening to a recording of a verse on the tape, CD or any other recorded format.

Omitting a Verse of Sajdah

Q. Is it permissible to omit a verse of Sajdah while reciting the Holy Qur'ān to avoid having to perform the Sajdah?

A It is Makrooh to omit a verse of Sajdah for the above reason.

Sajdah Tilāwat upon a Child

Q Is Sajdah Tilāwat Wājib on a child when he listens to the Holy Qur'ān?

A No, Sajdah Tilāwat is not Wājib on a child, an insane person or a woman in the state of Haidh (menstruation) or Nifās (post-natal bleeding).

Qadhā Umri

Q Nowadays some scholars are saying in their commentary of the Holy Qur'ān and sermons regarding performing Qadhā Salāh that, all the Salāh one has missed can be compensated by offering Tawbah (repentance) only. Furthermore, there is no need to perform all the missed Salāh again. Would you explain in the light of the Shari'ah whether it is necessary or not to perform all the Salāh one has missed during his lifetime.

Secondly, do any of the four Imāms differ on this matter or hold the view that if a person misses a large number of Salāh, then it is enough for him to offer Tawbah only and he doesn't need to perform the Qadhā Salāh at all? I would also like to know if it is necessary to perform the missed Salāh of all previous years and what is the correct method of doing so?

A A similar question was posed to Mufti Taqi Uthmāni Sāhib and I think it is sufficient to quote the answer he has given. The detailed answer includes all the points you have raised.

In Saheeh al-Bukhāri, Sayyidunā Anas Ibn Mālik ﷺ has quoted the Holy Prophet ﷺ as saying, "A person who forgets to offer his Salāh, it is compulsory upon him to offer it whenever he remembers it. There is no other Kaffārah (penalty) for it except this." (Bukhāri)

In Saheeh Muslim, the Holy Prophet ﷺ has been quoted as saying, "When anyone of you goes to sleep or due to negligence, misses his Salāh, then whenever he remembers it, he must offer that Salāh. For Allāh ﷻ has said in the Holy Qur'ān, **"Establish Salāh for My remembrance."** (20:14)

In Sunan Nasai it is mentioned that the Holy Prophet ﷺ was asked about the person who goes to sleep at the time of Salāh or misses it due to negligence. The Holy Prophet ﷺ said, "The Kaffārah for that is to offer that Salāh whenever he remembers."

In all these Ahādeeth, the Holy Prophet ﷺ has stated the principle that if a person does not offer a Salāh on time, then it is compulsory upon him to offer it whenever it comes to mind. This is apparent from the aforementioned statement, "The Kaffārah for that is to offer that Salāh whenever he remembers."

The Salāh may have been missed due to negligence or because he went to sleep, or because he forgot about it. In the Ahādeeth related in Saheeh Muslim, Sunan Nasai and by referring to the verse 20:14, the Holy Prophet ﷺ has made it clear that this verse is also regarding the order of offering Qadhā Salāh. The meaning of the verse is that whenever a person thinks of this Fardh, this order of Allāh ﷻ, then he must offer it necessarily. On the basis of the order of offering Qadhā Salāh which the Holy Prophet ﷺ has given in the above stated Hadeeth, all the scholars have stated that the Qadhā of all missed Salāh, as many as they are, must be necessarily offered. All the different schools of thought; Hanafi, Shāfi'ee, Māliki and Hanbali, unanimously agree upon it.

Thus it is completely wrong , misleading and contrary to the clear orders of the Holy Qur'ān, Hadeeth and the unanimous decision of the scholars to say that if the number of Salāh is too many, then there is no need to offer their Qadhā at all.

Saying such a thing is similar to putting an end to a very important Fardh as Salāh on the basis of ones opinion. It is completely wrong to say that it is enough to offer Tawbah (repentance) only for all the Qadhā Salāh. For the essential condition for Tawbah to be accepted by Allāh ﷻ, a person must offer as much atonement as he possibly can for the wrong he committed, along with offering repentance.

It would be appropriate here to mention the fact that in some books of the principles of Hadeeth, whilst explaining the signs of Mawdhoo (fabricated) or unauthentic Hadeeth, the example of the Hadeeth of Qadhā-Umri has been given. The Ahādeeth of Qadhā-Umri which have been called unauthentic or Mawdhoo are those Ahādeeth which declare one or a few Salāh to serve for all the missed Salāh of a lifetime. Besides the fact that there is no proof of such Hadeeth, the reason for their being unauthentic has also been given by Mulla Ali Qāri ﷺ as, one or a few Salāh cannot compensate for the ones missed over the years.

Upon this there is a consensus of opinion amongst all Muslim jurisprudents and scholars. Thus if due to these Mawdhoo or unauthentic Ahādeeth, a person believes that the entire conception of Qadhā-Umri is baseless and that the offering of all previously missed Salāh is not necessary then his belief is based on nothing but sheer ignorance.

The correct method of offering Qadhā-Umri:

In the light of the Holy Qur'ān, Sunnah and unanimous agreement of Islamic jurisprudents, it is established beyond any shadow of a doubt that the Muslim who has not offered Salāh in the early years of his life due to negligence or carelessness and later offers repentance, it is essential upon him to make a careful calculation of all his missed Salāh and then try to offer them as soon as possible.

Some scholars for further convenience, have suggested that a person should offer one Qadhā Salāh along with each Fardh Salāh he is offering. In this way he will have offered five Qadhā Salāh in a day. But whenever he gets the opportunity, he should offer more. Moreover, one must be careful when making the intention of the Qadhā Salāh. The intention must be clear and exact. For example, if a person is offering the Qadhā Salāh of Fajr, he must make intention for Qadhā of the first Fajr Salāh which is Fardh upon him.

Conclusion:

Thus it is compulsory upon a person to offer Qadhā of all the Salāh he has missed. Mere repentance is not enough to absolve a person of this duty. Even if the Qadhā Salāh may be great in number, it is essential for him to offer them.

If a person starts offering five Qadhā Salāh daily and whenever he gets the chance, he offers more than five and makes a will that after his death, Fidyah (compensation) be given from his estate for the number of Salāh he could not offer in his lifetime, then it is hoped that Allāh ﷻ shall accept this act of his and forgive him. This is the correct method of offering Qadhā-Umri. It is misleading to say that there is no need to offer Qadhā-Umri and that only repentance is enough.

Sunnats of Eid-ul-Adhā

Q On Eid day we observe people doing so many different things. Some people follow the Sunnah whilst many others commit different kinds of evil. What should a true Muslim do on that day?

A Eid-ul-Fitr and Eid-ul-Adhā are Islamic festivals. Muslims should only do those things that are permitted in Islām. The occasion of Eid does not give anyone the licence to commit sins.

Sins will remain sins whatever the occasion may be. We should try to adhere to the Islāmic guidelines in regards to Eid festivals as much as possible if we want to achieve success in both the worlds.

The Sunnats of Eid are as follows:

1.   Wake up earlier than usual.
2.   Brush the teeth with Miswāk.
3.   Have a bath.
4.   Be well dressed in an Islamic manner
5.   Dress in one's best clothes, not necessarily new.
6.   Use Itr (perfume).
7.   Perform Eid Salāh at the Eidgah.
8.   To eat something sweet, preferably dates before the Eidul-Fitr Salāh. Whereas to delay in eating until after the Eidul-Adhā Salāh.
9.   Go to the place of Salāh early.
10.   Walk to the place of Eid Salāh if it's within walking distance.
11.   Recite the Takbeer on the way to the place of Eid Salāh.
12.   Use different routes to and from the place of Eid Salāh.

Takbeer Tashreeq

Q It has become a custom to recite Takbeer Tashreeq thrice in the Masjid in the days of Tashreeq. What is correct, once or thrice?

A To recite the Takbeer once is Wājib (essential). It is not Sunnah to say it thrice. It is written in Majmaul Anhār: "If a person says it more than once, then he has opposed the Sunnah." Therefore this custom should be stopped and the correct way should be adopted.

Imāms of the Masājid should inform their followers regarding the correct way of reciting the Takbeer Tashreeq.

Janāzah Salāh upon a Person who Commits Suicide

Q If a person consumes poison and kills himself, then is there a Janāzah Salāh upon that person?

A Even though a person committed suicide which is a major sin in Shari'ah, he will be given full burial rites. This means that he will be given Ghusl (bath), Kafn (shroud) and Janāzah Salāh will be performed for him. The person will also be buried in a Muslim cemetery.

It is stated in Fatāwa Ālamgheeri, "He who takes his own life intentionally, he too will be given full burial rites and Janāzah will also be performed for him. This is the view of Imām Abū Haneefah ﷺ and Imām Muhammad ﷺ and this is the most authentic view."

The same verdict is mentioned in Fatāwa Shāmi, "He who kills himself (i.e. commits suicide), even though it is done intentionally, he will be given Ghusl and Janāzah Salāh will also be performed for him."

Allāh ﷺ Knows Best

6. CHAPTER ON
ZAKĀT

Meaning of Zakāt

Q What is meant by Zakāt and what is it's status in Islām?

A Zakāt is the name given to that portion of money or ones wealth, which is given to the poor and needy, making them the full owners of it, as commanded by Allāh ﷻ. In other words, Salāh and fasting are physical forms of worship, whereas the giving of Zakāt is a monetary form of worship. Giving Zakāt is Fardh (obligatory) when one fulfils all its criteria. The verses of the Holy Qur'ān and Ahādeeth prove that it is Fardh. A person who denies the obligation of Zakāt is a disbeliever.

Zakāt Money to a Student

Q A student came from abroad to study in England. After paying the first term's fee, he had no money left neither in England nor back home to pay the 2nd term's fee. Is it permissible for him to receive Zakāt money?

A In the mentioned case, if the student genuinely has no money whatsoever with him and furthermore he does not have any spare assets (which are surplus to his needs) and which do not reach the Nisāb threshold value, then it is permissible for such a student to receive Zakāt money to pay his fees.

Disclosure of Zakāt

Q Is it necessary to disclose to the recipient of Zakāt that Zakāt money is being given to him?

A No, it is not necessary. It is permissible to give Zakāt money under the pretext of a reward or a gift as long as the giver makes the intention of Zakāt in his heart.

Zakāt Money to Islamic Institutes

Q Is it permissible to give Zakāt money to Islamic institutes?

A It is only permissible to give Zakāt money to those students of an Islamic institute who fulfil the criteria of receiving Zakāt. Zakāt money can also be given to the management of such Islamic institutions for being spent on the poor students.

However, it would not be permissible to donate Zakāt money towards the construction, utilities, facilities, the building etc. of the institute itself. This is because one of the conditions for the fulfilment of one's Zakāt is that the recipient must have full ownership of the Zakāt money. Recipient being the needy person, not the institute's management. By donating towards the construction etc. the recipient does not have the full ownership of it. Hence, it will only be permissible to give it to the students (that are rightfully entitled to Zakāt).

Differences between Hibah, Hadyah and Sadaqah

Q Can you please explain the differences between Hibah, Hadyah and Sadaqah.

A Hibah, Hadyah and Sadaqah are similar from the point of view that in each of these cases a person makes some other person the owner of some item of his possession and then under normal circumstances does not have the option of taking it back. But in each of these three, there are some differences in the motive of the giver.

The Definition of Hadyah
A Hadyah is a gift that a person gives to someone as a sign of respect or out of love.

The Definition of Sadaqah
Sadaqah or Khairāt is something given to someone purely with the intention of reward from Allāh ﷻ.

The Definition of Hibah
The literal meaning of Hibah is giving and in the Shari'ah it means giving someone else some item of ones possession without taking anything in return and making him the owner.

Different Types of Charities and their Recipients

Q Can you please explain to me the different types of charities? I have become confused by words like Zakāt, Sadaqah, Lillāh, Fitrah.

A Below is an explanation of the different terms of charities:

Zakāt

Zakāt is obligatory upon every wealthy Muslim (who possesses wealth equivalent to or more than the Nisāb level, which is surplus to his/her basic needs) who must pay 2.5% (1/40) of the value of the specified assets after deducting liabilities and after the lapse of one lunar year.

<u>Recipients:</u> Can only be given to Muslims that are poor and destitute.

Sadaqah

The word Sadaqah is given to charity which is given voluntarily. i.e. Nafl.

<u>Recipients:</u> Nafl Sadaqah (optional charity) can be given to Muslims, non-Muslims, the rich, the poor, friends or family.

Lillāh

Literally means 'for the sake of Allāh ﷻ'. It is also a form of optional charity given for the humanitarian needs or the Deen of Allāh ﷻ. e.g. the building of a Masjid, maintaining the Masjid, payment of salaries, purchasing Islamic literature, building hospitals and Madrasahs etc.

Fitrah

Fitrah is compulsory upon every Muslim who has sufficient basic necessities for himself, his family and dependents for the day of Eid-ul-Fitr and after deducting his debts, he possesses wealth equivalent to the Nisāb for that day. (Nisāb means the minimum amount of wealth in ones possession which makes Zakāt liable on a person). It does not have to be possessed for one lunar year.

Amount of Fitrah: 1.633 kg of wheat or 3.266 kg of barley or the market value thereof.

<u>Recipients:</u> Poor and needy Muslims. It may however not be given to one's parents, grandparents, children or grandchildren.

Nazr (Vow)

This is when a person makes a vow that he would give a specified amount in charity if a certain task is fulfilled. Once the task is fulfilled it becomes compulsory to discharge the relevant amount.

Recipients: Same as those of Zakāt.

Fidyah
When a person is permanently ill with no hope of recovery, or if a person due to extreme old age and weakness cannot fast, he has to give Fidyah as compensation for every missed fast.

The same would apply to a person who could not perform Salāh due to the above reasons. Fidyah is also given for the missed Salāh of a deceased (dead person).

Amount: Same amount as Fitrah, and it is given for each Salāh or fast missed.

Recipients: Same as those of Zakāt.

Kaffārah
A penalty to compensate for a Ramadhān fast broken without a valid reason.

Amount:

1. To fast for sixty consecutive days for previously missed fasts even though it is one fast missed.

2. In the event of one being unable to fast due to severe illness, weakness, etc then one should give meals to sixty poor people.

3. Or give the equivalent in cash or kind.

Sadaqah Jāriyah (Continuous Charity)

Q Which acts are 'Sadaqah Jāriyah' (continuous charity) for me when I die? Is building a road for the public in a poor country Sadaqah Jāriyah?

A The following Hadeeth covers some of the main acts which would be regarded as Sadaqah Jāriyah.

The Holy Prophet ﷺ said, "From those actions and good deeds (the rewards of which) a believer will receive after his death are, the sacred knowledge he taught and conveyed; the pious child he left behind; a copy of the Holy Qur'ān which he left as a legacy; the Masjid which he constructed or a house which he built for the traveller; a stream which he set flowing; or voluntary charity which he gave from his wealth while he was alive and healthy, will continue to reach him after his death." (Ibn Mājah)

Thus from the above Hadeeth, we can deduce that the building of a road in a poor country or any other place for travellers, seeking the reward from Allāh ﷻ is also Sadaqah Jāriyah.

The Punishment for Neglecting Zakāt

Q What is the punishment for not giving Zakāt? Nowadays people are very careless regarding this obligation.

A Imām Bukhāri ﷺ narrates a Hadeeth in which he mentions that the Holy Prophet ﷺ has said, "The person on whom Allāh ﷻ has bestowed wealth and he does not give Zakāt, on the Day of Judgement his wealth will be turned into a venomous bald serpent which will coil around his/her neck and bite his/her jaws and say, 'I am your wealth, I am your treasure'."

In another Hadeeth, it has been mentioned that on the night of Mi'rāj the Holy Prophet ﷺ passed by a group of people whose private parts had been covered, front and back by rags. They were grazing like animals and eating from Zaqqoom and the stones of Hell (Zaqqoom is a tree with bitter thorny, fruits). The Holy Prophet ﷺ asked, "Who are these people?" Sayyidunā Jibreel ﷺ replied, "These are the people who did not give Zakāt of their wealth. They have not been oppressed neither does Allāh ﷻ oppress His servants." (Tabarāni)

Zakāt is Fardh at the rate of 2.5% (e.g. £2.50 for every £100).

Correct Amount of Sadaqatul-Fitr

Q On whom is Sadaqatul-Fitr Wājib and what is the correct amount?

A It is Wājib (compulsory) upon a person who possesses the value of Ni-sāb in cash or equivalent e.g. merchandise, gold, silver, shares or goods, which are not merchandise, but which exceeds one's needs and are used only occasionally throughout the year like some clothes, crockery etc. and which reach the threshold value of Nisāb.

The total amount of Sadaqatul-Fitr can be given to one person, or one Sadaqatul-Fitr can be shared between a few people.

Sadaqatul-Fitr is the equivalent of 1.633kg of wheat or 3.266kg of barley or the market value thereof.

Allāh ﷻ Knows Best

7. Chapter on
Ramadhān
& Fasting

Definition of Fasting

Q What is fasting?

A Fasting means to abstain from eating, drinking and sexual intercourse from Subah-Sādiq (true-dawn) until sunset, with the intention of fasting for the purpose of pleasing Allāh ﷻ .

The Obligation of Fasting

Q When does fasting become Fardh (obligatory)?

A If a person fulfils the following conditions then fasting will be Fardh:

1. To be a Muslim.
2. To be mature (Bāligh).
3. To be sane.
4. To have knowledge that it is the month of Ramadhān.

Not Waking up for Sahree

Q Is fasting valid if one does not wake up for Sahree?

A The fasting is valid if one does not wake up for Sahree. Although the fast will be valid, the person will be deprived from its blessings. It is Sunnah to have Sahree before Subah-Sādiq. The Holy Prophet ﷺ said, "Have Sahree because there is Barakah (blessing) in having Sahree." The Holy Prophet ﷺ has also said, "Verily Allāh ﷻ and His Angels send blessings upon those who eat Sahree."

There are many benefits of Sahree:

1. The meal provides strength for the day.
2. It gives one an opportunity to perform Tahajjud Salāh.
3. It gives one an opportunity to make Du'ā.
4. It enables one to perform Fajr Salāh on time.
5. It helps in removing bad temper which results due to hunger.

Eating in Public in the Month of Ramadhān

Q Was fasting compulsory upon the previous nations? What is the ruling regarding a person who intentionally misses fast? My friend openly eats in front of us on the days of fasting. What is the state of his Imān?

A The Holy Qur'ān clearly mentions that fasting was compulsory upon the previous nations and it is also obligatory upon us. Allāh 🕮 says, "**O you who believe! Siyām (fasting) has been ordained for you the way it was compulsory on the previous people so that you may attain Taqwā (piety)." (2:183)**

Fasting is amongst the fundamental pillars of Islām. It has been ordained by Allāh 🕮 for the development of Taqwā (piety) in the believers. Fasting is extremely effective for the acquisition of Taqwā. One who denies the Fardhiyyat (obligation) of fasting, no longer remains a Muslim. The one who does not fast without a valid reason during the month of Ramadhān is a Fāsiq (a very sinful person) of the highest order. Such a person should repent sincerely and make up for his fasting before he exposes his Imān to the brink of Kufr (disbelief). You should advise your friend seriously on this matter.

Intention Not Made at Night

Q I forgot to make my Niyyat (intention) during the night, but without breaking my fast I made the intention in the morning. Is my fast valid?

A It is preferable to make the Niyyat for the fast of Ramadhān during the night, i.e. prior to the entry of Subah Sādiq (when the fast begins). If the intention was not made during the night, the fast will be valid if the intention was made before Zawāl (midday). The exact time limit for the validity of the intention for fasting is the time of Nisf-Nahār (midday).

Nisf-Nahār is determined by dividing the day into two, the time duration from Subah-Sādiq to sunset and adding the result to Subah-Sādiq time.

Example:

Subah-Sādiq - 6:00am.
Sunset - 6:00pm.
Time duration from Subah-Sādiq to sunset is 12 hours.
12 hours divided by 2 = 6 hours.
Add this result to Subah-Sādiq: 6:00 + 6:00 = 12:00pm = Nisf-Nahār.

If intention is made for the fast before 12:00pm (in the above example) the Ramadhān fast will be valid.

Note: One must not regard 12:00pm the only time of Nisf-Nahār always. The aforementioned was just used to illustrate an example to facilitate ones understanding. Otherwise, the time varies depending upon which season of the year Ramadhān occurs.

Fasting without Niyyat

Q **Is a fast in Ramadhān valid without the intention?**

A The Niyyat for fasting is necessary. If a person abstains from eating, drinking and cohabitation from Subah-Sādiq (true dawn) to sunset without the Niyyat of fast, then the fast will not be valid. It is not necessary to express the Niyyat verbally as Niyyat means to intend. Thus the intention in the heart will suffice. However, it is recommended to express the Niyyat verbally as well.

To Observe Fast after the Completion
of Ramadhān

Q **I kept my fast of Ramadhān and performed the Eid Salāh in Britain. Thereafter, I travelled abroad where a day of Ramadhān remained. Should I fast that one day and perform the Eid Salāh or not?**

A Although your obligation is over, it will be necessary for you to observe the fast with the rest of the Muslims and perform the Eid Salāh with them to honour the blessed month of Ramadhān and the special occasion.

Having a Bath whilst Fasting

Q Is it permissible to have a bath whilst fasting?

A Yes, it is permissible. However, caution must be taken when gargling due to the fear that water may accidentally slip down the throat resulting in the fast breaking.

Applying Oil whilst Fasting

Q Does applying oil on the hair break the fast?

A No, it doesn't.

Gargling whilst Fasting

Q When I was gargling at the time of Wudhu, water went down my throat accidentally. Does this break my fast or not?

A Yes, the fast will break if water went down the throat at the time of gargling. Qadhā will be necessary but not Kaffārah.

Fasting and Haidh (Menstruation)

Q What is the ruling regarding fasting whilst a woman is experiencing Haidh?

A A woman must not fast during the time she is experiencing menstruation. Instead she will have to observe these missed fasts as Qadhā later on after the completion of her Haidh. If the bleeding of Haidh started while she was fasting, her fast will break even if there was a very small portion of the fast remaining. Since the fast is not valid, it will be necessary for her to repeat it.

If a woman starts menstruating on the day when she was fasting, thereby causing her fast to break, she should not eat or drink anything for the remainder of that day. It is necessary for her to appear to others as if she is fasting. If the bleeding stops after Subah-Sādiq (true dawn) in Ramadhān even though she has not eaten anything, her fast is not valid even if she makes an intention to fast.

Qadhā becomes necessary for that particular fast as she was in the state of impurity (Haidh) for a certain part of the day. If bleeding stopped before Subah-Sādiq, then she should make an intention and keep the fast.

Nifās (Postnatal Bleeding) and Fast

Q What is Nifās? What should a woman do if she is in Nifās and the month of Ramadhān arrives?

A Bleeding from the womb after childbirth is called Nifās. Its maximum period is forty days and if bleeding continues for more than forty days, the extra days are not regarded as Nifās but Istihādah instead. There is no minimum period for Nifās. It may last for either one day or a little while and sometimes a woman may not even bleed a single drop after a child is born. There is a general misunderstanding that Nifās is for the full forty days. Whereas this is the maximum period, not the exact marked period. Due to this misunderstanding Salāh, fast etc. is neglected.

Fasting cannot be observed during Nifās. However, Qadhā fasts should be kept as fasting is not pardoned. The fast will break as soon as a child is born and Nifās begins. She may take food and medicine if necessary otherwise she should remain and appear as if she is fasting. If she becomes purified from Nifās after Subah-Sādiq (true dawn) she should not fast on that day but observe Qadhā later. If she becomes clean before Subah-Sādiq, then she should make the intention and observe the fast of that day.

Wet Dream

Q Does a wet dream break the fast?

A No, a wet dream does not break the fast.

I'tikāf

Q Every year some people stay in the Masjid for the last 10 days of Ramadhān for I'tikāf. What is the ruling on this matter? Is it necessary?

A I'tikāf means that a person remains in the Masjid for a certain period of time with the Niyyat of I'tikāf. There is no time limit prescribed. Thus whatever time is spent in the Masjid with the intention of I'tikāf will constitute Nafl I'tikāf.

There are three types of I'tikāf:

1. Wājib (compulsory)
2. Sunnat-e-Muakkadah
3. Nafl (optional)

Wājib I'tikāf
An I'tikāf of Nazr (vow) or Sunnah I'tikāf that was broken, in both cases, I'tikāf becomes Wājib. It is also nesessary to fast whilst observing this category of I'tikāf.

Sunnat-e-Muakkadah
I'tikāf of the last 10 days of Ramadhān is Sunnat-e-Muakkadah-alal-Kifāyah. This means that if one person, who lives in a particular area in which the Masjid is situated, performs I'tikāf, then the responsibility is absolved from all the Muslims of that area. But if no one performs it, then everyone will be sinful for neglecting this Sunnat-e-Muakkadah.

Nafl (Optional)
This form of I'tikāf is not fixed with time, fasting, day or night. On the contrary, a person will receive the reward of I'tikāf if he enters the Masjid with the intention of I'tikāf at any time and for whatever period. This is such an easy action that it neither requires much time nor effort, and one receives great reward. Hence, whenever a person visits the Masjid for any worship, he should make the intention of I'tikāf so that he can receive great rewards.

The Reward of I'tikāf

Q What is the reward for I'tikāf?

A Sayyidunā Husain ⚘ reports that the Holy Prophet ⚘ said, "If anyone observes the I'tikāf of the last ten days of Ramadhān, then he will get a reward equal to that of performing Hajj and Umrah twice." (Baihaqi, Targheeb)

Sayyidunā Abdullāh Ibn Abbās ﷺ narrates that the Holy Prophet ﷺ said regarding those who observe I'tikāf, "The person who observes I'tikāf is safe from all sins, receives so much reward as though someone is doing righteous deeds (inspite of not having done these deeds)." (Mishkāt)

In another Hadeeth, Sayyidunā Abdullāh Ibn Abbās ﷺ reports that if anyone observes I'tikāf for only one day seeking Allāh's ﷻ pleasure, then Allāh ﷻ will put between him and Hell, three trenches the width of each trench being greater than the distance between the Heavens and the Earth.

(Targheeb)

The conclusion drawn is that the Mu'takif (person who performs I'tikāf) will be kept very far away from Hell, meaning that he will enter Paradise.

Cutting Nails whilst in I'tikāf

Q Is it permissible for a person performing I'tikāf to cut his nails?

A The Mu'takif (a person performing I'tikāf) is permitted to cut his nails, trim his moustache, ensuring that the nails or hair do not fall inside the Masjid. This can be done by placing a cloth.

Bringing Food from Home
whilst in I'tikāf

Q Is it permissible to bring food from home in the state of I'tikāf?

A It is permissible to go home and bring the food if no one is available to bring it. He can wait for a short while until the food is ready, he then should return to the Masjid instantly.

I'tikāf for Women

Q Can a woman perform I'tikāf?

A Yes, and she will get the same reward for performing I'tikāf as a man does. Before performing I'tikāf, the woman should take permission from her husband. She will perform her I'tikāf where she performs her Salāh.

If no place is fixed, then she should fix a corner of a room, somewhere in the house for I'tikāf. She may put a bed in that place for sleeping. If there is no one to bring the food for her, she may go to the kitchen and bring the food to the place of I'tikāf.

Allāh ﷻ Knows Best

8. CHAPTER ON
HAJJ & UMRAH

Control of Menstruation During Hajj

Q Does Islām allow for the control of menstruation with the aid of medication at the time of Hajj?

A One basis for prohibition in Islām is 'Harm'. Anything which is harmful in nature or injurious will be prohibited in terms of the principles of Islām. Poisonous substances are unlawful because of their capacity to harm. Hence, it will not be permissible to use any harmful substance unless it is confirmed by an expert and qualified medical practitioner. Controlling menstruation is not normally permissible because of the following two reasons.

Firstly, it is harmful to the body. Anything which interferes with the natural functions of the body is usually harmful to the body.

Secondly, it falls within the scope of the general application of the Quranic verse, **"(Shaytān said to Allāh): I shall most certainly command them (people) to change the creation of Allāh." (4:119)**

Controlling menstruation is an interference with the nature of the creation of Allāh ﷻ. Such interference is not allowed in Islām. However, if there is a real need for this measure only then will it be temporarily permissible. For instance, Tawāf-e-Ziyārat is Fardh (obligatory) in Hajj, without the Tawāf having been performed one remains in the state of Ihrām. Control of menstruation would be permissible for this purpose only. Control of menstruation for other acts such as honeymoon etc. will be forbidden.

Many of our Muslim sisters worry a great deal about the occurrence of menses during Hajj and Umrah. It must be borne in mind that our mothers; the wives of the Holy Prophet ﷺ and the Sahābiyyāt (female Companions) performed Hajj and Umrah without the use of such medication. It is therefore necessary that a woman intending to go for Hajj should learn the rulings regarding menstruation and this important pillar of Islām before she departs.

Pelting the Jamarāt (Stones) for Women in Hajj

Q I took my wife with me to perform Hajj. On the 10th of Dhul-Hijjah my wife accompanied me for stoning the big Jamarāt.

But when we approached the place of stoning, there was an intense crowd and the situation was very chaotic. I had to escort my wife to a safe place and then on my own I carried out the stoning on her behalf. On the 11th and 12th we were successful in carrying out the stoning. What is the Islamic ruling?

A The point that you have mentioned often occurs because of the lack of organisation. But Rame-Jamarāt (pelting of the stones) can only be carried out by another person if the person concerned is very ill or is too weak to reach the place of Jamarāt either by walking or by transport. (Muallimul-Hujjāj)

But in reference to your situation where there is an intense crowd, another person cannot perform the Rame-Jamarat on behalf of the woman. If she cannot do the Ramee, then she should give dam (sacrifice of an animal). In the evening and night there are less people. Although it is Makrooh to carry out the Ramee at those times, for women and excused people, it is permissible for them to do the Ramee without any Karāhat (dislike).

The Obligation of Hajj

Q When does Hajj become Fardh? What will happen if a person delays his/her Hajj?

A The conditions that make Hajj Fardh are as follows:

1) To be a Muslim.
2) To be mentally fit (not insane).
3) To be physically fit (not disabled).
4) To be mature (to be physically mature).
5) Security of journey and route.
6) To have sufficient provisions for dependents for the duration of absence; to possess all requirements for travel and be financially independent.
7) A woman must be accompanied by her husband or a Mahram (a male member of her family whom she cannot marry according to Islām i.e. brother, father, son etc).

If any of the above mentioned conditions are not found, Hajj will no be considered Fardh.

When the conditions that make Hajj Fardh are found, then it becomes Fardh upon that person to perform Hajj immediately (during the first available Hajj period). However, Hajj is Fardh only once in a lifetime.

One is not permitted to delay the Hajj until the following year without a valid reason. If one delays the Hajj, then he/she will be committing a very grave sin.

The Holy Prophet 鐮 said, "One who intends to perform Hajj, then verily he must hasten." (Abū Dāwood)

He also said, "Hasten in performing Hajj, for indeed one never knows what will befall him."

To Pass Away whilst Performing Hajj

Q My brother went to perform Hajj but whilst still in the state of Ihrām he passed away. What will happen to his Hajj?

A It is mentioned in a Hadeeth that whosoever dies while in the state of Ihrām, he shall rise up from his grave on the Day of Judgement reciting the Talbiyah (Labbaik). In another Hadeeth the Holy Prophet 鐮 said, "The one who went for Hajj then died, Allāh 鐮 will write the reward of Hajj for him continuously up to the Day of Judgement and the one who went for Umrah and died, Allāh 鐮 will write the reward of Umrah for him continuously till the Day of Judgement."

In one Hadeeth, it is mentioned that when a person goes for Hajj or Umrah and passes away on the way, he shall not be brought before Allāh 鐮 for judgement nor will he have to account for his actions. It shall be said to him, "Enter into Paradise".

NB: If Hajj was already Fardh upon him but he passed away before fulfilling this obligation of Hajj, then Hajj should be carried out by someone else on his behalf from one-third of his estate.

Female's Ihrām

Q What is the Ihrām of a female?

A The female who intends to perform Hajj or Umrah will wear her normal sewn garments, stockings, etc. Her head must be fully covered, not a single strand of hair should be exposed.

Her face and her hands up to the wrists may be exposed. But it is compulsory upon the female to cover her face when there is a fear of Fitnah (corruption) or any Ghair Mahram (strange men) are in front of her. In such situations, the face will have to be covered in such a manner, that the covering does not touch the face e.g. by using a cap with a veil over it.

The Three Types of Hajj

Q Hajj has become Fardh upon me and I have come to know that there are three types of Hajj. What are they and which one should I perform and will my obligation be absolved by performing any one of them?

A The three types of Hajj are: Qirān, Tamattu and Ifrād.

1. Qirān: In this type of Hajj, the intending Hāji (pilgrim) makes intention for both Hajj and Umrah together by wearing the same Ihrām for both. The person who performs Qirān is called a Qārin.

2. Tamattu: This type of Hajj is when the intending Hāji (pilgrim) combines the Hajj and Umrah in such a way that he wears the Umrah Ihrām from the Meeqāt and does not combine the Ihrām for Hajj with it. A new Ihrām is worn for Hajj. In short the Hāji performs Hajj and Umrah with two separate Ihrāms. The person who performs Tamattu is called a Mutamatti.

3. Ifrād: This is where the intending Hāji makes intention for Hajj only. He does not combine the Hajj with Umrah. A person who performs Ifrād is called a Mufrid.

It is up to the person which one he chooses. However, Qirān is the most virtuous and more rewarding, thereafter Tamattu and lastly Ifrād. A person will be absolved from the responsibility by performing any of the above types of Hajj.

Meeqāt

Q **What is meant by Meeqāt?**

A Meeqāt refers to the boundaries around the holy city of Makkah which were fixed by the Holy Prophet ﷺ for a non-resident of Makkah from which point wearing the Ihrām is necessary.

It would not be permissible for a non-resident of Makkah to go beyond the fixed boundaries without Ihrām.

Places of Wearing Ihrām

Q **Where should I commence my Ihrām?**

A It will depend upon from where you are entering Makkah. There are different boundaries (Meeqāt) for different people.

1) Zul-Hulaifah (Bir-Ali) - This is the Meeqāt for those pilgrims who are coming from Madinah. It is approximately 450km north of Makkah.

2) Juhfa - This is the Meeqāt for those pilgrims who are coming from the northwest of Makkah, i.e. through Syria. This is situated 204km northwest (near the town of Rābigh) of Makkah.

3) Yalamlam - This is the Meeqāt for those pilgrims who are coming from the south of Makkah, i.e. through Yemen. Yalamlam is a mountain situated 54 km south of Makkah.

4) Qarnul-Manāzil - This is the Meeqāt of those pilgrims who are coming from the east of Makkah, i.e. through Najd. It is situated about 94km east of Makkah.

5) Zātul-Irq - This is the Meeqāt for those pilgrims who are coming from the northeast of Makkah, i.e. through Iraq. It is situated 94km northeast of Makkah.

6) Hill - This is the Meeqāt for those people who are residing between the Meeqāt and the boundaries of the Haram.

7) Haram - This is the Meeqāt for those pilgrims who are residing within the boundaries of Haram. These pilgrims can wear their Ihrām anywhere within the Haram. However, if they are performing Umrah, their Meeqāt is the Hill.

Note: The boundaries fixed for the people living in England is Juhfa.

40 Salāh in Madeenah

Q Our elders say that it is compulsory to complete 40 Salāh in Masjid Nabawi when one visits Madinah. Is this a necessary act whilst performing Umrah or Hajj?

A No, it is not necessary. Even the visit to Madeenah is not compulsory, nor is it a part of the compulsory acts of Hajj or Umrah.

However to visit Madeenah Munawwarah is a highly recommended act. A person who visits Madeenah and the grave of the Holy Prophet ﷺ will receive tremendous rewards. The Holy Prophet ﷺ said, "My intercession is obligatory for the one who visits my grave." (Bazzār, Dār Qutni)

When the visit of Madeenah itself is not necessary, how can it be said that performing 40 Salāh is compulsory. However, if someone can stay in Madeenah for at least 8 days, it is advisable for him to complete 40 Salāh in Masjid Nabawi because the eminent companion Sayyidunā Anas Ibn Mālik ﷺ narrates that the Holy Prophet ﷺ said, "Whoever performs forty Salāh in my Masjid, destined for him is the freedom from the Fire of Hell and salvation from the punishment, and he becomes immune from hypocrisy."

This Hadeeth mentions great reward for a person who performs 40 Salāh in the Masjid of the Holy Prophet ﷺ. Therefore, every Muslim who gets the opportunity to visit Madeenah, should not miss out on this great reward.

The Method of Performing Hajj

Q I am intending to perform Hajj this year and I have not performed Hajj previously. Therefore it will be a completely new experience for me. Please can you explain the method of performing Hajj?

A To explain the full method of performing Hajj would require a full book and Alhamdulillāh, now there are many authentic books available pertaining to the Masāil of Hajj. It is advisable that you consult your local scholars for authentic publications regarding the topic of Hajj. Nevertheless, I will briefly outline the most important acts during the five days of Hajj.

1st Day - 8th Dhul-Hijjah
After putting on the Ihrām one will proceed to Minā after sunrise and perform all the five Salāh there i.e. Zuhr, Asr, Maghrib, Ishā and Fajr of the next day (9th Dhul-Hijjah).

2nd Day - 9th Dhul-Hijjah
After sunrise, proceed towards Arafah and begin to make Wuqoof (stay there) after Zawāl. Zuhr and Asr Salāh will be performed in Arafah. Both of the prayers will be combined in the time of Zuhr. However, this will only take place when both the Salāh are performed in Masjid Nimra (in Arafah). Otherwise, if both Salāh are not offered in the Masjid but are performed in the tents etc. then both Salāh will not be combined but will be performed in their stipulated times.

A person should engage himself in Du'ā, Dhikr, recitation of the Holy Qur'ān etc. until sunset. (Maghrib Salāh will not be performed in Arafah). Immediately after sunset the Hujjāj will proceed towards Muzdalifah. Here they will perform Maghrib Salāh and Ishā Salāh at the time of Ishā regardless of whether they are performed in the Masjid or not. The night will be spent at Muzdalifah.

3rd Day - 10th Dhul-Hijjah
After performing Fajr Salāh in Muzdalifah, set-off back to Minā before sunrise. On this day four important rites have to be performed:

1) Ramee of Jamaratul Aqabah (stoning the big Shaytān only).
2) Zabah (to sacrifice an animal).

3) Halq or Qasr (shaving or trimming the hair of the head).
4) To perform Tawāf-e-Ziyārat.

Note: It is compulsory that the first three acts are performed in their correct sequence as stated. If there is any change in their order then Dam (sacrificing a goat or sheep) will be necessary as a penalty.

4th Day - 11th Dhul-Hijjah
All three Shaytāns have to be pelted on this day and the nights will be spent in Minā. Ramee (i.e. the pelting time) begins after Zawāl and ends before sunset.

5th Day - 12th Dhul-Hijjah
Perform Ramee, i.e. pelt all three Shaytāns after Zawāl. Thereafter a person may now proceed to Makkah. If one wishes to remain in Minā on the 13th of Dhul-Hijjah, then he may do so but he should pelt the three Shaytāns before proceeding to Makkah. The pelting on this day is permissible throughout the day (including the period before Zawāl).

Note: For those people who are performing Hajj for the first time or may not be aware of the rituals of Hajj, it is advisable to accompany a group in which there is a learned scholar to guide them through the different rituals of Hajj.

Meezāb

Q What is the Meezāb-Rahmah?

A Meezāb is the gutter on the roof of the Holy Ka'bah on the side of the Hateem.

Hateem

Q Where is the Hateem situated?

A The Hateem is a semi-circular area surrounded by a shoulder high wall next to the Ka'bah. The Hateem is a part of the Ka'bah.

Maqām Ibrāheem

Q Where is the Maqām Ibrāheem? Is it true that the footprints of Sayyidunā Ibrāheem ﷷ are imprinted on the Maqām Ibrāheem?

A Maqām Ibrāheem is the stone on which Sayyidunā Ibrāheem ﷷ stood when he built the Holy Ka'bah. Allāh ﷻ loved the work of Sayyidunā Ibrāheem ﷷ so much that he caused the trace of his footprints to remain as a reminder to the believers amongst his descendants.

Sayyidunā Saeed Ibn Jubair ؓ narrates that the Holy Prophet ﷺ said, "The stone is the station of Sayyidunā Ibrāheem ﷷ, Allāh ﷻ made it soft and made it a mercy. Sayyidunā Ibrāheem ﷷ would stand on it and Sayyidunā Ismāeel ﷷ, would hand the stones up to him.

Sayyidunā Anas ؓ narrated that Sayyidunā Umar Ibn Khattāb ؓ said, "My opinion was supported by my Lord in three cases. Amongst them was when I said, 'O Messenger of Allāh ﷺ, why do we not take the Maqām Ibrāheem as a place of Salāh?" Then this verse was revealed, **"And take the Maqām of Ibrāheem as a place of Salāh."** (2:125)

At the time of Sayyidunā Ibrāheem ﷷ, the Maqām Ibrāheem was attached to the Holy Ka'bah until it was moved back by Sayyidunā Umar ؓ to the place where it is now.

Sa'ee in the State of Menstruation

Q If a woman after finishing Tawāf, starts her menstruation, can she perform Sa'ee between Safā and Marwā?

A In the above situation, it will be permissible for the woman to perform Sa'ee as to be free from Haidh (menstruation) or Janābat (major impurity) is not a condition for the validity of Sa'ee. However, it is Mustahab to perform Sa'ee in the state of purity. But due to the reason that the Mas'ā (the place of Sa'ee, Safā and Marwā) is now included within Masjidul-Harām, at the present time it will not be permissible for a woman experiencing menstruation to enter the Masjid in order to perform Sa'ee.

Umrah and Menstruation

Q What should a woman do if she experiences menstruation whilst in Umrah?

A All Umrah activities are allowed during menstruation except Tawāf. Tawāf is not allowed because firstly it is Wājib to be in the state of purity when performing Tawāf. Secondly, it is performed in the Masjid for which purity is an essential condition for entering the Masjid. Since a menstruating woman is not in a state of purity, Tawāf cannot be performed. Also, the woman will not perform Sa'ee between Safā and Marwā because they have now become part of the Masjid and for a woman to enter the Masjid in the state of menstruation is prohibited (as mentioned previously).

If a woman is on her way to perform Umrah and she experiences menstruation then there is no harm. She should put on her Ihrām, make intention and read Talbiyah (Labbaik). Thereafter, she will remain in the state of Ihrām and will not perform Tawāf nor Sa'ee until her mensturation ends. Once it ends then she is able to do them both.

If Haidh starts during the Tawāf, she should stop the Tawāf and leave the Masjid immediately. It is sinful to complete the Tawāf or stay in the Masjid after the occurrence of Haidh. However, if she has completed four or more rounds of the Tawāf and thereafter her menstruation begins then the Tawāf is regarded as complete, but she should give Sadaqah for each of the remaining rounds (this Sadaqah is same as Sadaqatul-Fitr). If less than four rounds are complete, then the whole Tawāf is regarded as invalid and Qadhā is necessary when she becomes clean from her Haidh. If she fails to do Qadhā of the Tawāf after attaining purity then as a penalty she must give Dam.

Warning to One Who Neglects Hajj

Q A person has enough gold or cash with which he can perform Hajj, but he/she does not perform it. What will be their consequences regarding this in the Islamic point of view?

A Once a person has cash, gold, silver, shares, excess property etc with which one can perform Hajj at an average cost then Hajj becomes Fardh (compulsory). He must perform Hajj immediately and waste no time. If anyone is able to perform Hajj but does not perform it then severe warnings have been mentioned in the Ahādeeth. One cannot be sure how long one will live, hence Hajj should be performed immediately when it becomes Fardh.

Sayyidunā Abdullāh Ibn Abbās ﷺ narrates that the Holy Prophet ﷺ said, "A person who intends to perform Hajj then he must hasten." (Abū Dāwood)

The Holy Prophet ﷺ has instructed the people on whom Hajj is Fardh to quickly perform it before it is too late. It often happens when it is delayed, obstructions and hindrances occur and such people remain deprived from performing their Fardh Hajj.

Sayyidunā Umar ﷺ used to say, "Whosoever has health and (sufficient) wealth to take him to Hajj and still does not go for Hajj and dies without performing it, then on his forehead the word 'Kāfir' (disbeliever) shall be written on the Day of Judgement." Therefore, when Hajj becomes compulsory it should be performed immediately. In Fatāwa Ālamgheeri it is written: When Hajj becomes compulsory it must be performed in the same year. It is a sin and Makrooh-e-Tahreemi (close to Harām) to delay Fardh Hajj without a valid reason.

In Fatāwa Mahmoodiyah it mentions: It is necessary for a husband who is going for Hajj to take his wife also if Hajj is Fardh on her too. The husband cannot refuse to take her.

Ruling of Ihrām

Q Can you explain the ruling of Ihrām for females? What can she wear and what can't she wear? Is there any difference between the male and the female Ihrām?

A 1. The rulings of Ihrām for a woman are like the rulings of Ihrām for a man. The differences are that it is Wājib for a woman to cover her head, but she is not allowed to let any cloth touch her face, and she is allowed to wear stitched garments.

2. A woman is not allowed to appear before a male stranger without wearing a veil. Therefore, she must have something over her forehead that may support a veil to hide her face without touching it, such as a cap.

3. It is permissible for a woman to wear stitched garments in a state of Ihrām. She may even wear coloured clothes but they must not be dyed with saffron; if they are then she must wash them thoroughly so that the fragrance vanishes from them.

4. A woman is allowed to wear jewellery, socks and gloves while she is in a state of Ihrām. However, it is better that she does not wear them.

5. A woman is not allowed to recite the Talbiyah in a loud voice. She may, however recite it in a voice audible to herself only.

6. A woman should not observe the Idtibā (the covering of the body in a manner that the left shoulder, left arm and back are covered and the right arm exposed), nor Ramal (to walk hastily, taking shorter steps lifting the legs forcefully, keeping the chest out and moving the shoulders simultaneously) during the Tawāf. She should neither walk at a faster pace between the two green columns and fluorescent lights during Sa'ee, but rather she should walk at her normal pace.

If there is a crowd of men, she should not climb the Safā and Marwā. Similarly, in the case of large crowds of men around the Black Stone she should not attempt to kiss it or touch it. Similarly, if there are too many people at the Maqām Ibrāheem, she should perform the two Rak'āts of Tawāf at some other place in the Masjid, not at the Maqām Ibrāheem.

7. A woman is not allowed to shave her head. Therefore, in order to release herself from the Ihrām, she should cut her hair from the tips, the amount equivalent to the first joint of a finger.

8. During menstruation, a woman is permitted to perform every act of Hajj, but she is not permitted to perform Tawāf. If she experiences menstruation before she commences the Ihrām, even then she should have a bath, commence the Ihrām and go through all the acts except Tawāf and Sa'ee.

9. If she has to delay the Tawāf Ziyārah due to menstruation she will not be liable for Dam (sacrifice of sheep), even though in normal circumstances Dam is compulsory as a penalty on the account of delaying.

10. If she experiences menstruation at the time of returning home and she cannot perform the Tawāf Widā then too, the Dam will not be Wājib on her but it is better that she waits until purified and return only after performing the Tawāf Widā. (Muallimul-Hujjāj)

Allāh ﷻ Knows Best

9. CHAPTER ON QURBĀNI

Sending Qurbāni (Sacrifice) Money Abroad

Q What is better, to sacrifice the animal of Qurbāni oneself or send its cost to some other place? Many of us send the money of Qurbāni to poor countries. Is there any fault in this?

A In the above mentioned case, sacrifice is correct without any fault. But it is preferable that one selects an animal himself and if possible slaughters it himself as this animal will be a means of great reward in the Hereafter. If one cannot slaughter the animal himself, then one should at least be present at the place of slaughter.

It is stated in Tabarāni that the Holy Prophet ﷺ said to Sayyidah Fātimah ﷺ, "O Fātimah! Be near the sacrificial animal because for each drop of its blood, your former sins will be pardoned. Hence to be present at the time of such divine favour is better and will be reckoned as appreciation of divine bounty."

Sayyidah Fātimah ﷺ asked, "O Messenger of Allāh ﷺ, is this divine favour special for us, the members of your family or is it common for all?" He replied, "(It is not special for us) but it is for us as well as for every Muslim."

It is Mustahab to partake of the meat of ones own sacrifice. If possible, one should partake of this meat of ones own sacrificed animal on the very day of Eid and feed it to neighbours, relatives and other poor people. One is deprived of these blessings if one gets the sacrifice done at other places. If it is done like this on account of some disability or valid reason, then one can hope for the full or even more reward, for all depends on the correct method and intention. One can arrange Qurbāni at one's birth place to fulfill the rights of ones relatives.

Distributing Qurbāni Meat

Q How should we distribute the meat of Qurbāni?

A It is recommended that the meat be divided into three parts.
1.   One part for oneself.
2.   One part for the family, relatives and friends.
3.   One part for the poor and needy.

Nevertheless, it is also permissible to give all the meat away or to keep all the meat for oneself as well.

Distributing Qurbāni Meat to Non-Muslims

Q Can we give Qurbāni meat to non-Muslims?

A Yes, it can be given to non-Muslims.

Aqeeqah

Q What is Aqeeqah and when should the Aqeeqah take place? Is there any difference in the Aqeeqah of a male child and a female child?

A When a child is born, male or female, it is Sunnah that the child be given a name on the seventh day of birth. When the hair of the head of the baby is shaved, a sacrifice is also offered which is called Aqeeqah. By performing Aqeeqah, all impurities of the child are removed and the child is saved from all calamities by the grace of Allāh ﷻ.

The method of performing Aqeeqah is that for a male child it is Sunnah that two goats or sheep are sacrificed whereas for a female child only one goat or sheep is sacrificed. If an animal of seven shares (cow or camel) is used for Aqeeqah then two shares will be taken for a male and one for a female.

It is also a Sunnah that the hair of the child is shaved. Silver, equal to the weight of the shaved hair should also be given in charity.

Aqeeqah should be performed on the seventh day of the birth of a child. If not done on the seventh day, then on the following seventh day of the following week and so on whenever possible. For instance if the child was born on a Friday, then Aqeeqah should be performed on the following Thursday (the 7th day after birth). If it is not performed on this Thursday, then any other Thursday. According to the Hanafi school of thought Aqeeqah is Sunnah. The Holy Prophet ﷺ has said, "The child is pawned against its Aqeeqah, hence an animal should be slaughtered on its behalf on the 7th day and it should be given a name and its head should be shaven."

The word 'pawned' (bonded) has been explained differently:

1. It has been stated in the Ahādeeth that an infant will intercede on behalf of its parents, but if the Aqeeqah is not performed in spite of having the ability to do so and the child dies in infancy, it will then not intercede on behalf of its parents. Just as a pawned article is of no use to a person, this child too, will be of no use to its parents.

2. Without the Aqeeqah, the child remains deprived of safety as well as blessings i.e. as long as the Aqeeqah is not performed, it is near illness and disease and away from safety.

3. Without the Aqeeqah, the child remains in dirt and is away from cleanliness, as the Holy Prophet ﷺ has said, "For the child there is Aqeeqah, so therefore sacrifice an animal and remove his dirt." (Bukhāri)

It is also stated that the Holy Prophet ﷺ performed Aqeeqah for his grandson, Sayyidunā Hasan ؓ by slaughtering a goat and ordered Sayyidah Fātimah ؓ to get the child's head shaved and give silver equal to the weight of the shaven hair in charity. Sayyidah Fātimah ؓ complied with the order. The weight of the hair was one Dirham or less. (Tirmizi)

Sayyidunā Abū Burdah ؓ reports in another Hadeeth, "During the Days of Ignorance (pre-Islamic era) we used to slaughter a goat on the birth of a child and apply the goats blood onto the infant's head, now that Allāh ﷻ has favoured us with Islām, we slaughter a goat on the 7th day of the child's birth, shave its head and apply saffron to the shaven head." (Abū Dāwood)

Hence applying a thin paste of saffron on the shaven head is also praiseworthy and proven from the above Hadeeth.

Every wealthy person should perform Aqeeqah. If one does not possess sufficient money, then it is permissible for such a person to sacrifice only one goat for a male child as this is also proven from Hadeeth. There is no harm if Aqeeqah is not performed provided one does not have the means for Aqeeqah.

Those animals that are not permissible for Qurbāni, are also not permissible for Aqeeqah. Requirements for the animals of Qurbāni and Aqeeqah are the same. It is permissible to distribute the meat of Aqeeqah, raw or cooked and it can also be served to guests.

Allāh ﷻ Knows Best

10. CHAPTER ON
DEATH
& INHERITANCE

Distribution of Wealth

Q My father passed away in India and we would like to distribute his wealth according to the Islamic Law. My father left behind the following relations:

1) 2nd wife (1st wife passed away long time ago).
2) 3 sons (2 from 2nd marriage and 1 from 1st marriage).
3) 1 sister.

I will be most grateful if you would kindly advise me as to how we can distribute my late father's wealth according to the Islamic Law.

A In reference to your question, after the burial expenses, clearing all outstanding debts and will (which will be executed from only one third of his wealth), your father's wealth will be divided into twenty four parts. Three parts will be given to the second wife and each son will receive seven parts.

Note: The sister will not receive any wealth in the presence of the sons.

Engraving on the Slab Stone

Q Is it permissible to engrave the name, date of birth and death of the deceased on a slab stone?

A It is permissible to engrave the name of the deceased and his date of birth and death on a slab stone. It is stated in Noorul-Eedha (a famous book of Fiqh). There is no fault in writing on it so that its sign does not fade and it is not trampled on. The same ruling is given in Shāmi (a famous book in jurisprudence): There is no fault in writing to preserve the sign of the grave and so that it is not disrespected. But it is not recommended to write if the need does not arise. Even though the Fuqahā have permitted writing in the cases of necessity, it is better not to inscribe anything.

Constructing Solid Graves

Q Is the constructing of solid graves permissible? Nowadays many Muslims are erecting tombs and grave stones etc.

A It is not permissible to build solid graves. It is prohibited in the light of the Ahādeeth. It is mentioned in a Hadeeth of Saheeh Muslim that the Holy Prophet 鐴 has forbidden the construction of solid graves, the erecting of a building on it and sitting on top of it.

Hence the Fuqahā (jurists) have prohibited the placing of solid bricks in the grave, building a solid platform around it and from taking fire and solid articles of fire near it. (Raddul-Muhtār)

It is beneficial for the dead body if the grave remains earthy. An earthy, neglected and uncared grave is worthier of divine blessings and mercy and more effective for the visitors' hearts. Observing such graves reminds the visitor of death and the scenes before his eyes capture the decline and abhorrence of worldly belongings and thus achieves the objectives of visiting graves.

The love and affection one cherishes for the deceased does not make it necessary that the grave should be made solid and decorated. The love and devotion of the Companions 鐴 for the Holy Prophet 鐴 is outstanding. They would not let his ablution water fall on the ground but would take it into their hands and anoint it over their faces and yet, in spite of this unparalleled love and reverence, they did not erect a solid grave for their most beloved Master. We, too should follow in their footsteps.

Note: There is much wisdom and many reasons in the laws and commands of Islām. If solid graves were not forbidden, then today there would have been graves everywhere and it would have become extremely difficult to find and obtain land for farming and living. We should therefore be very grateful to Allāh 鐴 for the Islamic Laws.

Du'ā after the Janāzah Salāh

Q In many places nowadays I have seen that after the Janāzah Salāh, Du'ā is performed in the standing posture whilst raising the hands. I have heard that it is incorrect to supplicate after the Janāzah Salāh. If it is, then what should a person do after the Janāzah Salāh?

A The Janāzah Salāh itself is a Du'ā for the deceased. After the first Takbeer Thanā (praises) is recited, after the second Takbeer Durood Shareef is recited followed by the third Takbeer after which the Du'ā, that comprises invoking of forgiveness for the deceased and of safety of Imān (faith) for the living is read. Thereafter the fourth Takbeer is said and then the Salāh is concluded by the two Salāms. The words of this Du'ā have been taught by the Holy Prophet ﷺ. The method of detaining the dead body after the Janāzah Salāh for collective Du'ā is not proven from the Holy Prophet ﷺ nor from the Companions ﷺ. Hence this method should be given up. The Holy Prophet ﷺ has stated, "Anyone who does any work which we have not ordered or practiced is Mardood (rejected)." (Muslim)

Sayyidunā Huzaifah ﷺ reports, "You should not perform any Salāh which the Companions ﷺ of the Holy Prophet ﷺ did not perform."

From the time of the Holy Prophet ﷺ till this day, the Fuqahā (jurists) have continuously issued the verdict that Du'ā after the Janāzah Salāh is forbidden and Makrooh.

1. In Khulāsatul-Fatāwa it is written, "Do not stand for Du'ā and recitation of the Holy Qur'ān before and after the Janāzah Salāh."

2. In Fatāwa Sirājiyah, Shaykh Sirājuddin Awshi ﷺ states, "When one has finished the Janāzah Salāh, one should not pause for invoking."
(Fatāwa Sirājiyyah and Qādhikhān)

3. In Fatāwa Bazāziah it is written, "Since one has already performed Du'ā once, one should not stay for Du'ā after the Janāzah Salāh because the major part of the Janāzah Salāh itself is Du'ā."

4. In Bahrur-Rāiq, Shaykh Ibn Nujaim Misri ﷺ writes, "One should not perform Du'ā after the termination of the Janāzah Salāh."

5. Mulla Ali Qāri ﷺ writes in his famous commentary of Mishkāt-Mirqātul-Mafātih; "One should not make Du'ā for the dead after the Janāzah Salāh because it creates doubts of exceeding the Janāzah Salāh."

After the Janāzah Salāh, people should hasten towards burying the deceased instead of wasting their time in such acts which are clearly contrary to the Sunnah.

It is established from correct and authentic Ahādeeth that after the burial, the people should engage themselves in the recitation of the Holy Qur'ān and in asking forgiveness near the grave for as much time as would be required for slaughtering a camel and distributing its meat. This is Mustahab and the deceased benefit from it.

Etiquettes of Ta'ziat (Condolence)

Q What is the ruling and etiquettes of Ta'ziat. Can you explain the period of Ta'ziat as well please?

A The word Ta'ziat means to sympathise with the bereaved. It is from the teachings of the Holy Prophet 📿 that one should console and comfort a Muslim who is in distress. The Holy Prophet 📿 has said, "He who consoles the one in distress shall be rewarded as much as the bereaved."

Etiquettes of making Ta'ziat:

1. Be very humble and sympathetic.
2. Express one's grief and sorrow.
3. Speak little about worldly affairs.
4. Avoid joke and laughter.
5. Offer help and guidance.
6. Mention only good acts of the deceased and abstain from the evil ones.
7. Do not enquire too extensively regarding the deceased.

The period of Ta'ziat is three days after the time of death. It is Makrooh (undesirable) to make Ta'ziat after three days, except in cases where one is not present at the funeral or one is coming from a far off place. Ta'ziat can be made before burial.

Dying with Imān

Q What Du'ā or act can I perform to ensure that I die with Imān. i.e. being able to recite the Shahādah at the time of death?

A Pray to Allāh 🕌 to keep oneself steadfast on Imān and always abstain from sins. Shaykh Ashraf Ali Thānwi 🕌 has written in his book 'Remedies from the Holy Qur'ān' that if one recites verse number 8 of Sūrah Al-Imrān after every Fardh Salāh, then Inshā-Allāh one will die with Imān.

"Our Lord, do not allow our hearts to deviate after You have guided us and grant us Mercy from Your Presence. Indeed You are the Bestower." (3:8)

Female Kafn (Shroud)

Q Is it true that a female burial shroud (Kafn) consists of a long Qamees (shirt), a simple Salwār (trousers) and a material to wrap the body in? Should this Salwār Qamees be white and one that she wore whilst alive and prayed in? How many yards should the material be?

A According to the Sunnah, the burial shroud (Kafn) for a woman is made of five pieces of cloth. They are as follows, a Qamees (shirt) that is from the neck to the feet without any sleeves or tapering at the bottom, an Izār (wrapper) from head to toe; a Lifāfah (outer wrapper), this will be sufficiently long in order to exceed the head and the feet so that it can be tied above the head and below the feet; a Orni (veil) for her head and face, and a Sinaband (cloth), the width of which is from her breasts to at least her navel in order to cover her breasts.

The quality of the cloth should be equivalent to what she wore on Eid days whilst alive. It is better if the material used for the burial shroud is white cotton. The burial shroud should not contain sleeves, nor tapered at the ends, and neither should the ends be folded over. (Marāqil-Falāh)

As the burial shroud will have no sleeves, nor is there a Salwār within the burial shroud, it can be deduced that an existing Salwār Qamees cannot be used. The material itself does not have to be new; a used, washed material will be sufficient. The length of the material would depend on the size and height of the deceased.

Sending the Dead Body to One's Native Land

Q What is the Islamic ruling regarding sending the deceased to one's native country?

A The Islamic ruling is that after the death of a Muslim occurs, male or female, the body should be given a bath, shrouded and the Janāzah Salāh performed as soon as possible.

When death occurs, then the bathing, shrouding and the burial should be hastened in respect of the deceased, which is clearly mentioned in many Ahādeeth. It is improper that the body of a Muslim be delayed in its burial.

It is Sunnah and desirable to bury the deceased in the graveyard of the locality where the death occurred. It is Makrooh Tahreemi (near forbidden) to transport the body to another town or country (without a valid excuse).

If there is no graveyard for Muslims at the place of death or there is a valid excuse, then in such circumstances it will be permissible to transfer the body to the nearest graveyard. In transporting a deceased person to another country, many prohibited things are committed e.g.

1. The burial of the deceased is delayed while Islām requires that the burial should take place as soon as possible.

2. Delay in burial results in the deceased developing unpleasant odours and physical decay.

3. At the death of a husband, the wife is required to observe Iddat (a period of waiting for 4 months and 10 days). Contrary to this, the wife sometimes also travels with the coffin. This is prohibited.

4. Heavy costs are incurred without a valid reason.

5. The coffin is stored and carried like other luggage which is highly disrespectful to the dead body.

6. Health regulations of both of the respective countries require the body to be injected with certain substances due to which the honour and dignity of the deceased is not upheld. It is compulsory to respect and honour the dead body in the same way as it is compulsory when alive.

7. In some places, the internal organs of the deceased are removed. If this is correct, then this is not permissible at all. It is a great injustice to dispose the internal organs of the deceased in this manner.

8. The Janāzah Salāh should be performed once only. In transportation of the body, the Janāzah Salāh is usually performed again.

These are some of the reasons for which transportation of the dead body is not permissible. Hence, it is necessary to bury one's deceased in the nearest cemetery.

What to Recite in the Graveyard

Q What is the best Du'ā that may be read in the graveyard?

A There are numerous Du'ās which can be recited in the graveyard. The most virtuous is the recitation of the Holy Qur'ān. Stand facing the grave and recite as much Holy Qur'ān as possible and make Du'ā for the forgiveness of the deceased.

Recite Sūrah al-Ikhlās 11 times. It is related in a Hadeeth that whoever visits the graveyard and recites Sūrah Al-Ikhlās 11 times and then supplicates for the deceased, he will be rewarded as many as the number of dead people in the graveyard. It has been related in another Hadeeth that whoever visits the graveyard and recites Sūrah Al-Fātihah, Sūrah Al-Ikhlās and Sūrah At-Takāsur and then prays for the deceased, the people of the graveyard will also ask Allāh ﷻ for such a person's forgiveness.

We have to remember that we should only adopt the method and practice shown to us by our beloved Prophet ﷺ. The Ahādeeth of the Holy Prophet ﷺ only mentions salutations and Du'ās for the deceased and remembering death. Placing wreaths, flowers, paying homage, etc. are incorrect and have no basis in Islām.

Lighting Lamps & Decorating the Grave

Q What is the ruling regarding placing a cloth over the grave and lighting lamps at the side of graves?

A It is against the Sunnah and impermissible to place a cloth over the grave. This practice was never done at the time of the golden era - the era of the Holy Prophet ﷺ, the Companions ؓ, Tābi'een ؓ, or the era of the four Imāms ؓ.

Regarding the lighting of lamps, Sayyidunā Abdullāh Ibn Abbās ؓ relates, "The Holy Prophet ﷺ cursed those people who make the graves a place of worship and those who light lamps there." (Mishkāt)

Mulla Ali Qāri ؓ mentions in the commentary of this narration: "The reason for the prohibition of lighting lamps at the gravesides is either because it is a waste of money, since it is not beneficial to anyone, and also because fire is a sign of Jahannam (which should be kept far from graves), or this prohibition is in order to prevent excessive respect being granted to the graveyard, just as it is prohibited to make the graves a site for worship."

It is stated in Raddul-Muhtār, "It is Makrooh Tahreemi to place a cloth on a grave."

Giving Bath to the Deceased

Q What are the virtues of giving bath to the deceased? Nowadays people are scared and reluctant to carry out this duty.

A There are many virtues of giving bath to the dead body. Sayyidunā Abū Umāmah ؓ relates that the Holy Prophet ﷺ said, "If anyone gives a bath to the dead and conceals it (does not disclose its faults) then Allāh ﷻ will conceal his sins (he will not be disgraced in the Hereafter because of his sins). Furthermore, he who shrouds the dead will be clothed by Allāh ﷻ in the Hereafter with silk garments." (Kanzul-Ummāl)

We can realise how virtuous this act is according to the above Hadeeth. Thus a person should not be scared to handle the dead or consider it an ill omen or bad luck. He should undertake the task of bathing the dead with a willing heart and receive the great rewards mentioned in the Ahādeeth.

In another Hadeeth, Sayyidunā Ali ؓ relates that the Holy Prophet ﷺ said, "If anyone bathes the dead, shrouds him and applies Hanoot (perfume) to him, carries his Janāzah, performs his Salāh and does not disclose his defects that he witnesses, then his sins will be removed from him as he was when his mother gave birth to him." (That is his minor sins will be forgiven).

(Kanzul-Ummāl)

Women Visiting the Graveyard

Q What is the ruling regarding women visiting the graveyard?

A According to a group of scholars, it is not permissible for women to visit the graveyard because the Holy Prophet ﷺ said specifically regarding women, "Allāh ﷻ has cursed the female visitors to the grave." (Mishkāt)

Therefore it is impermissible and prohibited for women to go to visit graves or shrines in any condition and at any place.

However, in another Hadeeth, the Holy Prophet ﷺ said, "I used to forbid you from visiting the grave. (Now that this prohibition has been lifted). Visit them now, because it lessens the desire for this world and reminds one of the Hereafter." (Mishkāt)

The Holy Prophet ﷺ in order to save his Ummah from the ignorant practices of grave-worship etc. initially forbade them from visiting the graves. After these evil practices were eradicated from the people, the Holy Prophet ﷺ gave consent for the visiting of the graves.

Hence from this Hadeeth, it can be deduced that it is permissible for both man and woman to visit the graveyard.

Shaykh Ashraf Ali Thānwi ﷺ states in Imdādul-Fatāwa: "What is the purpose of women going to the graveyard? If they are going only for crying out loud, or to perform irreligious acts, or to honour their oaths and pledges, then it is impermissible and prohibited for them to go for these things. And if they are going for taking heed and for sending reward, then it is permissible for them to go provided that they are aged and stable. It is Makrooh for young women to go to the graveyard."

Nowadays, women in our localities are not in their Hijāb, and the graveyard is a place of solitude. Instead of visiting graves for taking heed, many acts contrary to Islām are committed there. Acts of Shirk (polytheism) are being committed besides the graves. For the above mentioned reasons, women will be forbidden from visiting the graveyard.

However, if at some places women are accompanied with their Mahram (close relatives to whom marriage is prohibited) to visit the graves and the women observe the full Hijāb and instead of crying and wailing, they respect the etiquettes of the graveyard, and furthermore there is full surety that they will abstain from the aforementioned vices, only then they will be permitted to visit the graveyard.

Attending the Funeral of non-Muslims

Q My next door neighbour who is a non-Muslim has died. Is it permissible for me to attend his funeral?

A If one has to join out of necessity or because of being a neighbour, then there is a scope of permissibility for it. However, they should not participate in any such ceremonies that are contrary to Islām.

It is permissible rather recommended to express your sympathy and give your condolences to your neighbours at times of grief and sorrow. Hence, show your full support and co-operation (within the perimeters of Islam) for them.

Right to Enter the Grave

Q Who has more right to enter the grave?

A The Wali (legal guardian) or the representative of the deceased has the highest right to enter the grave.

They should go down and others may follow them after obtaining permission from the representative. In the case of a woman, only her Mahram must enter the grave, if necessary her husband can also enter the grave.

The Wali or representative of the deceased will be accordingly; male children of the deceased i.e. the sons and in their absence, their male offspring i.e. the grandsons.

Then the deceased's father, paternal grandfather and great grandfather. Then his brothers, the paternal uncles and paternal cousins. In their absence, the husband of the deceased. In absence of all the above, any Mahram or in case of a deceased man, his neighbours will have the right. (Shāmi, Ālamgheeri)

Number of People Entering the Grave

Q How many people should enter the grave to lower the dead body and who has the most right to enter?

A According to the need, 2, 3 or 4 people can enter the grave. Islām has not fixed any specific number. The amount of people should be based on necessity. However in terms of authority, the Wali (legal guardian) has the most right to enter the grave. He should go down first and others can also go after seeking permission from the Wali. In the case of a woman, only her Mahram relatives should enter the grave, if necessary, her husband can also enter the grave. A Wali of the deceased will be accordingly: male children of the deceased, e.g. son and in his absence, his male offspring etc. then the deceased's father, paternal grandfather etc. then his brothers, then paternal uncles and paternal cousins. In their absence, the husband of the deceased. In absence of all of the above Mahram or in the case of a deceased male, his neighbours will have the right to enter the grave. (Shāmi)

Punishment in the Grave

Q Is there punishment in the grave before Qiyāmah (Day of Judgement)? What is the proof?

A The life of the Hereafter has two stages. From death to resurrection known as 'Ālame Barzakh'.

From resurrection to eternity known as 'Ālame Mahshar'.

It is proven from the Holy Qur'ān and Ahādeeth that a person is sometimes punished during the period between death and resurrection. Death means the separation of the soul from the body. The soul is then transmitted to another world. Muslims should firmly believe in all the detailed explanations given by the Holy Prophet 鬱 with regard to the grave and Qiyāmah.

The Holy Qur'ān says, **"The Fire; they are exposed to it, morning and afternoon, and on the Day when the Hour will be established (it will be said to the angels): 'Enter Pharaoh's people to the severest torment'."** (40:46)

This verse proves the two stages of punishment. Barzakh (life of the grave) and Mahshar (Day of Judgement). In another verse, Allāh 鬱 says, **"Because of their sins they were drowned, then they were made to enter the Fire, and they found none to help them instead of Allāh."** (71:25)

In this verse we learn that the people of Nooh 鬱 were admitted into the fire immediately after being drowned. Surely this is before Qiyāmah (Mahshar). Moreover, Allāh 鬱 states in the Holy Qur'ān regarding the Shuhadā (martyrs), **"Think not of those who are killed in the way of Allāh as dead. Nay, they are alive, with their Lord well provided."** (3:169)

The pious servants of Allāh 鬱 are in peace and comfort even before Qiyāmah. The Holy Prophet 鬱 has said that a voice comes from the Heavens, "My servant was truthful, spread for him the carpets of Jannah and dress him in the clothing of Jannah and open for him the doors of Jannah." The doors of Jannah are opened for him and he begins to enjoy the cool and fragrant breeze of Jannah and his grave is widened for him as far as his eyes can see. These verses of the Holy Qur'ān and the Ahādeeth prove that there is reward and punishment in the grave.

Cutting the Nails and Hair of the Deceased

Q Is it permissible to cut the nails and hair of the deceased when giving a bath?

A After a person passes away, everything should be left as it is. Hence the hair should not be cut nor combed and the toe and finger nails should not be clipped. (Sharhul Bidāyah)

Janāzah Salāh with Shoes on

Q Can Janāzah Salāh be performed with shoes on or by standing on them?

A It is permissible to perform Janāzah Salāh with shoes on or whilst standing on them with the condition that the shoes are free from impurities. If they are not clean then the Janāzah Salāh will not be valid. If you are unsure then it is preferable to remove them.

Language of the Questioning in the Grave

Q In which language is the deceased in the grave questioned?

A It is stated in the Kitāb "Sharhus-Sudoor Fi-Sharh-Hālil-Mawtā-wal-Quboor" written by the great scholar Imām Jalāl-ud-Deen Suyūti ﷺ that according to some scholars the questioning is done in the Syriac language. However, Hāfiz Ibn Hajar's ﷺ analysis is that the Ahādeeth explicitly and clearly state that the questioning is done in the Arabic language. It is also possible that each individual will be questioned in his/her mother's tongue.

Stillborn Child

Q What is the Islamic ruling regarding a stillborn child?

A If a child is stillborn and there are no signs of life at the time of birth, then he will be given a Ghusl (bath) in the normal way. However, he should not be wrapped in the normal Kafn. Instead, the child should be wrapped in a piece of cloth and buried without performing the Janāzah Salāh.

It is Mustahab to name the child. But if a child died after being born alive, then he should be given Ghusl and Kafn as normal. Janāzah Salāh will also be performed upon him and he will be buried in the normal way. Also the child will be named.

If a woman had a miscarriage and the infant's limbs i.e. its hands, feet, face, nose etc. are not formed, then it should not be bathed nor shrouded in a Kafn. Instead, it should be wrapped in a piece of cloth and buried. Nevertheless, if any of its limbs are formed then the same rule will apply as that of a stillborn baby. That is, it will be given a name and Ghusl will be performed. But it should not be given the normal Kafn nor should Janāzah Salāh be performed upon it. Instead, it should be wrapped in a cloth and buried.

At the Time of Death

Q I was present at the death bed of my father during his last moments. What should a person do in such a sorrowful situation?

A At the time when a person is in his last moments of life, those present should recite Sūrah Yāseen and Sūrah R'ad. The Talqeen should be done (Talqeen is to remind the dying person of the two Shahādah). Those present should remember that the Muhtadar (a person on whom the signs of death are visible) must not be ordered to recite the Kalimah but must be helped to recite it. This can easily be done by those present in the room reciting the Kalimah aloud. Once the departing person recites the Kalimah, all who are present should remain silent.

The dying person should not be drawn into any worldly discussions, but if he discusses any worldly affairs, then the Talqeen should be repeated. It is recommended that a scholar or a pious person is present in the room so that the mercy of Allāh ﷻ descends.

Any person who is in the state of Janābat, Haidh or Nifās should not be in the room.

Compulsory Acts of Janāzah Salāh

Q What are the compulsory acts of Janāzah Salāh?

A There are two Fardh in Janāzah Salāh:

1. To stand and perform the Salāh.
2. To perform the four Takbeers.

The Place of the Imām in Janāzah Salāh

Q Where should the Imām stand in Janāzah?

A The Imām in Janāzah Salāh will stand in line with the chest of the deceased. The body of the deceased will be placed with his head on the right side of the Imām.

The Muqtadis (followers) will make an odd number of rows. The rows for Janāzah Salāh should be close to one another because there are no Ruku or Sajdah to be made.

Late Arrivers in Janāzah

Q How should I complete my Janāzah Salāh when the Imām has already called out one Takbeer or more?

A Whoever arrives after the Imām has called out one or more Takbeers should wait and join the Imām when he calls the next Takbeer and continue with the Imām. After the Salām he should then complete the missed Takbeers, by just saying the Takbeer 'Allāhu Akbar' once for every Takbeer missed.

Between these Takbeers, no Thanā, Durood Shareef or Du'ā should be read. If the Imām has completed the fourth Takbeer (before he has said the Salām) then too, the late comers should join and complete all missed Takbeers after the Salām.

Allāh ﷻ Knows Best

11. CHAPTER ON
LAWFUL & UNLAWFUL

Medicine Containing Harām Ingredients

Q I have recently discovered that the insulin used by diabetics to maintain their sugar level is obtained from the pancreas of a pig. Would this be acceptable (i.e. to use this insulin) under Islamic law, considering the fact that the diabetic needs the insulin to maintain his sugar level for survival and pain relief. To the best of my knowledge, there is no alternative. Please can you provide me with any evidence from the Holy Qur'ān and Ahādeeth.

A It is stated in the Holy Qur'ān, **"He (Allāh ﷻ) has forbidden for you, only the Maytah (dead animal), blood, the flesh of swine and that which is slaughtered as a sacrifice for other than Allāh ﷻ (or has been slaughtered for idols etc.). But if one is forced by necessity neither rebelliously nor transgressing the limits, then there is no sin for him. Truly Allāh ﷻ is Forgiving and Most Merciful."** (2:173)

From this verse an injunction can be deduced that to use forbidden products for medical purposes in exceptional circumstances is permissible. However, only under the following extreme conditions can prohibited medicine be permissible:

1. In a critical state where life is in danger.
2. The health is so critical that by not consuming such medicine, the health will severely deteriorate permanently.
3. There is no alternative Halāl medicine available.
4. The Harām medicine used is effective as a cure for that particular illness or disease.
5. There is no carnal desire involved during the usage of the Harām product other than for the cure.
6. Only the amount needed should be used (not to exceed the limits).
7. An expert doctor informs that there is no alternative cure other than that substance.

If all the aforementioned conditions are met then in such a critical condition, Harām products can be used for medical purposes.

However, in this day and age, because the usage of Harām medicine are endemically found, the Fuqahā (jurists) have given permission to use them in usual conditions of illness when no other Halāl medicines are available.

(Ma'āriful Qur'ān, vol.1 pg. 426-427)

It is stated in Durrul Mukhtār that the Fuqahā have differed regarding seeking a cure through Harām products. The stronger verdict is Harām. But the present Ulamā have given permission if it is discovered that the Harām product is the only cure, and no other medicine is known.

Coloured Contact Lenses

Q Is it permissible to wear coloured contact lenses?

A To wear coloured contact lenses without the intention of pride, deceiving and showing-off is permissible.

Measles Injection

Q Are children allowed to have the measles injection?

A The measles injection can be taken if one is at risk, otherwise it is preferable to refrain from it.

Post-Mortem

Q Is post-mortem permissible in Islām? Sometimes post-mortems lead to information that may help save other lives. Many times a post-mortem is done to discover the reason of a mysterious and suspicious death. What is the Islamic verdict?

A All things and practices have their advantages as well as their disadvantages. Islām has outlawed many of those practices that consist of more harmful effects inspite of their benefits.

While acknowledging the benefits of post-mortems, Islām does not permit this form of mutilation of the body in normal circumstances due to the following reasons:

a) The human body is sacred and an object of honour and respect. Cutting it, dissecting it and mutilating it is not permissible no matter what beneficial results may stem from such post-mortems.

b) The human body does not belong to any person, hence man has no right to use and misuse the human body.

Islām has declared unlawful the cutting and the dissecting of the body of a human in normal situations. However, Islām has made some exceptions to this law in extreme critical circumstances e.g.:

1) A pregnant woman dies and the baby is alive inside her. In this case, it is compulsory to cut open the body and remove the baby. However if the baby is already dead, then it is not lawful to cut the dead body. (Fatāwa Ālamgheeri)

2) A person unlawfully takes possession of another person's property and thus swallows it e.g. a precious stone and dies. In this case if the owner demands his wealth it will be paid from the estate of the deceased. If the deceased has left sufficient wealth to compensate for the liability, it will not be permissible to operate on him to remove the article.

However, if he does not possess sufficient wealth to compensate for the item which he had swallowed and the owner demands his wealth, the body will be cut and the item returned to its rightful owner.

These are some exceptions allowed in Islām because the rights of others are involved. Under normal circumstances post-mortems are not permissible. Another important point to remember is that Islām has ordained many rules and acts applicable for the Mayyit (deceased). For instance, bodies used for experimental purposes by medical students are deprived from the holy rituals such as Ghusl (bath), Kafn (shroud), Dafn (burial) etc. The teachings of Islām regarding this matter are all abandoned in cases of mutilation or experiments on bodies.

Perfume or Cream Containing Alcohol

Q Is it permissible to use perfumes or creams which contain alcohol?

A Those perfumes or creams that contain alcohol will either contain original or artificial alcohol. Perfumes or creams that contain original alcohol are not permissible at all to use. However, if they contain artificial alcohol then they are usually permissible to use. It is recommended that you enquire regarding each product to determine its permissibility.

Honeymoon

Q What does Islām say about a couple celebrating honeymoon?

A Islām does not recognise the concept of honeymoon.

Hypnotism

Q Is it permissible for Muslims to get hypnotised?

A No, this is not permissible in Islām.

Smoking

Q Is smoking Harām or is it Makrooh? Scientifically it is proven that smoking is seriously harmful to the health and may even be fatal. But the majority of the Ulamā say that smoking is Makrooh. Please can you explain fully with proof of what your opinion is.

A Smoking is prohibited according to Islām due to the disastrous affects it has upon the human body. The earlier Ulamā who had ruled that smoking was Makrooh did so only on account of it being an offensive odour. If they were aware of the harmful affects of smoking, then undoubtedly they would have issued a different ruling to prohibit this harmful practice. Smoking did not exist at the time of the Holy Prophet ﷺ but our religion Islām has laid down general principles from which many laws are derived. From these principles, the Fuqahā (jurists) have come to the conclusion that smoking is prohibited.

Allāh ﷻ describing the mission of the Holy Prophet ﷺ says, **"He commands them to do good and prevents them from evil and makes Halāl for them that which is pure and makes Harām for them that which is impure." (7:157)**

This verse clearly denotes pure things to be Halāl and impure things to be Harām (forbidden). An intelligent person would no doubt regard smoking to be from amongst the impure things. The literal meaning of impurity is a bad thing which has a bad taste and smell. These two qualities are found in a cigarette.

In another verse Allāh ﷻ says, **"And do not squander (your wealth). Indeed the squanderers are the brothers of Shaytān." (17:27)**

Another verse of the Holy Qur'ān states, **"And do not waste, for Allāh does not love those who waste." (6:141)**

It is stated in a Hadeeth, "Verily Allāh ﷻ has prohibited for you disobedience to parents, burying daughters alive, to deny what you owe and demand what you have no right to and has disliked for you hearsay (gossip), excessive questioning and the squandering of wealth." (Bukhāri, Muslim)

Without any doubt, purchasing cigarettes is destruction, wasting and squandering of wealth. This is not permissible according to the consensus of the Jurists.

The Holy prophet ﷺ said, "Whoever eats (raw) garlic or onion should keep away from us, keep far away from our Masājid and should sit at home."

This is concerning the odour of the two vegetables, so what about the offensive stench of cigarettes which harms the smoker and irritates other people? Its foul smell is worse than the smell of garlic and onion.

Smoking causes fatal illnesses i.e. lung cancer, bronchitis etc. Allāh ﷻ states in the Holy Qur'ān, **"And do not throw yourself into destruction with your own hands." (2:195)**

In another verse of the Holy Qur'ān, Allāh ﷻ says, **"And do not kill yourselves." (4:29)**

The Holy Prophet ﷺ said, "Whomsoever drinks poison, thereby killing himself will sip this poison forever and ever in the fire of Jahannam (Hell)."

Cigarettes consist of many poisonous substances, furthermore the smoker indulges in a slow suicidal act by inhaling this poison.

In another Hadeeth it is stated, "A person should not commit such an act which is harmful and cause harm to others."

Smoking is purely a combination of harming oneself and causing harm to others.

The difference of opinion between the Muslim scholars is that smoking is either Harām or Makrooh Tahreemi. Nevertheless, people misunderstand the term 'Makrooh'.

In Raddul-Muhtār, it is stated: Makrooh Tahreemi is a terminology which is used to denote its closeness to Harām, infact some have said it is another term used for Harām.

There is no difference between the Ulamā that something considered to be Makrooh consists of a sin, just as something Harām involves a sin. In fact to think of an act of sin as something small makes it worse than Harām. To abstain from smoking is necessary just as it is necessary to refrain from any other sin.

We should not be confused and deceived by the word 'Makrooh'. I have mentioned earlier with an ample amount of evidence that smoking is an act of sin irrespective of it being classified Harām or Makrooh-e-Tahreemi. To refrain from it is essential as it is for other prohibited acts.

Islām and the Beard

Q Some people do not keep a beard saying that if we keep a beard and do some wrong action, we will be disgracing those who keep beards and showing disrespect to the beard. They say that when we start praying, fasting etc. and become good Muslims, then we will keep the beard. What is the ruling with regard to such people?

A The feeling of such people outwardly may seem very pleasing and also convincing. It seems as if they desire to uphold and honour the status of the beard, but in reality if we ponder slightly deeper, we will realise that this is an evil deception.

Through this very trick, Shaytān has deceived many and involved them in sins. Understand this from the following example: A Muslim has deceived a certain person, consequently the name of the entire Muslim brotherhood becomes stained. Now, if Shaytān deceives such an individual to think, 'Because of me, the Muslims are being dishonoured. Hence, (Allāh 🕮 Forbid) I shall now renounce Islām', so can this ever be justified? Surely this is an action which he should never ever think of doing! Instead he should become a true Muslim and desist from his misconduct.

Similarly if Shaytān provokes a person saying, "If you grow a beard and commit evil then the beard would be disrespected and those who are keeping beards will be disgraced. Hence, abandon this Sunnah." He should never ever do this, rather he should grow his beard and save himself from misconduct. A person should never forsake a good deed for a bad, but rather abandon a sin for the sake of good.

If such people really intend to uphold and honour this sign of Islām, then logically, and from an Islamic point of view, they should lengthen their beards and refrain from misconduct and major sins. Furthermore, pray to Allāh 🕮 to grant them the ability of upholding this great symbol and sign of Islām, so that on the Day of Judgement they can be resurrected in the state of an Islamic appearance and consequently be blessed with the intercession of the Holy Prophet 🕮. Sayyidunā Abū Hurairah 🕮 narrates that the Holy Prophet 🕮 said, "Everyone from my Ummah will enter Jannah except those who reject." The Sahābah 🕮 asked, "Who are those who reject?" The Holy Prophet 🕮 replied, "The person who follows me will enter Jannah and the person who disobeys me has rejected."

Ruling of the Beard

Q What is the ruling of the beard; is it Wājib or Sunnat? Is it permissible to shave the beard? Many people are of the opinion that keeping the beard is Sunnah. If somebody keeps the beard, it is good and he is following the Sunnah of the Holy Prophet 🕮 just as in the other Sunnats e.g. wearing the turban, using the Miswāk etc. However, if the beard is not kept, then there is no sin. To what extent are these opinions correct?

A It is a misconception to regard the beard as merely an act of Sunnah. In-fact the majority of the scholars and even according to the four schools of thought i.e. Hanafi, Māliki, Shāfi'ee and Hanbali it is stated, that to keep a beard is Wājib (compulsory). Therefore, shaving or trimming the beard (to less than a fist length) is forbidden and a sin. In this regard there are numer-ous Ahādeeth.

1. Sayyidah Ā'ishah ﷺ relates that the Holy Prophet ﷺ said, "Ten things are of nature, in which cutting the moustache and growing of a full beard are mentioned." (Abū Dāwood)

Commentary: From the above mentioned Hadeeth we learn that the cut-ting of the moustache and the lengthening of the beard is a requirement of human nature and the lengthening of the moustache and the cutting of the beard is against the norms of nature. Those people who are involved in this are (indirectly) deforming the nature of Allāh's ﷺ creation (as understood from the above mentioned Hadeeth).

It is mentioned in the Holy Qur'ān that when Shaytān, the accursed, was humiliated in Allāh's ﷺ court he vowed, **"And surely I will lead them astray and I will fill them with vain desires, and I will command them so that they will alter the creation of Allāh." (4:119)**

It is mentioned in Tafseer-e-Haqqāni, Bayānul Qur'ān and other Tafseers that the shaving of the beard is also included as one form of the deforma-tion of the nature of Allāh's ﷺ creation. Allāh ﷺ has naturally bestowed the masculine face with the beauty and dignity of a beard. Hence those people who shave their beards due to the temptations of Shaytān are mutilating not only their faces but their entire nature.

Since the conduct of the Prophets ﷺ is the only criterion for the correct nature for human beings, the word 'Fitrah' refers to their way and their Sun-nah. In this context it means that to trim the moustache and to lengthen the beard is a unanimous Sunnah of approximately 124,000 Prophets ﷺ, who are that blessed group, which the Holy Prophet ﷺ was ordered to follow. It is mentioned in the Holy Qur'ān, **"These are the ones that Allāh guided, so follow their guidance." (6:90)**

Therefore those who shave and cut their beards are opposing the ways of the Prophets. This Hadeeth warns us that the shaving of the beard constitutes of three sins:

a) Opposing human nature.
b) Through the temptations of Shaytān, disfiguring of Allāh's ﷻ creation.
c) Opposing the manner of the Prophets ﷺ.

Because of these three reasons, to shave the beard is prohibited.

2. It is reported from Sayyidunā Abdullāh Ibn Umar ؓ that the Holy Prophet ﷺ said, "Trim the moustache and lengthen the beard." (Bukhāri)

Commentary:
In the above Hadeeth, the order of clipping the moustache and the lengthening of the beard is mentioned. Obedience to the command of the Holy Prophet ﷺ is Wājib (compulsory) and to oppose it, is forbidden. Therefore it is Wājib to lengthen the beard and forbidden to shave it.

3. Sayyidunā Abdullāh Ibn Umar ؓ narrates that he heard the Holy Prophet ﷺ saying, "Oppose the fire worshippers, lengthen the beard and trim the moustache." (Bukhāri)

Commentary:
From this Hadeeth we understand that the keeping of the beard and the clipping of the moustache is a distinguishing feature of a Muslim. On the contrary, to lengthen the moustache and to shave the beard is the feature of a fire worshipper and the idol worshippers.

The Holy Prophet ﷺ has emphasised to his Ummah the inculcation of the features of the Muslims and emphasised the opposing of the fire worshippers and the Mushrikoon. Abandoning the features of a Muslim and taking up traits of other nations is forbidden.

Concerning this the Holy Prophet ﷺ said, "Whomsoever resembles a nation is from amongst them." (Abū Dāwood)

Therefore those who inculcate the practice of others (concerning which the Holy Prophet 🌸 has commanded us to oppose) should fear the grave warning of the Holy Prophet 🌸 that they will be resurrected amongst such people (whom they emulate) on the Day of Judgement.

4. Sayyidunā Zaid Ibn Arqam 🌸 narrates that he heard the Holy Prophet 🌸 saying, "Those who do not trim the moustache are not from amongst us." (Ahmad, Tirmizi, Nasai)

Commentary:

In the above Hadeeth it is mentioned that those who do not clip their moustaches are not from amongst us. It is apparent that this very law will apply to the shaving of the beard as well! This is a very severe warning for those who merely follow their carnal desires and the deception of the Shaytān in shaving their beards. This is why the Holy Prophet 🌸 announced the exclusion of such individuals from his Ummah. Is it possible for anyone having some relationship with the Holy Prophet 🌸 to ignore this warning.

The Holy Prophet 🌸 disliked the shaving of the beard so much so that he even disliked looking at the ambassadors of the king of Persia when they entered the gathering of the Holy Prophet 🌸, in the condition that their beards were shaved off and their moustaches were long.

The Holy Prophet 🌸 addressing them said, "Woe unto you! May you be destroyed! Who has ordered you to do this?" They replied, "Our Master (i.e. the king of Persia) has ordered us." The Holy Prophet 🌸 remarked, "My Lord has commanded me to lengthen the beard and clip the moustache."

Those who violate the command of the Lord of the Holy Prophet 🌸 and follow the lord of the fire worshippers, should repeatedly consider how they will show their faces in the courts of Allāh 🌼 and the Holy Prophet 🌸 on the Day of Judgement?

If the Holy Prophet 🌸 was to say to them, "Because of distorting your appearance you are excluded from our group." Then whose intercession will they hope for?

It has also been derived from this Hadeeth that the lengthening of the moustache and trimming or shaving of the beard is forbidden and a sin. The fact that the Holy Prophet ﷺ has warned that such a person is not one of us, portrays that carrying out such a sin is in fact very severe.

5. Sayyidunā Abdullāh Ibn Abbās ﷺ relates that he heard the Holy Prophet ﷺ saying, "Allāh's ﷻ curse be on those men who emulate women and Allāh's ﷻ curse on those women who emulate men." (Bukhāri)

Commentary:
In this Hadeeth, the Holy Prophet ﷺ has cursed the men who resemble women. In the commentary of this Hadeeth, Mulla Ali Qāri ﷺ, the author of 'Mirqāt' writes that the words 'Allāh's ﷻ curse' could be, a curse which would mean 'May Allāh's ﷻ curse be upon such people' or it could be an informative sentence which would then mean 'Allāh ﷻ curses such people'.

Besides the above mentioned evils of shaving the beard, another evil is the resemblance of women. Allāh ﷻ made the beard a distinguishing feature between men and women. Hence, those who shave their beards eradicate the distinguishing features of men and consequently resemble women thereby incur the curse of Allāh ﷻ and His beloved Prophet ﷺ.

Bearing in mind all the Ahādeeth, the jurists have agreed upon the following facts:

1.   To lengthen the beard is Wājib (compulsory).
2.   It is a sign of Islām.
3.   To shave or trim the beard (shorter than a fist length) is forbidden and a sin.

Organ Transplant

Q Is organ transplant permissible in Islām? Organ transplant involves removing either whole organs or parts of organs and tissues from either animals or other humans and transplanting them into a patient who is desperately in need.

The purpose of organ transplant is either to save a life or to improve the quality of life and to prevent further deterioration of it e.g. heal different bone tissues, allow one to see, feel better etc. Can you answer in detail please?

A Blood and organs are vital for every human being in order to sustain life. The contemporary Jurists unanimously agree that it is permissible to obtain an organ from an animal in the case of Iztirār (extreme necessity where life is at risk) and Hājat (need where health will deteriorate permanently). However, the jurists differ with regards to the permissibility of surgically transferring an organ of a healthy person into a patient.

The basis of the difference between the Jurists is whether transplanting an organ into another person is a degradation of a human being's honour or not. This is because Allāh 🕮 has sanctified and honoured the status of a human being over many of his other creations. Those jurists who view organ transplant to be prohibited is because, in their opinion it violates the sanctity of a human being, and above all every organ and limb belongs to Allāh 🕮. Hence, no human being can employ it in any way he/she wishes.

On the other hand, some jurists for instance Shaykh Khālid Saifullāh agree in the permissibility of organ transplant arguing that transferring an organ into another body to save a person's life is not an infringement of a human being's honour. In fact to contribute an organ to save someone's life is considered an act of honour and reverence as Allāh 🕮 states in the Holy Qur'ān, **"And whosoever saves a human being then it is as though he has saved the whole of humanity."** (5:32)

Shaykh Khālid Saifullāh further argues that although Allāh 🕮 has honoured and esteemed mankind, the Holy Qur'ān and the Ahādeeth of the Holy Prophet 🕮 have not clearly set any boundaries of honour.

In such cases, the jurists will refer to the 'custom' which in the terminology of Shari'ah is known as Urf or Ādat. This will be taken into consideration and some juristic issues can be deduced from this type of source where there is no clear mention in the Holy Qur'ān or Hadeeth. Urf or custom will be considered as long as it does not contradict the fundamental principles of Islām.

The evidence of the reliability of Urf is mentioned in the Hadeeth related by Sayyidunā Abdullāh Ibn Mas'ood ☬ that the Holy Prophet ﷺ said, "Whatever the Muslims consider to be good then that will be good in the eyes of Allāh ﷻ." (Musnad Ahmad)

Some jurists have mentioned that this Hadeeth was not the words of the Holy Prophet ﷺ but stated by Sayyidunā Abdullāh Ibn Masood ☬. However, the jurists have still accepted it. In another Hadeeth, it is related that the Holy Prophet ﷺ had prohibited all the bad and corrupt customs and instructed all the good customs (Hujjatullāhil-Bāligah). However, if any custom contradicts the fundamental principles of Islām then all the jurists unanimously agree that such a custom will not be accepted and neither can any ruling of a particular issue be deduced from it.

Customs and traditions vary from time to time whereby different injunctions will be given according to the suitability of time. Islām has not set any boundaries or limits of how and when a human being's esteem is violated. Hence, the time and the tradition will be taken into consideration. Mufti Kifāyatullāh ☬ states that at this present time the progress of technology, new surgical methods of obtaining organs have emerged whereby the society usually considers it an honour to save someone's life. For this reason organ transplant should be permitted. (Kifāyatul Mufti)

Shaykh Khālid Saifullāh further states that the jurists agree with the permissibility of blood transfusion in the state of Iztirār (extreme necessity where life is at risk) and Hājat (need where health will deteriorate permanently). The jurists do not regard it as an act of infringement of mankind's honour when blood from someone's body is being transferred into another person's body. So how can organ transplant infringe the dignity of a person?

Furthermore, the jurists have stated that the injunction of its permissibility is based upon the juristic principle of, "Iztirār makes prohibited acts permissible."

This means that at the time of Iztirār prohibited things become permissible to use. This principle is deduced from the Holy Qur'ān where Allāh ﷻ states, **"But if anyone is forced by necessity neither rebelliously nor transgressing the limit then there is no sin." (2:173)**

In short, organ transplant is permitted in the case of Iztirār and Hājat and in doing so one will not be violating the honour and sanctity of mankind. In fact saving another human being's life is an honour itself. If in the state of Iztirār and Hājat blood transfusion is permitted then organ transplant should also be permitted.

Abortion

Q Is abortion permissible in Islām?

If it is, then is there a time limit for terminating the intra-uterine life? Many a times the doctors proclaim that the mother's life will be in danger if the abortion does not take place or the child will be born handicapped etc. What is the Islamic verdict?

A Life in general and human life in particular is sacred. It does not matter where the life exists, whether the life is extra-uterine or intra-uterine, its location has no significance on its sanctity.

This sanctity applies not only to human life, but to human body also. Hence according to Islām, the physical body of the human being after death is just as sacred as it was before death. The degree of sanctity of life is greater than that for the body.

Islamically, once the soul enters the foetus after 120 days, it will then hold the same sanctity as that of a human being. Thus a being existing within the uterus is just as sacred as a human being living apparently. Islām does not discriminate between intra-uterine life and extra-uterine life. Both are equally sacred. The mother has no priority in regard to existence over her baby who still happens to be within her. The authoritative book of jurisprudence, Al-Bahrur Rāiq states, "Islām does not allow the killing of one life in order to sustain another."

In Jawāhirul Fiqh, the following ruling is recorded, "It is not lawful for a Muslim to save his own life with the life of another who is just as sacred as himself."

In Islām, sanctity of life applies to all human beings, whether they are Muslims or non-Muslims. It is therefore not permissible for a Muslim to take the life of any human being apart from the exemptions made by Allāh ﷻ. Infact he is not allowed to take any animal life unnecessarily. The Holy Qur'ān states, **"Do not kill any life which Allāh has ordained sacred except (by the demands) of justice." (17:33)**

The Fuqahā (jurists) have determined the foetus to be lifeless prior to 120 days of pregnancy. Hence after 120 days the foetus obtains life. This injunction has been inferred from a long Hadeeth narrated by Sayyidunā Abdullāh Ibn Mas'ood ؓ that the Holy Prophet ﷺ said, "Verily the creation of each one of you is brought together in his mother's womb for 40 days in a form of Nutfah (semen), then he is a clot of blood for a similar period (i.e. another 40 days), then becomes a morsel of flesh for a similar period (another 40 days totalling 120 days altogether), then an angel is sent to him to breathe life into him." (Bukhāri, Muslim)

The Rooh (soul) enters the foetus on or around 120 days, from that time onwards the foetus is no longer a lifeless organ, but it is a human being. After the entry of the Rooh, under no circumstances will abortion be permissible. It is written in Raddul-Muhtār, "After entry of the Rooh, abortion is not permissible."

In Fatāwa Ālamgheeri, it is mentioned, "In the case of a complication in birth where the emergence of the baby is not possible other than by abortion, and there is danger to the life of the mother (because of complications), it (abortion) will be permissible only if the baby is lifeless (i.e. prior to 120 days). If it becomes a living organism (after 120 days) then abortion is not permissible."

In Shāmi, the following ruling is given, "After entry of the Rooh, abortion is not permissible. However, there is a difference of opinion amongst the authorities regarding abortion before entry of the Rooh. (i.e. before reaching the 120 days period)."

In short, abortion is unlawful after 120 days whatever the circumstance may be. Prior to the entry of the Rooh, i.e. before 120 days, abortion is Harām, but becomes permissible for the protection of health and life of the mother which may become gravely endangered on account of the pregnancy.

Although some authorities are of the opinion that abortion, irrespective of the period of pregnancy is not permissible for any reason, the contemporary Ulamā have accepted the view of permissibility of abortion in a case of extreme necessity (i.e. for life or health) provided that the 120 day period has not yet expired.

Considering the fact that there is a difference of opinion amongst the scholars regarding the permissibility of abortion even within the 120 day period, doctors should be extremely cautious and only proceed if the continued pregnancy constitutes a serious threat to the life of the mother.

Responsibilities of Children towards Parents

Q **What do the scholars say regarding the following situation? An old mother has some sons and daughters but none of them are prepared to look after her. The sons and daughters after consulting amongst themselves, decided to send their mother to a nursing home (Allāh 🕮 forbid). So can you kindly shed some light regarding the responsibilities of the sons and daughters towards their mother. Can you also mention Quranic verses and Ahādeeth to prove the point and to create awareness.**

A The Holy Qur'ān in many verses mentions that showing kindness to the parents is not only necessary but also an act of piety. It will be sufficient here to mention just two verses, **"Your Lord has decreed that you worship none but Him, and unto parents show kindness and if either of them or both of them attain old age with you, say not to them a word of contempt, nor shout at them but speak to them in terms of honour. And lower unto them the wing of submission out of mercy and say: 'O my Lord have mercy on them as they had raised me in (my) childhood'." (17:23-24)**

Similarly, the Ahādeeth of the Holy Prophet 🕮 are full with injunctions and exhortations regarding the rights of parents. It is reported in a Hadeeth by Sayyidunā Abdullāh Ibn Mas'ood 🕮, that showing reverence and kindness to parents is one of the three dearest acts in the sight of Allāh 🕮:

1) Offering Salāh on time.
2) Showing kindness and reverence to parents.
3) Striving in the way of Allāh ﷻ.   (Bukhāri, Muslim)

In another Hadeeth, Sayyidunā Abū Hurairah ؓ reports that the Holy Prophet ﷺ said, "May he not prosper, may he not prosper, may he not prosper, he whose old parents are alive, one of them or both of them but he does not enter Paradise." (i.e. does not take good care of them nor treats them politely so that he becomes entitled to enter Paradise).

Sayyidunā Abdullāh Ibn Abbās ؓ says that the Holy Prophet ﷺ said, "A person who obeys Allāh ﷻ in the matter of his parents (i.e. discharges his obligations towards them) then if both his parents are alive, two doors to Paradise are opened for him and if only one of the parents is alive, one door to Paradise is opened for him. However, if he disobeys them, then if he disobeys both of them, then two doors towards Hell are opened for him and if he disobeys one of them then one door towards Hell is opened for him."

On one occasion, someone asked the Holy Prophet ﷺ if this calamity will befall a person even if he has been unfairly treated by his parents? The Holy Prophet ﷺ replied thrice in the affirmative. It is mentioned in Ibn Mājah on the authority of Sayyidunā Abū Umāmah ؓ that a person once asked the Holy Prophet ﷺ as to what were the rights of parents over their children? The Holy Prophet ﷺ replied, "Your parents are your Heaven or Hell."

In short it is incumbent upon the sons and daughters to take good care of their parents and to see that they are neither wronged, offended nor disobeyed as long as the commands of Allāh ﷻ and the rights of others are not infringed. This general rule of obedience towards parents also applies to those parents that are disbelievers.

It is reported by Sayyidah Asmā ؓ, the daughter of Sayyidunā Abū Bakr ؓ that her mother came to meet her while she was still a disbeliever. She enquired from the Holy Prophet ﷺ if she could give her some (monetary) help and the Holy Prophet ﷺ replied in the affirmative.

From the mentioned Quranic verses and Ahādeeth, we can understand the importance and significance of looking after the parents and treating them with kindness. Besides the aforementioned, there are numerous Ahādeeth concerning the rights of parents.

Regarding your question about nursing homes or old peoples' homes, it is wrong for a Muslim to send his or her parents to such places. The sons and daughters should ponder over these Ahādeeth and beseech forgiveness from Allāh ﷻ and from their mother. They should at once retrieve their mother from the old peoples home and plead to her for forgiveness, otherwise there is a danger of incurring the wrath of Allāh ﷻ upon them and possibly not reciting the Kalimah at the time of death. Furthermore, there is a higher likelihood of them suffering a calamity in this world as well as in the Hereafter. This calamity can be in the form of anything i.e. their future children being disobedient or experiencing a bad death etc. May Allāh ﷻ protect us from such calamities.

I conclude my answer with a text from the authentic Hanafi Fiqh Kitāb, 'Al-Hidāya':

It is necessary upon a person to spend upon his parents and grandparents if they are not well off, even though they are disbelievers. Regarding the parents, Allāh ﷻ says in the Holy Qur'ān, **"Stay well with them in this world."** This verse was revealed regarding non-Muslim parents. It is highly unpleasant that one enjoys a luxurious life and the bounties of Allāh ﷻ whilst one forsakes them to die in poverty. (Al-Hidāya)

Calling Someone Rahmān

Q **My brother is called Abdur Rahmān and many people abbreviate the name and call him Rahmān only. Is this permissible as I know that Rahmān is the name of Allāh ﷻ only.**

A It is very unfortunate that many Muslims do not pay attention to this critical matter. Many times names are abbreviated in a manner that their accurate sense is totally changed and they fall in the scope of Shirk (polytheism).

Abdur Rahmān and other compound names like Abdur Razzāq, Abdur Rabb are often abbreviated as Rahmān, Razzāq and Rabb which are the holy names of Allāh ﷻ. These are exclusive for Him alone and cannot be used for anyone else. It is not permissible to call a human being with these names without the prefix of Abdul etc.

Gheebat (backbiting)

Q Gheebat is committed so frequently that it has become a habit and a pass time for many. We read and listen very often to the Hadeeth that backbiting is worse than adultery but even then we do not restrain our tongues from committing this evil sin. Is there any easy way of stopping this sin?

A What you have mentioned is regrettably true. The tongue is a great gift of Allāh ﷻ and a marvellous creation. Its size may be small but the capacity to obey or disobey can be great. Kufr (disbelief) can't be distinguished from Imān except through the testimony of the tongue. Imān and Kufr are the ultimate limits of obedience and disobedience. The tongue has a very broad function range. There is a large amount of good that can be performed and a large amount of evil that can be inflicted. If one releases his tongue, Shaytān will take him everywhere till he ultimately makes him fall. The only way to be saved from the evils of the tongue is to restrain it from all prohibited talk. The tongue should be used only for what is beneficial in this life and the Hereafter.

The Holy Prophet ﷺ said, "Whoever gives me surety in safeguarding what is between his jaws and what is between his legs, I guarantee for him entrance into Paradise."

'What is between his jaws' in the Hadeeth refers to the tongue and 'what is between his legs' refers to the private parts.

Imām Nawawi ﷻ commentating on this Hadeeth states, "Be aware that it is necessary upon every mature person to guard his tongue against all kinds of talk except when it is clear that the talk will be beneficial. When speaking and remaining silent are both equal, as a precaution, the correct thing is to abstain from speaking because often even permissible talk may lead to unlawful or disgraceful matters."

The Holy Prophet ﷺ said, "When the son of Ādam عليه السلام gets up in the morning, all the parts of his body seek refuge from the tongue saying, 'Fear Allāh ﷻ regarding us, we follow you, if you are upright we shall also be upright and if you go astray, we shall also go astray'."

The prohibition of Gheebat is clear in the Holy Qur'ān. Allāh ﷻ mentions in Sūrah Al-Hujurāt, **"O you who believe! Refrain from excessive suspicion. Verily, some forms of suspicion are a sin. Never spy and never backbite each other. Does any of you like to consume the flesh of his dead brother, which you abhor? Fear Allāh, as Allāh is the Most Pardoning, Most Merciful."** (49:12)

In a verse of Sūrah Banee Isrāeel it is mentioned, **"And do not pursue what you have no knowledge about. Verily, questioning shall take place with regards to the ears, the eyes and the hearts."** (17:36)

Everything uttered by the mouth is instantly recorded and written down by the angels. Allāh ﷻ says in the Holy Qur'ān, **"Not a word does he utter, but there is a watcher by him ready (to record it)."** (50:18)

Imām Ahmad Ibn Hanbal ﵀ narrates a Hadeeth on the authority of Sayyidunā Jābir Ibn Abdullāh ﵁ who relates, "While we were with the Holy Prophet ﷺ we smelt a rotten smell. The Holy Prophet ﷺ then asked, 'Do you know what this smell is? This is the smell of those who backbite the believers'." (Ahmad)

Sayyidunā Anas ﵁ narrates that the Holy Prophet ﷺ said, "When I ascended (on the night of Mi'rāj). I passed by some people who had copper nails and they were scratching their faces and chests with them. I asked, 'Who are these people, O Jibreel?' He replied, 'These are the people who eat the flesh of human beings and disgrace them'." (Ahmad, Abū Dāwood)

To overcome this spiritual illness we must realise how grievous Gheebat is. The Holy Prophet ﷺ defined Gheebat very clearly. He said, "Do you know what is meant by Gheebat?" The Companions ﵃ said, "Allāh ﷻ and His Messenger ﷺ know best." He replied, "To say something about your brother which he dislikes." One asked, "Even if what I say is true about my brother?"

He replied, "If such defects you say are true about him, then you have back-bitten against him and if he doesn't have (the defects) what you say, then you have committed slander against him (which is worse than backbit-ing)." (Muslim, Abū Dāwood, Tirmizi)

Backbiting is not only restricted to the tongue as commonly understood by many people. To describe any defect through one's actions e.g. a wink, sig-nal, hint, nod or any movement are different forms of Gheebat and thus Harām. Writing the defects of someone also comes under the category of Gheebat.

Sayyidah Ā'ishah ﷺ said, "A woman came in our house. When she left, I moved my hands indicating that she was short. The Holy Prophet ﷺ said, 'You have backbitten against her." (Abū Dāwood, Ahmad)

When the Holy Prophet ﷺ saw Sayyidah Ā'ishah ﷺ imitating a woman (in an inappropriate manner), he is reported to have said, "I would not like to imi-tate anybody even if I was given such-and-such."

(Abū Dāwood, Tirmizi, Ahmad)

Regarding how to desist from backbiting, we must firstly turn to Allāh ﷻ in repentance and deeply regret the offence committed against Allāh ﷻ.

Secondly, we have committed an offence against the servant of Allāh ﷻ (Huqooqulibād) and have violated their right. Hence, if the Gheebat has reached the person, then forgiveness must also be sought from him and regret must be expressed too.

However, if the Gheebat didn't reach the person, then he should pray for the person's forgiveness and not tell him something he didn't know anyway, fearing that some evil may result from telling him.

A person backbiting must immediately give up the sin for it is amongst the most destructive sins. The following are a few noteworthy points that we should always consider before speaking. This will Inshā-Allāh enable us to safeguard our tongues from backbiting:

- The backbiter incurs the anger and punishment of Allāh ﷻ.

- His good deeds are transferred to the person he gossiped against. If the backbiter or the gossiper does not have any good deeds in his account then he will receive the bad deeds of the victim into his account. Whoever remembers this will hopefully not commit Gheebat.
- A person should look into his own faults and strive on correcting them. Doing this, he should be too embarrassed to criticise others.
- The backbiter should remember that backbiting his own Muslim brother is like eating his flesh.
- If the backbiter doesn't have the fault he wants to talk about in others, he should thank Allāh ﷻ for that. Furthermore, he should not pollute himself with the grave sin of Gheebat.
- The backbiter should refrain from talking unnecessarily. We should defend our Muslim brothers and sisters in there absence.
- We should always remember the verse of Allāh ﷻ and the Ahādeeth regarding the severity of Gheebat.

It is a right of a Muslim to speak up and oppose Gheebat made against his Muslim brother or sister. There are great virtues for one who fulfils this obligation.

Sayyidah Asmā ﵂ relates that the Holy Prophet ﷺ said, "Whoever defends the honour of his brother in his absence, will be entitled to Allāh's ﷻ protection from the Fire." (Ahmad)

In another Hadeeth, the Holy Prophet ﷺ has said, "Whoever defends the honour of his brother, Allāh ﷻ will protect his face from the Fire on the Day of Judgement." (Ahmad, Tirmizi)

I will conclude this answer by relating a statement of Sayyidunā Eesa ﵇ which he said to his Hawāriyyoon (disciples), "Tell me if you came across a person while he was sleeping and the wind had uncovered a part of his Satr (private parts), would you cover him?"

They said, "Yes." He said, "No, you would even uncover the rest." They said with surprise, "Subhān-Allāh! How would we uncover the rest?" He said, "Isn't a person mentioned to you and then you say the worst you know about him? So you indeed uncover the rest of the clothes from his Satr (private parts)."

Mahram whilst Travelling

Q I accompanied my wife up to the airport and her brother waited for her in India at the airport. She only lacked a Mahram during the flight hours. Is this permissible?

A In the above mentioned situation, the woman is travelling for a distance longer than that of a Shar'ee journey (48 miles). Hence, the rules applicable to a Musāfir (traveller) will apply to her such as that of Qasr Salāh (shortening of every four Rak'āt Fardh Salāh). Therefore, the rules of accompanying a Mahram will also be compulsory. If a Mahram does not accompany her on such a flight, it will be wrong for her to travel even though the flight may be for a short period of time.

Travelling for Education whilst Leaving the Wife at Home

Q I am intending to go abroad and study for a degree in further education. But I am at the same time worried about my young wife who I will be leaving behind at home. Is it permissible for me to embark on this journey for the pursuit of further education or not?

A It is compulsory for a husband to provide maintenance for his wife and it is also compulsory that he has sexual relations with her at least once in four months. It is therefore permissible for the husband to be on a journey only if he will not be infringing the compulsory rights of his wife. Nevertheless, it will not be permissible for him to leave her if he fears that she will become prey to sins.

However, if she happily gives consent in leaving her for a period longer than four months and her maintenance etc. has been arranged then it will be permissible for him to travel as long as he has no fear of her falling into sin.

Oral Sex

Q What does Islām say about oral sex? When the husband and wife are in a state of purity, is the area of the private parts clean or not?

If at the time of intercourse the wife takes the husband's private parts orally, or the husband does the same to his wife, is this type of act acceptable or not? One feels shy to ask this type of question. However necessity makes one ask these types of questions?

A Islām being a complete way of life has answers to all problems and queries. Regarding Masāil of Deen (religious verdicts) one should never be shy. If on the account of shyness one does not enquire an Islamic ruling on a particular matter then how will we know the religious verdict on such issues.

For Allāh ﷻ has said in the Holy Qur'ān, **"Allāh does not shy away from the truth."** (33:53)

Therefore, one should not hide behind a veil of shyness in asking about religious verdicts.

Concerning your question, without doubt, the external private parts are clean as long as there are no impure stains on it. However, it is not natural that everything clean can be taken orally. The matter inside the nose is considered to be clean. Does it mean that one can lick someone's nose or suck and kiss the matter that comes out of the nose? Is it permissible to do this? The external part of the back passage is also clean, but is it permissible to make oral contact with this? No.

In the same manner for a husband to take the wife's private part orally and lick it or for the wife to do the same to her husband is not permissible and unnatural. It is strongly undesirable and an act of sin.

If the couple have intense sexual desires then they should have sexual intercourse in order to fulfil their desires.

Consider, the mouth that takes the blessed name of Allāh ﷻ, recites the Holy Qur'ān, Durood etc. yet it is also used to intake that flesh from where impurity ejaculates? How can our hearts be satisfied with the remembrance of Allah ﷻ whilst committing such an immoral act?

As a poet once said, "Washing the mouth a thousand times with rose water even then taking Your blessed Name is disrespectful."

Intercourse During Menstruation

Q My husband demands me to have intercourse whilst I am experiencing menstruation. Is it permissible for me to comply with his demand or not?

A In the state of menstruation intercourse is strictly forbidden. This is clearly mentioned in the Holy Qur'ān, **"And they ask you about (sexual relation) in menstruation. Tell them that it is impure, thus abstain (sexually) from women during menstruation. Do not approach them (for sexual relations) until they become cleansed."** (2:222)

From this verse it is clearly understood that sexual intercourse is completely Harām whilst a woman is experiencing menstruation. Scientifically, it is an accepted fact that the blood of menstruation is of a specific type, both in composition and in colour from normal blood. It could be contaminated with blood-borne infections that could be detrimental if they gain entry into the body of the male. The menstrual blood is unclean and contains the leftovers of the lining of the womb. During intercourse, the male sexual organ would be making direct contact with the contaminated blood. This very act is a possible contributing factor towards the transmission of fatal venereal diseases. Contaminated blood of the vaginal lining can be so contagious that they can be passed on to the baby during natural delivery causing fatal illnesses in the child.

The Holy Prophet ﷺ has mentioned, "A person who has intercourse with a woman during her menstruation or has anal sex with her or approaches a fortune teller, believing in him, has rejected all that which has been revealed upon Muhammad ﷺ." (Tirmizi)

What a stern warning by the Holy Prophet ﷺ that a person who indulges in these prohibited acts would transgress the boundaries of Islām and would step into the pits of disbelief and would discard the teachings brought by the Holy Prophet ﷺ.

Islām allows a husband to be intimate with his wife in the state of menstruation apart from the area between the navel and the knees.

Anal Intercourse

Q Is anal sex allowed with one's wife?

A The Holy Prophet ﷺ has stated, "One who has anal sex with his wife is Mal'oon (cursed)." (Tirmizi)

"One who has anal intercourse has disbelieved in the commands sent upon the Holy Prophet ﷺ." (Tirmizi)

Sayyidunā Abdullāh Ibn Abbās ؓ explaining the verse, **"Your wives are your tilling fields. So approach your tilling fields as you desire." (2:223)** states that the Holy Prophet ﷺ has stated that only carry out intercourse from the front passage and not any other way.

This verse indicates two reasons for not permitting intercourse from the back passage.

1. Intercourse is described as farming. Contrary to this, the back passage is a place to relieve heavy solid waste. The Quranic verse implies that the woman's vagina is a means of cultivating the woman, as this is the only place through which sperm can fertilise the woman's egg. Thus it is permissible according to the Holy Qur'ān to enter the woman from any direction only in the vagina. It is worth noting that when Allāh ﷻ has not permitted intercourse from the front on the days of menstruation due to impurities being released from there, then how can He permit intercourse from the back passage, which is regularly discharging impure solid waste.

The anus is not for increasing the human population. Furthermore, this act also deprives the woman from satisfying her sexual pleasures.

2. The anal passage is not made for intercourse. For intercourse, the vagina is the only suitable place. Those who transgress and revert to the anus, in reality are disobeying the Divine Law and the vast wisdom of Allāh ﷻ.

By committing this unnatural act, the woman could have in the long run, physical and psychological problems about her sexual confidence, which may ultimately have implications on the physical and sexual well-being of her relationship with her husband.

Contraception

Q **Is the practice of contraception allowed in Islām?**

If so, under what circumstances? Nowadays it is fashionable to have small families, and the government of different countries encourage or even restrict the amount of children each couple can have. In the poor countries, contraception is practiced on the basis of not being able to provide for a large family. Governments of different countries are worried that if the population keeps on increasing at this speed, there will not be a sufficient food supply for all the people on Earth. What does Islām say regarding this issue?

A Contraception is permissible on a limited scale for valid reasons, those reasons that Islām has considered to be valid. Man made queries or doubts are not acceptable. There are two methods of avoiding conception (birth).

1. Temporary Reversible Contraception

Some reversible contraceptives prevent pregnancy by creating a barrier between the male sperm and the female egg, others either stop the fertilised egg from attaching to the womb or provides a chemical state by which the woman's body feels that it is already pregnant. There are various methods of reversible contraception. A few are mentioned as follows:

a) The Pill
The pill has two hormones called oestrogen and progestogen similar to those which occur naturally in the body. It works by preventing the release of the egg each month. The pill has revolutionised contraception.

b) Injection
It is possible to provide many months of protection from pregnancy by an intra muscular injection of progestogen.

c) Intra-Uterine Device (I.U.D.)
Intra-uterine devices are often described as the loop, the coil or the curl. They are inserted into the woman's womb and prevent a fertilised egg from attaching itself in the womb.

d) Condom (Sheath)

A condom is a tube of fine rubber closed at one end, and is worn by the man on his penis during intercourse. When the man ejaculates the condom retains the semen, thereby preventing it from reaching the woman's womb. It is known by a variety of names, including sheath, rubber etc.

e) Diaphragms and Caps

These are round dome shaped contraceptives made of rubber which are inserted in the vagina and cover the neck of the womb, preventing any sperm from entering the womb.

f) The Rhythm Method

This is known as the safe period or periodic practice of abstinence. This method depends on the woman calculating the time of ovulation every month by keeping a record of her periods and working out the average length of her menstrual cycle.

g) Spermicides

Spermicides create a barrier between the man's sperm and the woman's egg (the ovum). They contain chemicals which kill the sperm when they come into contact with them. Spermicides come in the form of a cream, jelly or pessary.

h) Azl (Coitus Interruptus or the Withdrawal Method)

In this the man withdraws his penis and ejaculates the sperm outside the vagina. This method was practiced at the time of our beloved Prophet ﷺ.

All modern day reversible contraception that only create a barrier in order to prevent the sperm meeting the egg will come under the same ruling as Azl (coitus interruptus). In other words it is undesirable to use them in normal circumstances. However, they are permissible.

2. Permanent Irreversible Contraception

When a couple decide never again to have a baby, not even if anything were to happen to their children or their marriage, then they often opt for a sterilisation operation.

a) Male Sterilisation (Vasectomy)

This is a quick operation performed on the male which can be done under local anesthetic. Two little cuts are made at the top of the scrotum and the sperm duct is cut on each side which carries the sperm to the outside.

b) Female Sterilisation (Tubectomy)

This operation involves cutting, tying, clipping or blocking the fallopian tube. It is often done through a sort of telescope and can render a woman incapable of reproducing ever again.

The circumstances which permit reversible and permanent contraception differ.

Reversible Contraception

Among the reasons accepted by Islām as valid for practicing reversible contraception are:
1. Physical weakness.
2. Sickness.
3. The wife maintaining her beauty or figure for the sake of her husband.
4. The couple being on a journey or in a distant land.
5. Adverse political conditions, e.g. children are forcibly separated from their parents.
6. The wife is immoral.
7. The couple decide to separate in the near future.

The above reasons are valid without Karāhat (dislike) for practicing reversible contraception. Otherwise in general circumstances it is Makrooh Tanzeehi (undesirable) to do this kind of act.

Poverty or the fear of poverty is not a valid reason for contraception, nor is it permissible to practice contraception on account of not being able to provide for a large family. According to the Holy Qur'ān, **"There is not a living creature, but its provision is the responsibility of Allāh." (11:6)**

Similarly, intention to control sexual desire which may be derived out of piety is not lawful grounds for contraception. If practiced for any reason which is unlawful in Islām, then the contraception will likewise be unlawful e.g. for indulgence in illicit sex.

Likewise it will be unlawful for economical reasons so that the few children first born can have the best of everything. Contraception is also not permissible on the basis that it is fashionable to have small families. The fashion to have small families is the practice of other nations. The Holy Prophet ﷺ said, "Whoever imitates a group becomes one of them." (Abū Dāwood)

In addition, small families is in direct conflict with the instruction of the Holy Prophet ﷺ who said, "Marry those women who are affectionate and reproduce in abundance. Verily, I will compete with you (your large numbers) over the other nations on the Day of Judgement." (Mishkāt)

Thus, it does not befit Muslims to adopt a custom or fashion which is in opposition to the expressed desire of the Holy Prophet ﷺ.

Furthermore, many couples practice contraception for professional reasons so that a wife can pursue a career. It should be borne in mind that it is not permissible for this reason. The true Islamic career for a woman is her role at home as a wife and mother. Allāh ﷻ has appointed the affairs of life between man and woman. The affairs of the home are the duties of women.

Nevertheless, if the wife is immoral or she refuses to nurture the children and the father feels that he may not be in a position to make adequate arrangements with suitable people to take care of the upbringing of the children, then only the reversible method of contraception will be permissible.

It will also be permissible for the couple to use contraception for spacing children so that each child receives adequate attention.

Permanent Contraception
Permanent contraception is only permissible if the woman's life is in danger or her health is seriously threatened permanently.

Sterilisation (vasectomy or tubectomy) etc. is a means of permanent prevention of reproduction which is strictly forbidden in Islām. Sterilisation should be viewed in a very grave manner. In view of the gravity of the crime in Islām, it is compulsory that the Muslim doctors do not treat it lightly. It is allowed only in severe cases. It should be carried out only as a last resort. Such action is forbidden in the Holy Qur'ān and it is described as transgression.

Once when the Holy Prophet ﷺ condemned sterilisation and warned against it, he recited in support the following verse from the Holy Qur'ān, **"O you who believe! Do not make Harām the pure things which Allāh has made Halāl for you, and do not commit transgression. Verily, Allāh does not like the transgressors." (5:87)**

The Ahādeeth of the Holy Prophet ﷺ prohibit sterilisation or the elimination of the ability to reproduce most severely. Imām Badruddin ﷺ states in his commentary of Bukhāri, "Termination of reproduction is unanimously Harām."

A Muslim who is aware of the exhortation of the Holy Prophet ﷺ regarding reproduction in abundance, can never look with favour towards any act which cuts and terminates reproduction.

A Muslim doctor should ponder over the following points before inclining towards prescribing permanent contraception.

The Holy Prophet ﷺ said, "Marry those women who are affectionate and reproduce in abundance. Verily, I will compete with you (your large numbers) over the other nations on the Day of Judgement." (Mishkāt)

Sterilisation as well as reversible contraception resorted to unnecessarily come, within the general ruling of the following verse from the Holy Qur'ān, **"(Shaytān said to Allāh) I will most certainly command them (people) to alter (interfere and transform) the creation of Allāh." (4:119)**

Sterilisation is thus an act whispered into the heart of man by Shaytān who has promised at the time of his expulsion from Heaven that he will mislead mankind.

Amongst the ways of misleading, is his trick of influencing man to interfere with and alter the natural and physical capacities, forms and attributes which Allāh ﷻ has created in His creatures. Reference to this is made in the above-cited Quranic verse.

In short, sterilisation is totally against the teachings and spirit of Islam. Unnecessary adoption of these practices is a major sin. Temporary reversible contraception is disliked in normal circumstances (as mentioned previously).

Accepting Funds from non-Muslim Donors

Q Is it permissible to accept donations from a non-Muslim individual or non-Muslim organisations for the purpose of constructing a Masjid or Madrasah?

A Donations for a Masjid, Madrasah or similar projects can be accepted from a non-Muslim individual or organisations with the condition that such donations are not, in any manner harmful to the interests of the Muslims. For example, if there is any doubt that the donors will try to interfere with the management of the Masjid or Madrasah or the donation will ultimately be detrimental to the prestige and honour of the Muslims, then such donations should not be accepted.

Fur and Leather Garments

Q Can a man or woman wear clothes made of fur or leather derived from the hides of wild animals like tiger and fox etc?

A The use of fur or leather products like clothes, hats and shoes etc are permissible in Islām for both men and women. The basic principle is that the skin of every animal will become pure after it is tanned or medically treated, except the skin of the pig and human being. Hence, the skin of every animal except the pig and human being can be used for any lawful purpose.

Halāl Mortgage

Q I was thinking of purchasing a house, but due to the reason that taking a mortgage is Harām, I have always restrained myself from taking a loan. Now recently I have heard some banks and companies are offering Halāl mortgages, which pleased me and at the same time confused me. Can you explain to me how a mortgage can be Halāl?

A The dictionary definition of mortgage is:

1. A conveyance of property by a debtor to a creditor as security for a debt (especially one incurred by the purchase of the property on the condition that it shall be returned on payment of the debt within a certain period).

2. The deed affecting such a transaction.

3. The loan itself.

In a conventional mortgage, what you are really doing is taking out a loan where your property is used as a security by the lender. Any payment will be due back on the loan with interest.

In the Islamic system, no money is lent nor is a loan given so there's no question or issue of interest. In effect, it is not a mortgage at all just a home purchase plan.

The system which is adopted by these companies and banks are of two types:

<u>1st Type</u> - The bank or the company buys the property from the seller and then sells it onto the purchaser with profit. This is based on the principles of trading and is normally referred to as Murābahah (Arabic for trading).

In this situation, the bank or the company is simply the middle man buying and selling to make a profit. This is just like any other business buying from a supplier and then selling onto the consumer. The higher price (selling price to the consumer) is calculated depending on the value of the property, the number of years one wishes to repay over and the amount of deposit given initially.

<u>2nd Type</u> - In this situation, the bank or the company buys the property from the seller and then agrees to sell it on to the purchaser at the same price. The bank/company will remain the owner of the property until the full purchase price of the property has been paid.

During this period (whilst the purchaser is paying for the house) the bank/company will charge the buyer rent for making use of the property it (the bank/company) owns. This type of option is based on the principles of leasing and is normally called Ijāra (Arabic for leasing). In this option, the bank or the company simply acts as the landlord and the buyer as the 'tenant' whilst the property is being paid for.

Thus, if any bank/company offers a mortgage through these two methods and they also comply with all other regulations of Islām, then it will be permissible to purchase homes through them.

Aftershaves Containing Alcohol

Q Can we use aftershaves, lotions and sprays which contain alcohol? Please elaborate.

A Generally those aftershaves, lotions and sprays containing alcohol cannot be used. Severe punishment has been narrated in Ahādeeth for the person who deals with alcohol.

The Holy Qur'ān states, **"O you who believe! Indeed liquor, gambling, idols and arrows are filth from the acts of Shaytān, so abstain from them so that you may be successful." (5:90)**

In the Hadeeth, the Holy Prophet ﷺ has cursed the person who drinks wine. In another Hadeeth, he cursed ten people who deal with wine and intoxicants.

However the aforementioned rule will only apply to natural alcohol whose compound structure has not changed. However, if it is artificial alcohol or its compound structure has changed (like synthetic alcohol or alcohol denat) then it can be used.

Note: As a precaution it is advisable that one inquires directly from the company about the alcohol ingredient.

Shaking Hands with the Opposite Gender

Q Many times, there are occasions where we have to shake hands with the opposite sex whilst working in offices or schools. In the event of refusal, they take it as disrespect and against good character. Does Islām permit shaking hands with the opposite sex in these particular situations?

A Men shaking hands with women or women shaking hands with men is not permissible. Sayyidah Ā'ishah ﷺ narrates that the Holy Prophet ﷺ never touched the hand of a Ghair Mahram (strange woman). (Bukhāri)

It is advisable to decline in a polite manner and explain the Mas'alah if the need arises.

Photos of Scenery

Q Are Muslims allowed to take photos of sceneries?

A Yes, it is permissible.

Clothes with Pig-Skin Lining

Q Is it permissible to wear shoes or jackets which have pig-skin lining?

A It is not permissible.

Human Cloning

Q What is human cloning & what does Islām say about this matter?

A The purpose of human cloning is to effect a change in either the physical appearance or in the personality of the human being or in both. This aim and purpose is in conflict with the law and the created system of Allāh ﷺ.

Any act which interferes with the natural process created by Allāh ﷺ, or which brings about alteration in the natural attributes and appearance of a human being, will come under the ruling of the following verse of the Holy Qur'ān, **"Allāh cursed him (Iblees). He (Iblees) said: 'I shall most certainly take a fixed share from your servants. I shall most certainly mislead them; I shall give them vain hopes; I shall command them to pierce the ears of animals and I shall most certainly order them to change the created forms of Allāh'. Whoever takes Shaytān for a friend besides Allāh, verily, he has incurred a manifest loss (destruction and ruin in both worlds)."** (4:118-119)

From this verse it is clear that changing the created forms of Allāh ﷻ is an un-Islamic act. It is Shaytān who induces man to embark on such activities which interferes and changes the natural process which Allāh ﷻ has created. In the Ahādeeth several examples of such acts of change are given. Among these acts are the following:

1. Men cutting or shaving their beards.
2. Women cutting their hair.
3. Women filing their teeth for beauty.
4. Tattooing.
5. Castration of human beings.
6. Using black dye to conceal white hair for the sake of deceiving others.

If a person resorts to plastic surgery or any other type of surgery to alter his appearance because he feels dissatisfied with his natural looks, then such changing will be Harām since it will come within the scope of the aforementioned verse. The prohibition applies regardless of whether such change is effected after birth or before birth, i.e. in the embryonic stage.

While the aspect of change is the main factor of prohibition, there are other factors also. Even non-Muslims in their presentation of ethical reasons against cloning mention such factors.

Life Support Machine

Q A person received a very severe injury to a vital part of his brain. The doctor has pronounced him being 'Brain-Dead'. The concept of 'Brain Death' has been evolved whereby the doctor can judge that the patient has received such a severe injury to vital parts of his brain that if the life support machine which is keeping him alive is switched off, the patient will definitely die. The machine is only turned off after organs have been removed from the body. These organs are only being kept 'alive' or 'perfuse' whilst the machine is on. What is the Islamic view?

A Death according to Islām is the same as what all mankind has understood it to be since the very beginning of man on earth.

There is no need for any new theory to guide Muslims regarding the event of death. Death is not a new occurrence and for understanding it, there is no need for any academic definition. So far as Islām is concerned, death is the end of man's life on earth. This end arrives when his soul permanently leaves his physical body. When all physical functions in a man's body cease operation, death has arrived. The man will then be regarded as dead. Termination of his physical functions is the consequence of the separation of the Rooh (soul). Without the Rooh, the body is lifeless.

The slightest sign of physical movement in the body indicates life, or the presence of the Rooh, even if his breathing is artificially sustained. He will be regarded as being alive according to Islām as long as he breathes or as long as any other physical activity remains in his body. Therefore, the Brain Death concept is not valid according to Islām. Even if vital parts in his brain are irreparably damaged, he will still be alive according to Islām as long as he breathes even if such breathing is with the aid of a machine. The fact that he is being perfused by a machine is a clear indication of the existence of the Rooh in his body. A dead man cannot be perfused or kept alive by any means.

According to the Holy Qur'ān, death comes by the command of Allāh ﷻ at its appointed time. Death cannot be advanced nor delayed by a second. This is the absolute teaching of the Holy Qur'ān. Any contrary belief is Kufr (disbelief). Therefore the means of sustaining a mans breathing i.e. by the way of a machine, are also matters decreed by Divine Permission. The switching on and off of the life-sustaining machine will be determined by Divine Commands, which operates in ways unknown to us.

Such matters and affairs belong to the Takweeni field (the metaphysical realm) and cannot be logically explained. It is a matter of pure Imān in which the Muslim has no alternative but to accept and believe. Suffice to say that life cannot be prolonged by any means beyond its divinely stipulated term.

Islām explains the arrival of death by the appearance of certain physical signs. The signs of death are as follows:

1. The legs become inactive, unable to remain erect.

2. The nose tilts.

3. The temples wilt.   (Kabeeri, Shāmi, Fathul Bāri)

In brief Islām does not recognise the concept of 'Brain Death'. Thus based on this it would not be permissible to switch off the machine. Allāh 🕮 states in the Holy Qur'ān, **"Do not proclaim something about which you have no knowledge." (17:36)**

Genetic Counselling

Q **What does Islām say on genetic counselling e.g. the doctor nowadays can, by doing special tests, predict in advance that a couple have a very high risk of getting children with some dangerous illness. In such a case, if consulted, is a doctor allowed to counsel such couples not to have children or permit the wife to have an abortion if she is under 4 months pregnant.**

A It is permissible in this case to advise against having children. But this is a matter best left to the couple. These are personal matters. If they wish to have children, they should not be discouraged in such a case.

If the wife becomes pregnant, it will be permissible to resort to abortion for the reasons stated in the question. But an abortion will be permissible only before 120 days (within four months). It is best to advise the couple to use reversible contraception in such a case.

Artificial Insemination

Q **Does Islām allow insemination with the husband's semen? What if the artificial insemination was carried out by a donor's semen? Will the ruling differ in this matter?**

A Artificial insemination with the husband's semen is permissible if the following conditions are met:

1. The wife is unable to become pregnant in the normal way.

2. The semen must not be acquired by self-masturbation.

3. There must be absolute certainty that the semen which is being used is that of the husband.

If any of these conditions are lacking, artificial insemination will not be permissible.

Artificial insemination with a donor's semen is not permissible under any condition.

Gold Utensils

Q Is it permissible to drink water from a glass made of gold?

A It is not permissible to eat or drink from gold or silver utensils. Infact, it is not permissible to use these items for any purpose. Thus it is not permissible for both men or women to:

a) Eat and drink from gold or silver utensils.

b) Clean the teeth with a toothbrush made of gold or silver.

c) Sprinkle rose water with a gold or silver utensil which has been made for such a purpose.

d) To keep Surmah (antimony) in a gold or silver utensil which has been made for such a purpose.

e) Apply oil that is kept in a gold or silver utensil.

f) To keep betel-leaves in a container made out of gold or silver.

Allāh ﷻ Knows Best

12. CHAPTER ON
MARRIAGE

Polygamy

Q If a person marries a second time but does not do justice between his wives and neither does he treat them with fairness, what does Islām say regarding this matter?

A According to Islām, although a man is permitted by Allāh ﷻ to marry a second time, he must understand that another marriage brings about added responsibilities upon him. It is compulsory for him to follow the path of high standards of justice and equality between them.

It is reported by Sayyidunā Abū Hurairah ؓ that the Holy Prophet ﷺ said, "A husband who does not do justice nor equality between his wives, will rise on the Day of Judgement with half of his body paralysed."

This is not the end of his punishment. Therefore, a man should never rush into a second marriage but only when there is a need and in addition, he is fully confident that he will be able to do justice between them. It is incumbent on the husband to give his wives equal rights and equal expenses. In this he has absolutely no choice.

Amongst the equal rights includes; if he spends three nights with one wife, he is obliged to spend three nights with the other, too. If he spends one week with one wife he has to spend the same time with the other. If he went to one wife from Maghrib, it will be (injustice) a sinful act of inequality to commence from Ishā for the other.

If he buys a pair of shoes for one wife he is compelled by Islām to buy a pair of shoes of the same quality and price for the other wife. In the matter of time and finance he is not permitted to show preference to one over the other even if he naturally loves one more than the other.

Husbands must remember that the consequence of inequality and injustice are very grave in this world and the Hereafter.

In the Holy Qur'ān, Allāh ﷻ also forbids the husband to show injustice.

Allāh ﷻ states, **"You will never be able to maintain perfect justice (i.e. in terms of natural affection) between wives however much you desire to do so, so do not incline too much to one of them (by giving her more of your time and provision) so as to leave the other hanging (i.e. neither divorce nor married). And if you do justice, (and all that is right) and fear Allāh (by keeping away from all that is wrong) then Allāh is ever Forgiving, Most Merciful."** (4:129)

The Holy Prophet ﷺ practically displayed justice amongst his wives. Sayyidah Ā'ishah ﷺ says, "The Holy Prophet ﷺ gave equal rights to his wives (in spending nights etc.) He used to supplicate, 'O My Lord! This is my equality in spending nights etc. in which I am capable of. Do not hold me responsible for what I am not capable of.'"

Refraining from Sexual Intercourse whilst Married

Q If a husband and wife do not have sexual intercourse, are they still considered as a married couple?

A Yes.

Interacting with a Future Partner

Q Is it permissible to interact with your future husband before the Nikāh?

A It is not permissible to interact with future marriage partners.

Marriage Between Cousins

Q Is marriage between cousins allowed?

A Marriage between cousins is permissible, whether paternal or maternal cousins.

Marriage with Step Mother

Q Can a person marry his step mother?

A It is not permissible to marry one's step mother. The Holy Qur'ān prohibits this shameful act. It states, **"And do not marry women whom your fathers married, except what has already passed. Indeed this is shameful, detestable and an evil path (to adopt)." (4:22)**

Shaykh Shabbir Ahmad Uthmāni ﷺ explains this verse in his commentary 'Tafseer Uthmāni', "The ignorant people would marry their stepmothers and other unlawful relatives. This shameful act was prohibited by this verse. It is an evil way and invites the wrath of Allah ﷻ."

Wise men in the days of ignorance considered it evil and sinful and this type of marriage was known as Maqt and the children born were known as Maqti. Fathers here include the grandfathers. This custom should be buried forever and never revived. (Tafseer Uthmāni)

Masā'il:

1. It is not permissible to even marry a woman to whom your father's marriage was solemnised. The Holy Qur'ān does not mention whether intercourse takes place or not. Mere Ijāb and Qabool (acceptance from both sides) will be sufficient and the son cannot marry that woman.

2. In the same way if the father committed adultery with a woman, then the son cannot marry that woman.

3. Similarly, the son's wife will be Harām upon the father even though intercourse did not take place. In the famous book of Fiqh, Raddul Muhtār, it is stated, "It is Harām upon a person to marry the wife of his father, grandfather etc. and the wife of his son, grandson etc. immediately after the solemnisation of the Nikāh whether intercourse takes place or not."

Exchanging Gifts at the Time of Seeing the Bride

Q Is exchanging Hadyah (gift) permissible at the time of seeing the bride?

A Giving and receiving Hadyah (gift) is proven from authentic Ahādeeth. It is permissible to give and take gifts at the time of seeing the bride. But it should be kept in mind that Ghair-Mahram (strange men) are not permitted to intermingle with the bride as it is the custom of these days. If they willingly want to give Hadyah, they should give it to a male relative of the bride, who then will forward it to the new bride.

Furthermore, giving gifts should not be included as a tradition in marriage as it is not necessary. It is not permissible to compel others or to criticise those who do not give anything.

Separation between a Married Couple

Q If a husband separates from his wife in anger for a year or more, is their marriage still intact?

A Mere separation does not invalidate the Nikāh, irrespective of the duration of the separation. The Nikāh remains intact so long as divorce does not take place.

Affair with Sister-in-Law

Q If a man had an affair with his wife's sister, is his Nikāh still intact?

A His Nikāh is still intact. However, such immoral deeds are the result of not maintaining Hijāb. Most people are misled by their Nafs (carnal desire), considering it unnecessary to adopt Hijāb from close relatives such as cousins and brother-in-laws etc. It is compulsory to maintain Hijāb from all such relatives. Abandonment of the Hijāb leads to evil & disastrous consequences.

Correct Time for Marriage

Q What is the correct time for marriage?

A The Holy Prophet 🕮 said, "When a child attains maturity let him get married. If he attains maturity and his father does not get him married and thereafter he commits a sin, then his sin will fall upon his father."

When a parent feels that his children are of marriageable age and can bear the responsibilities and duties of a family, he should get them married. The age will vary with different individuals.

Intention at the Time of Nikāh

Q What intention should a person make at the time of Nikāh?

A Indeed every deed is according to the intention made for it. Nikāh is a Sunnah, so the better a person's intention, the more reward he will receive.

It should also be kept in mind that for one deed several intentions can be made and for each intention a separate reward will be received. At the time of Nikāh, the following intentions can be made:

1. To get married is a Sunnah of the Holy Prophet ﷺ. If a person practices on a Sunnah he will be rewarded immensely especially in this day and age.

2. By marrying, a person saves himself from committing sins such as Zinā (fornication).

3. By means of Nikāh, a person's lust and desires are kept under control. His thoughts are controlled and his eyes are saved from looking at indecent scenes.

4. A married man receives more reward for his worship in comparison to an unmarried man. The intention for more reward can be made.

5. Allāh ﷻ will by means of Nikāh bless one with pious children.

6. Through Nikāh, the children born will be an addition to the Ummah of the Holy Prophet ﷺ.

7. Allāh ﷻ will bless the couple with such children who will strive for Islām. In this way, the Ummah will benefit and in addition the children will become a means of the parent's entry into Jannah and a means of their salvation from Hell. Apart from these, other good intentions can be made.

Allāh ﷻ Knows Best

13. Chapter on

Divorce

Divorce Issued by the Court

Q What is the Islamic ruling on the divorce pronounced by the court? Is the divorce issued in court approved in Islām?

A This is a common question which is asked very frequently by scholars and non-scholars alike. I recently came across a very detailed Fatwa on this issue by the Respected and Honourable Shaykh Mufti Ismāeel Sahib, an eminent disciple of Shaykh Muhammad Zakariyya ﷺ, which is in my opinion more than sufficient. I am therefore quoting the question that was posed to him and the detailed answer Mufti Sāhib gave which is as follows:

Question: I would like you to give me satisfactory answers with relevant quotes on the following issue:

Here, in the United Kingdom we have a considerable amount of Muslims who have made this country their home. By living here, they are obviously influenced by the culture and way of life, specifically in matters of marriage and divorce. Sometimes the man and at other times the woman files a petition for divorce, with the court issuing divorce proceedings and annulling the marriage. Mostly consideration of the woman is taken into account.

The following issues need clarification:

Is the divorce issued by the court approved and authorised? If the man or woman files a divorce petition, is the ruling in both cases the same or not? If the divorce takes place, what type of divorce takes place? When does the divorce take place in regard to the waiting period (Iddah)? In many cases, the woman is mistreated. What measures can be adopted to remove these circumstances?

Answer: Allāh ﷻ states in the Holy Qur'ān, **"Men are the maintainers (Qawwamuna or protectors) of women, because Allāh ﷻ has favoured one over the other, and of what they spend (i.e. men) of their property (on women)."** (4:34)

It is mentioned in a Hadeeth that the Holy Prophet ﷺ said, "Divorce (the authority) is given to the one who holds the branch."

From the Islamic viewpoint, the right of divorce rests in the hands of the husband who is sane and classed as an adult. It is mentioned in Durrul Mukhtār (meaning Chosen Pearls) and many books of Islamic jurisprudence, as follows, "The one who has the right to divorce is the adult and sane husband." For this reason, a man has either the right to divorce his wife or make someone his representative.

For specific reasons, Islām has not given this right to women. Hence, a woman cannot divorce her husband, nor make anyone her representative. If a woman divorces her husband or makes the judge her representative or files a petition to divorce him, then Islām does not recognise nor approves this. The woman still remains in the marriage of her husband.

However, if circumstances arise in a woman's marriage and she cannot live anymore with her husband nor fulfil his rights, then she is entitled to have the marriage annulled, on Islamic principles, by making an arrangement with the husband, giving some wealth and seeking divorce (which in Islām is referred to as Khul'ah). Likewise, if the husband abuses her, does not support her, leaves her or deserts her, then she can resolve this by following the directives mentioned by the scholars in the book entitled 'Al-Heelatun-Nājiza' authored by Shaykh Ashraf Ali Thānwi ﷺ.

We live in this country and have made it our permanent residence. This is not an Islamic country, neither are the Islamic laws implemented, but are devised for the successful governance of the country. It is necessary for us, as citizens, to abide by the laws to the best of our ability in order to live a peaceful life.

It is our duty to fulfil the contract and agreement we have made, morally and legally. At the same time, we should follow Islām but not break the laws of the country.

The above-mentioned issue has to be dealt with in a similar manner. Therefore, it is necessary to look at it in detail. Those who live in this country and are considered 'married' by either registering their marriage here or have come to this country as husband and wife, are the ones who can file petition for divorce through the county court.

The procedure is as follows: The man or woman (petitioner) has to write to the court giving reasons for wanting to separate from each other and annul the marriage. Thereafter, the judge sends a letter to the opposite party (respondent), titled 'Divorce Petition' and puts forward a few questions, which have to be answered. If the opposite party (respondent) acknowledges the letter by signing it, but does not answer it, then the judge processes the case according to the law, and finding sufficient causes, will write that the marriage has broken down irretrievably unless sufficient cause is shown to the court within six weeks and that there is no opposition between the parties. This is termed 'Decree Nisi'. If no one opposes this decree within this period, then the petitioner has to apply for final decree and the judge issues a final and absolute divorce, which is termed 'Decree Absolute'. According to the law of the country, both are separated and their marriage is completely annulled. They are now free to marry someone else.

Let us analyse the issues in the light of Islām:

1. If it is the case, where the man files a petition for divorce in the county court and demands a separation, then in this, as the man has the right to divorce, he can either pronounce it or make someone else his representative. So, it is as if he has made the judge his representative to divorce his wife. It is not necessary that the representative be a Muslim, as is the case in the court of this country. The divorce will take place issued by the judge and the woman can marry someone else after completing the waiting period (Iddah).

She does not need to take an Islamic divorce from her husband thereafter.

2. If it is the case, where the woman files a petition for divorce and when the court began proceedings, the man gave permission to the judge to proceed, in clear terms, then in this case also the divorce will take place.

3. The third issue is, if the man goes to his solicitors after having received the divorce petition to give a reply. Generally, the solicitor advises clients of no benefit in defending the case except delay with financial implications, with the court issuing the divorce in any case. Because of this, the solicitor writes that both husband and wife will separate or the husband signs and sends the divorce petition to the county court, willingly.

Therefore, in this case also the divorce will take place, because of the willingness of the husband. It is mentioned in 'Fatāwa Ālamgheeri', "If the man says, give divorce to my wife," then this man has become his representative and agent and it is mentioned on page 407 of the same book, "If the husband said to his wife, let's go to so and so (judge), in order that he divorces you, she goes and is divorced by so and so (judge), then this person has become a representative and agent for him to divorce her, even though he (judge) is ignorant of the person who made him the representative."

4. The fourth issue is, if the woman files for a divorce and the judge sends the divorce petition to the husband, but the husband defends his case and is not willing to divorce her, but despite this the judge issues a divorce.

5. The fifth issue is, the husband acknowledges and accepts his mistake and is willing to fulfil her rights, but the judge issues a divorce.

6. The sixth issue is, the man receives the divorce petition but does not proceed with the case nor does he do anything to show his willingness to divorce her, but the judge issues a divorce.

7. The seventh issue is if the woman files for divorce and the judge sends the divorce petition to the husband, but he refuses to defend his case and is not willing to divorce her, despite this the judge issues a divorce.

In the above four cases (4,5,6,7), both are considered separate, according to the law of the country, **but not Islamically** as they are still considered as a married couple. Hence, the woman cannot marry another man. If she does so, then the marriage will be void and both will be considered living in sin, because Islām has not recognised a woman to have the authority to issue a divorce or make someone else her representative. In the above cases (4,5,6,7) the woman should make the husband willing to give divorce or refer to an Islamic Council working with correct Islamic principles.

As previously mentioned, the right to divorce or terminate a marriage is given to the husband who is adult and sane, or the Muslim ruler because of his general authority or his authorised judge. Islām does not approve the right of authorisation to a non-Muslim judge or any secular court.

Where there is no Muslim judge or there is a Muslim judge who does not or cannot follow the dictates of Islām, then the people of the area or country should establish a group or council such as 'Islamic Council' that deals with such problematic issues. They should be referred to in such matters. It is necessary upon these councils to follow the guidelines and conditions mentioned in Al-Heelatun Nājiza, otherwise the cases dealt by them will not be authorised.

Another issue is the prevalent mental gap between old and modern minds, resulting in many incidents of divorce taking place. Shaykh Ashraf Ali Thānwi ﷺ mentions in Al-Heelatun Nājiza , "An agreement or written settlement (Iqrār Nāma) should be followed cautiously."

Regarding what type of divorce will take place, there are 3 types of divorce in Islām:

1. Talāq Raj'ee (Revocable Divorce)
2. Talāq Bā'in (Irrevocable Divorce)
3. Talāq Mughallaza (Final Irrevocable Divorce)

The wording of a divorce done through the courts is as follows:

"...be dissolved unless sufficient cause be shown to the court within six weeks from the making thereof why the mentioned decree should not be made absolute, and no such cause having been shown, it is hereby certified that the stated decree was on the........., made final and absolute and that the said marriage was thereby dissolved. Date: ...."

The summary of the wording is as follows:

No sufficient and satisfactory reason has been given, this is why the decree issued before will now be affected conclusively and marriage will be irretrievably broken down. Thus, Talāq Bā'in (Irrevocable Divorce) will take place. The ruling of Talāq Bā'in is that the marriage is terminated and the man cannot rejoin with her, unless by renewing the marriage. There is no need for Halālah. Nevertheless, if the woman does not wish to renew the marriage, then she can remarry another man after having completed her waiting period (Iddah - which is three menstruations normally or if pregnant then until she gives birth). Divorce does not take place through the issuing of a Decree Nisi.

However, it will take place at the moment and date when Decree Absolute is pronounced. The waiting period (Iddah) will also start from that moment and date.

Divorce in the State of Intoxication

Q Is divorce valid if it is uttered in the state of intoxication?

A Allāh ﷻ has bestowed mankind with numerous blessings. If we just take this one blessing, which is the intellect, then one will never be able to truly express his gratitude to Allāh ﷻ for it, even though he prostrates throughout his entire life. Now what a great injustice and oppression it is to destroy this God given blessing and to cloud it with the consumption of alcohol? Even if it may be for a few minutes or hours.

Hence, a person who consumes alcohol will be very sinful for this heinous crime. It is for this reason also that Islām has stipulated that if a man issues a Talāq to his wife, even when in the most severest state of intoxication, the Talāq is valid. This is because he is still responsible for his actions and he had willingly committed this sin. Islām is not responsible for his actions. There is no loophole for him in the Islamic Law.

In brief, Talāq issued in the state of intoxication is effected and is valid according to Islām. But not every state of intoxication is included here. If any of those intoxicant substances which are Harām in Islām like alcohol, drugs etc. are consumed, on the account of which one is intoxicated and in this state the husband divorces his wife, then this divorce will take place.

There are certain products that are not Harām in Islām, but they may intoxicate i.e. medicine. If a person is intoxicated by the consumption of such things, and he issues a Talāq to his wife, then his pronouncement of Talāq will not be valid.

Imām Shāmi ﷺ states in Raddul Muhtār, "The ruling is that if a person is intoxicated by using Harām means, then he is not absolved of the responsibility, and the ruling will apply to him. His words and dealings in Talāq, freeing slaves and business transactions will be binding."

He further states, "If his sanity is affected by a headache or with any Halāl thing, then the Talāq (given in this state) will not be valid."

Talāq in the Future Tense

Q My husband one day in an angry mood said to me, "I am going to divorce you." Will his statement result in a divorce?

A If the husband says (using the future tense), "I am going to divorce you," this is not Talāq.

This same rule applies if he says, "I intended to give you one Talāq," or "I will give you a Talāq," then in such instances no Talāq will take place, since he is only expressing his intentions for the future.

It is stated in Fatāwa Qādhi Khān, "If one says, I intend to divorce you, a Talāq will not occur."

Talāq whilst Joking

Q Is Talāq valid if the husband pronounced it as a joke?

A As far as Talāq is concerned, even joking takes the effect of a valid and true Talāq. The Holy Prophet 🕌 says, "Three things, their seriousness is serious and their joking is serious, marriage, divorce and Raj'at (taking a wife back)." (Tirmizi)

Hence, if a man whilst joking divorces his wife, then she is in actual fact divorced.

It is stated in Durrul Mukhtār, "As for (issuing Talāq) in joke, indeed a Talāq takes place according to Islām because the Holy Prophet 🕌 has stated that its joking is also serious."

Talāq in the State of Anger

Q My sister's husband in an angry mood pronounced three Talāqs. Afterwards when his anger cooled down, he realised his grave error. Now he greatly regrets what he has done.

My father has brought my sister to our house and he strictly prohibits my sister's husband to meet her. He claims that there is no way out and Talāq Mughallazah (final irrevocable divorce) has taken place for which the marriage is broken. What is the ruling according to the Holy Qur'ān and Sunnah regarding this situation?

A In this situation, three divorces (Talāq Mughallazah) have taken place. The woman will now have to sit for her Iddat (waiting period) after which she can marry someone else. It is stated in Hidāya:

Talāq Bid'ah or irregular divorce is when a husband divorces his wife with three divorces at once (either in one sentence or separately thrice within one Tuhr (term of purity). If a husband gives three divorces in either of these two ways, it will occur. He will also be sinful.

Talāq Mughallazah (final irrevocable divorce) means three Talāqs. There are two ways how three Talāqs might be given:

1. The first is where three Talāqs are given in three separate Tuhr (purifications) after menstruation. This will give both parties an opportunity (of about two to three months) to reflect.

2. The second is where three Talāqs are given at one instance. In this case there will be no time to think or reach a solution (as in the question). Consequently, this is the most objectionable way of giving Talāq.

It was brought to the attention of the Holy Prophet ﷺ that someone had given three Talāqs together at one time. He was enraged with anger and exclaimed, "What! In my presence, the Book of Allāh ﷻ (Holy Qur'ān) is being made fun of?"

If someone gives three Talāqs separately or together, whether it be in a state of anger or calm, joking or seriousness, whether the wife is in a pure state or in menstruation or whether divorce is actually intended or not, in all cases three Talāqs will occur and to issue a Fatwa (judicial verdict) of one Talāq would be wrong. In this case, the woman would not be lawful for the husband without Halālah and those men who cohabit with their wives without Halālah are committing adultery all their lives.

Halālah is the process wherein a woman is given three Talāqs, then she has to complete her Iddat, thereafter she has to marry someone else and cohabit with him at least once. Now, when this second husband gives her Talāq willingly and she completes this Iddat, she can then remarry her first husband.

Note: The above mentioned process of Halālah would only be permissible if the former husband and final irrevocable divorced wife did not pre-plan this process. The aforementioned was to only clarify a ruling for such a person. Otherwise, after pronouncing three Talāqs for both of them to pre-plan Halālah in order to rejoin is a great sin. Sayyidunā Abdullāh Ibn Mas'ood ﷺ relates that the Holy Prophet ﷺ cursed the Muhallil (the one who performs Halālah) and Muhallal lahu (upon whom Halālah is done). (Dārimi, Ibn Mājah)

Attending the Court to Establish Divorce

Q What is the ruling regarding the following Mas'alah: My husband in the presence of my parents and two witnesses gave me three divorces. Is it necessary for my husband to attend an office or a court to establish the divorce or can he himself give the divorce?

A According to Islām, it is not necessary for your husband to attend any court or office to establish the divorce. If he has given the three Talāqs as mentioned then it will be valid. It is not necessary (although recommended) to have any witnesses or to have someone present at the time of pronouncing the words of Talāq. The Talāq will occur immediately after it is pronounced. After three months (if she does not experience menstruation) or three menstrual cycles (if she experiences menstruation) or after the child is born (if she is pregnant) she will be out of the wedlock.

Forcing One's Wife to Leave Home after Divorce

Q A man has given his wife one Talāq and demands her to go out of his house straight away. What does Islām say on this matter?

A The Holy Qur'ān enjoins on the husbands, **"Do not turn them out of their homes and neither should they leave by themselves, unless they commit open indecency."** (65:01)

This injunction clearly shows that as long as they are legally husband and wife, the wife has a lawful right to live in their own house and the husband should not force her out. This is a moral and legal duty until they are legally separated. This right is not terminated by the pronouncement of divorce.

A woman enjoys the right to live in the house till the expiry of the waiting period and it will be clear aggression and oppression on the part of the husband if he turns her out before the expiry of the period. However if she is guilty of any open lewdness (adultery), he has the right to send her away even before the expiry of the term of waiting.

When the waiting period is coming to an end, both the parties are again advised to think again, settle their differences and forget their complaints and anger because soon the time limit will pass and they will have no chance to compromise.

At the end of the waiting period, whether the husband decides 'to take her back' or 'leave her', in both cases it is recommended that they arrange two witnesses. These witnesses must be men of integrity and good character. This is for the protection of the interests of both parties.

Allāh ﷻ says in the Holy Qur'ān, **"Then when they are about to reach their appointed term, either take them back in a good manner or part with them in a good manner. And take as witness two just individuals from amongst you (Muslims). And establish the testimony for Allāh. That will be an admonition given to him who believes in Allāh and the Last Day. And whosoever fears Allāh and keeps his duty to Him, He will make a way for him to get out (from every difficulty)."** (65:02)

Allāh ﷻ Knows Best

14. CHAPTER ON
WOMEN

Trimming the Hair

Q Is it permissible for women to trim their hair, if not, why?

A It is forbidden for women to cut their hair or even trim it. It is narrated by Sayyidunā Ali ﷺ that the Holy Prophet ﷺ stated that it is forbidden for a woman to shave her head. (Nasai)

In another Hadeeth, the Holy Prophet ﷺ states, "Allāh ﷻ curses those who imitate women and curse those women who imitate men." (Bukhāri, Mishkāt)

In this Hadeeth, it clearly states that if a woman imitates a man she shall be cursed. Cutting and trimming the hair which is similar to a man or any other un-Islamic culture can be classified as imitating a man and therefore the Holy Prophet ﷺ has prohibited this act. (i.e. cutting or trimming in such a way which is similar to a man or any other un-Islamic culture is Harām).

It is stated in Durrul Mukhtār that it is a sin for a woman to shave or trim the head even though the husband orders her to do so.

The Cutting of Women's Hair

Q What is the ruling regarding the cutting of a woman's hair?

A In general, the major classical Hanafi Fiqh books prohibit the cutting of hair for women. In a Hadeeth it is mentioned that the Holy Prophet ﷺ forbade women from shaving their hair. (Tirmizi, Nasai)

Imām al-Haskafi ﷺ mentions in his book based on the Hanafi Fiqh, "If a woman cuts her hair, she will be sinful and cursed." In al-Bazzāziyya it is mentioned, "Even with the permission of the husband, as there is no obedience to the creation in the disobedience of the Creator." (Durrul Mukhtār)

The main two reasons given by scholars for the impermissibility of women cutting their hair are, imitation of the non-Muslims, and/or imitation of men, both of which have been clearly prohibited in Islām. In the Hadeeth compiled by Imām Abū Dāwood ﷺ and others, the Holy Prophet ﷺ said, "Whosoever imitates a group is amongst them."

Regarding the imitation of men, the Holy Prophet ﷺ cursed those men who imitate women, and those women who imitate men. (Bukhārī)

For the above two reasons, the jurists have generally prohibited the cutting of hair for women.

In view of the above, it would generally not be permitted for women to cut their hair. To imitate the habits of the non-Muslim women that are contrary to Islām is not permissible. Unfortunately the haircuts prevalent amongst many Muslim women have a clear resemblance with the practices of non-Muslim women, thus it will be unlawful.

Similarly, to shorten the hair in a way that it resembles the hair of men is also prohibited. If a woman does so, she will incur the curse of the Holy Prophet ﷺ.

However, if a woman trims her hair slightly in a way that she does not contravene any of the above two reasons, then this would be (and Allāh ﷻ knows best) permitted. There are two conditions for this permissibility that must be understood properly, and not misused or taken out of context.

Firstly, there should be no imitation of non-Muslim women; the hair styles adopted by non-Muslim women, such as flicks, perms, fringes, etc. will not be allowed. Cutting the hair from the front will also be impermissible.

Secondly, there should be no imitation of men; cutting the hair in any way that it resembles the hair of men is unlawful (Harām), as mentioned previously. Therefore, if a woman cuts her hair from the lower end (at the back) slightly, in order to level her hair, then this will be permissible. Furthermore, the hair can be cut or shaved due to medical reasons, and split ends may be cut to allow the hair to grow properly.

It should be noted that if the hair is cut, then it should be well below the shoulders, and this permissibility is only to cut it slightly. If the woman is married, then this should be done with the consent of the husband.

Finally, it should be remembered that it is better for a woman not to cut her hair altogether, unless there is some genuine reason, as highlighted above.

Previously, a woman's beauty was considered in the length of her hair, and not imitating men. Nowadays 'fashion trends' have turned that around.

Cutting the Hair

Q A husband wants his wife to cut her hair. Is it permissible?

A It is not permissible. Obedience to the husband or to anyone in anything which is unlawful, is not permissible.

Shaving any Parts of the Body

Q Are women allowed to shave any parts of their body i.e. legs, arms, eyebrows etc.?

A It is permissible to shave the hair of their body except for the head and eyebrows. It is not permissible for a woman to shave or even trim her hair nor to shape her eyebrows. Sayyidunā Abdullāh Ibn Abbās ؓ relates that the Holy Prophet ﷺ said, "Cursed are those women who join (other) hair with their hair and those women that seek to join (other) hair with their hair, and (cursed are) those that pluck the hair of the eyebrows and those that seek to pluck their eyebrows, and those that tattoo and those who seek to be tattooed without any illness. (Abū Dāwood)

Removing Facial Hair

Q Is it permissible for a woman to remove facial hair?

A It is not only permissible but also desirable for a woman to remove her facial hair. (Shāmi, Fatāwa Raheemiya)

Shaping Eyebrows

Q Is it permissible for women to shape their eyebrows by shading and removing some hair? My husband insists that I do it.

A This act is not permissible. The curse of Allāh ﷻ descends on women who tamper in this way with their eyebrows and natural features.

Islām describes such tampering as the act of Shaytān. It is not permissible to obey the husband when he makes Harām demands.

Covering the Hair when Retiring to Sleep

Q Do women have to cover their hair when they go to sleep?

A No, it is not necessary at all.

The Ruling of Hijāb in Islām

Q Can you please explain the Islamic ruling regarding the wearing of a veil or Burqah by a woman in Islām.

A Hijāb (veil) with its established limits is a Divine Law and guidance based on the Holy Qur'ān and the Ahādeeth of the Holy Prophet ﷺ. It is on this basis that it has been practiced continuously at all times by the Muslim Ummah. It is not a fiction that was imposed by people nor given the status of Islamic Law in Muslim societies based on cultural practice.

It is stated in Surah Al-Ahzāb, **"O Prophet! Tell your wives and daughters and the believing women that they should cast their Jalābeeb (outer garments) over them. This is more close that they are recognised so that they are not molested." (33:59)**

The scholars of the Holy Qur'ān clarify that according to this verse, it is compulsory for a woman to wear Hijāb.

Hijāb literally means screen, curtain, partition and concealment. As a verb it means to conceal oneself or hide from view. In Islamic term it means to conceal oneself from the view of the Ghair-Mahram i.e. a man with whom marriage is permissible.

The Holy Prophet ﷺ said, "A woman is an object of concealment, thus when she emerges, Shaytān secretly pursues her (and lays in wait to create his immorality)." (Tirmizi)

"Allāh ﷻ curses the one who looks (at females) and the one to whom the look was directed." (Tirmizi)

The Holy Prophet 🕌 said, "Beware of mingling with (strange) women." A man from the Ansār asked, "O' Messenger of Allāh 🕌, what do you say regarding the brother-in-law?" The Holy Prophet 🕌 replied, "A brother-in-law is death." (i.e. intermingling with him is as dangerous as death).

(Bukhāri)

However, when a woman emerges from her home, it is compulsory upon her to observe the following conditions: She must be properly and thoroughly covered in a loose outer cloak which totally covers her entire body.

In the Holy Qur'ān Allāh 🕌 says, **"O' Prophet, tell your wives, your daughters and the women of the believers that they draw over their Jilbābs (outer cloak/Burqah), (that is the minimum requirement that they should adopt) so that they be recognised (as respectable and honourable ladies) and not be molested, (by shameless people with loose morals)." (33:59)**

Meaning of Jilbāb

The Jilbāb is an outer sheet or cloak (Burqah). At the time of the Holy Prophet 🕌, this sheet was so large that two women could easily be covered with it.

In the era of the Holy Prophet 🕌 women use to wear the Jilbāb in such a way that the cloak covered the entire body from head to toe. The term 'Yudneena' used in the verse which literally means they should lower or draw down, commands that the cloak should be drawn over from above and lowered in such a way that it covers the whole body.

Full covering was the standard and normal practice in the time of the Holy Prophet 🕌. In this regard Sayyidah Ā'ishah 🕌 narrates that during the occasion of Hajjat-ul-Widā, when people passed along side us, we would draw the Jilbābs over ourselves. (Abū Dāwood)

Another incident which is also narrated by Abū Dāwood mentions; a young Muslim man was martyred. His mother, fully covering her face and wearing a Jilbāb, came to the battlefield to enquire about her son. With her face fully covered, she came into the presence of the Holy Prophet 🕌.

People were surprised that inspite of such an emergency, she did not discard her face covering. When the mother of the martyred Muslim learned of their surprise, she said, "My son is lost, but not my shame and modesty."

These narrations are sufficient to indicate that it is essential for women to exercise extra precaution assuring that their attire conforms to the Islamic Laws.

Hijāb (Veil)

Q How should a Muslim woman dress when emerging from her home? Is Hijāb necessary for her when she goes out?

A Hijāb (Arabic word) and Pardah (Urdu and Persian word) means separation between males and females. Free and unnecessary intermingling of both genders is forbidden in Islām. When a Muslim woman has to emerge from her home for a valid reason, it is compulsory on her to cover her entire body, head to feet with a thick and loose outer garment. She should refrain from wearing jingling (sound making) jewellery, such as anklets.

Observing Hijāb

Q Is it compulsory for me to cover myself i.e. observe Hijāb from my cousin brother, brother in-law and other such male relatives?

A Yes, it is compulsory for a mature female to cover herself from all mature male relatives that are non-Mahram (those with whom marriage is permissible).

This includes:

1) All types of cousin brothers - Paternal uncle's son, paternal aunt's son, maternal uncle's son, maternal aunt's son.
2) All types of brother in-laws - Husband's brother, sister's husband, husband's sister's husband.
3) Paternal aunt's husband.
4) Maternal aunt's husband.
5) Husband's nephew, husband's brother's son, husband's sister's son.
6) Husband's paternal uncle.

7) Husband's maternal uncle.
8) Husband's paternal aunt's husband.
9) Husband's maternal aunt's husband.

Birth by Caesarean

Q If a child is born through a caesarean section, then what will be the Mas'alah regarding her Nifās?

A If a child is born through a caesarean section, then only the blood that flows from the vagina will be regarded as Nifās. The blood that flows from the area where the surgery was performed is not classified as Nifās. If no blood flows at all from the vagina, then she should immediately take a bath and start performing her Salāh. If she is unable to take a bath because of a valid reason, then she should perform Tayammum and start performing her Fardh Salāh.

Miscarriage

Q What is the ruling regarding the bleeding after a miscarriage?

A If no part of the foetus has yet been formed but only thick blood or flesh like substance is discharged as a result of miscarriage or abortion (performed due to a condition allowed in Islam), then this is not regarded as the birth of a child and whatever bleeding results from this is not regarded as Nifās.

If a woman remained pure for fifteen days or more before the miscarriage or abortion and if this bleeding (after miscarriage or abortion) continued for three days or more, then it should be regarded as Haidh and all laws concerning Haidh will apply to her. If this bleeding stops within three days and does not appear again, then it should be regarded as Istihādah.

If some form or shape of the child (finger, nail, hair etc.) has already been formed, then the bleeding that follows miscarriage is regarded as Nifās and the laws concerning Nifās will become compulsory. That is, that during the period of Nifās; Salāh, Fasting, recitation of the Holy Qur'ān and sexual intercourse are forbidden.

By the end of the fourth month of pregnancy, normally some parts of the body are usually formed already. Hence if the miscarriage or abortion takes place after four months of pregnancy , then the bleeding that follows will be regarded as Nifās.

Travelling without a Mahram

Q Many Muslim sisters travel to far towns and cities and even to different countries for higher education or employment without any Mahram. What is the ruling in Islām regarding this matter. Is it permissible for them to travel alone without a Mahram?

A In the authentic books of Ahādeeth, the Holy Prophet ﷺ has clearly prohibited females from travelling alone. In a Hadeeth of Muslim narrated by Sayyidunā Abū Saeed al-Khudree ؓ the Holy Prophet ﷺ says, "Let no woman travel for more than three days (equivalent to 48 miles today) unless accompanied by her husband or her Mahram." From this Hadeeth, we can deduce the Mas'alah that a woman is prohibited from travelling alone.

The majority of scholars have based their opinions on this very Hadeeth, when they ruled that travelling without a proper Mahram is not permissible even when going to perform Fardh Hajj.

In comparison to this, travelling for higher education or employment are of a lower degree in importance, especially when a Muslim woman is not obliged to carry out these objectives.

The reason is clear because Islām has placed the responsibility of a woman's maintenance on her father before her marriage and on her husband after her marriage, and has not allowed women to leave their homes without any urgent need. Therefore, travelling for higher education or for employment purposes without a Mahram is not permissible.

However, in case of a woman who has neither a husband, father or any other Mahram to support her financially nor does she have enough funds to take care of her needs, then under this circumstance, it is permissible for her to go out of her house with proper Hijāb and earn her livelihood to the extent of her need. But if this objective can be easily achieved in one's own town, then there is no need to travel to one that is more distant.

Old Woman Travelling without a Mahram

Q What is the ruling regarding an old woman travelling alone?

A When a woman has reached an age when she no longer has sexual passion (usually after the age of menopause), then it is permissible for her to travel without a Mahram.

Mahram & Ghair-Mahram

Q Who is a Mahram and who is a Ghair-Mahram?

A Mahram refers to the person with whom marriage is not permissible at all and with whom Hijāb is not necessary e.g. father, son, uncle etc. Ghair-Mahram refers to all those people with whom marriage is permissible. It is also compulsory to observe Hijāb with all Ghair-Mahrams e.g. cousin brothers etc.

Earliest Age for Menstruation

Q At what age is it possible for a girl to begin menstruating?

A Fuqahā (jurists) have written that if a nine year old girl bleeds from the womb, and if the bleeding lasts for three days or more then it will be regarded as Haidh (menstruation). (Shāmi)

A girl younger than nine years of age cannot get Haidh. If bleeding does occur it will be Istihādah, not Haidh. A female from the age of nine up to the age of fifty-five years is normally considered as a menstruating woman.

Iddat

Q What is Iddat?

A Iddat refers to the period of waiting during which a woman cannot remarry after being widowed or divorced.

The Wife's Travel Expenses

Q Who is responsible for the wife's travel expenses?

A If a woman is travelling with her husband, then he will be responsible for her travel expenses even though the journey is undertaken for her personal benefit. But if the husband is not accompanying her, then he is not responsible for her expenses.

Meaning of Āsiya

Q We have kept our daughter's name Āsiya. I want to verify if this name is permissible to keep or not. Please could you also mention the importance of keeping good names for children and if it has any influence on the child.

A Āsiya spelt with Ain (ع) and Swād (ص) will mean disobedient. Hence, not permissible. It is reported by Sayyidunā Abdullāh Ibn Umar 🙴 the well known Sahābi that one of his sisters was named Āsiya which means disobedient. The Holy Prophet 🙵 changed her name to Jameelah which means beautiful.

However, if Āsiya is spelt with Alif (ا) and Seen (س) then it will mean a lady doctor. Āsiya was also the name of pharaoh's (Fir'awn) wife who embraced Islām. Due to the reason that in the English language both names are pronounced and spelt the same, it is preferable not to keep such a name. Nevertheless, if one wishes to adopt it then there is no harm bearing in mind the correct Arabic spelling.

We should always keep suitable names for our children. The Holy Prophet 🙵 changed the names of several people because they carried a bad meaning.

Many scientists today have admitted that the name of a person may influence his life. But the Holy Prophet 🙵 has stated this fact to his followers more than 1400 years ago, when he advised the Muslims to select good names for their children. Names are also a source of identity of ones religion.

Therefore, we should keep our children's name after the Holy Prophet 🙵 and the pious people, thus their name will reflect their identity.

It is the child's vested right to be honoured with a good name. The Holy Prophet 🌸 said, "It is the right of a child that his father should give him a good name and when he comes of age should get him married and he should give him the education of the Holy Qur'ān." (Kanzul Ummāl)

The Holy Prophet 🌸 also said, "On the Day of Qiyāmah you will be called by your own names and the names of your fathers, therefore keep good names." (Abū Dāwood)

It was the practice of the Holy Prophet 🌸 to inquire the names of individuals and villages. If they were pleasant it became apparent on his noble face. If not, his displeasure could be seen. Once the Holy Prophet 🌸 called for a person to milk a camel. One person volunteered, the Holy Prophet 🌸 said to him, "What is your name?", he replied, "Harb." The Holy Prophet 🌸 told him to sit down and refused to accept his service because his name was 'Harb' (meaning war) which did not imply pleasantness. Then the Holy Prophet 🌸 asked, "Who will milk?" A second person stood up to milk, the Holy Prophet 🌸 asked him his name. He replied, "Ya'eesh," (meaning long life). The Holy Prophet 🌸 said to him, "Milk her."

Sayyidunā Abdullāh Ibn Umar 🌸 narrates that the Holy Prophet 🌸said, "Truly the most beloved names in the eyes of Allāh 🌸 are Abdullāh and Abdur Rahmān." (Muslim, Tirmizi, Abū Dāwood)

It is also reported that the Holy Prophet 🌸 said, "Keep the names after the Prophets 🌸 and the most desirable names in the sight of Allāh 🌸 are Abdullāh and Abdur Rahmān, the most truthful names are Hārith (planter) and Hammām (thoughtful) and the most disliked ones are Harb (battle) and Murrah (bitter)."

Allāh 🌸 Knows Best

15. CHAPTER ON INNOVATION

Shaking Hands after Eid Salāh

Q After the two Eid Salāh which take place every year, people shake hands and embrace each other. Did the Holy Prophet 🌷 and his Companions 🌸 shake hands and embrace after the Eid Salāh?

A Saying Salām, shaking hands and embracing are acts of Sunnah and are included in Ibādah (worship). But we should remember that an act of worship will be classed as worship when it is discharged in accordance with the Holy Qur'ān and Sunnah.

During the time of Sayyidunā Ali 🌸, when he was the Ameerul-Mu'mineen (Leader of the Muslims), a man intended to perform Nafl Salāh in the Eid-Gah (a place designated for Eid Salāh) on Eid day. Sayyidunā Ali 🌸 forbade him. The man replied, "O' Ameerul-Mu'mineen, I know well that Allāh 🌸 will not punish me for performing Salāh." Sayyidunā Ali 🌸 replied, "I also know that Allāh 🌸 does not reward any deed or work unless the Holy Prophet 🌷 has done it or has emphasised to do it. Hence your Salāh (at this moment) is useless and futile. So I am afraid that Allāh 🌸 may punish you for the reason that you did something against the Holy Prophet's 🌷 practice."

The Adhān is an act of Ibādah, a religious practice and an Islamic symbol. For the Friday congregational Salāh there are two Adhān and an Iqāmah, but for the two Eid Salāh there is neither Adhān nor Iqāmah, because they are not proven. Everyone knows that if Adhān or the Iqāmah is given in the Eid-Gah, it will be classed as an innovation.

Similarly, to make handshaking and embracing necessary straight after the Eid and other Salāh is an innovation.

It is written in the book Majālisul-Abrār, "But at any other time besides the times of meeting, as after the Jumu'ah Salāh and the two Eid Salāh, as the people of this era have become habituated to, so there is no mention of this in the Hadeeth. Hence this is an unproven act, and this is proven and confirmed at its own place that an act that has no proof is rejected and not worthy of acting upon."

It is stated in the famous book of jurisprudence 'Shami': The custom of hand-shaking after Salāh (any Salāh) is disliked (Makrooh). The evidence is that the noble Companions ﷺ did not shake hands after Salāh. Hāfiz Ibn Hajar ﷺ states that the people shaking hands after the five time Salāh - is an innovation (Bid'ah), there is no basis for this in Islām. Shaykh Ibnul-Hāj Makki ﷺ writes in his book Al-Madkhal, "It is necessary for the Imām to forbid the people who have innovated a new custom of shaking hands after the Fajr, Friday congregational and Asr Salāh, for this is an innovation (Bid'ah)."

According to Islām, the appropriate time of handshaking is at the time of meeting someone and not after the Salāh. Hence it should be done only on that occasion which Islām has fixed for it, and should prevent those who practice against the Sunnah.

Mulla Ali Qāri ﷺ (the commentator of Mishkāt) writes in his commentary Mirqāt-Sharh-e-Mishkāt, "No doubt the time of handshaking is at the beginning of meeting."

People meet without shaking hands, discuss religious affairs and then shake hands after having performed the Salāh. Where is this Sunnah from? Hence some scholars have clearly confirmed that this method is disliked (Makrooh) and an innovation.

On the basis of these clarifications, it is necessary that one abstains from the customary handshaking but at the same time one should not adopt any method whereby resentment and hatred may spread amongst the people.

On such occasions one should keep in mind the instructions of Mulla Ali Qāri ﷺ. He says, "When a Muslim extends his hands in an inappropriate time for handshaking, one should not hurt his feeling by withdrawing one's hands and be the cause of mistrust. Instead one should politely explain and inform him of the reality of the precept (Mas'alah)."

Shaking Hands after Salāh

Q Is shaking hands after each Salāh Bid'ah (innovation)?

A This is not an act of Sunnah and neither did the Sahābah ﷺ adhere to this, therefore to practice this as a custom and to consider it necessary is a Bid'ah.

Placing the Hands on the Chest after Musāfahah (Shaking Hands)

Q I have noticed many brothers placing their right hand on the chest after shaking hands. Is this correct or not?

A There is no evidence (from the Holy Qur'ān or the Ahādeeth) regarding this practice. Hence, there is no reason to place the hand on the chest after Musāfahah. It is a cultural practice. Similarly, many kiss their hands after Musāfahah. This is also disliked. In fact the famous scholar Imām Ibn Ābideen Shāmi ﷺ has condemned these acts and classed them as Makrooh Tahreemi. (Shāmi)

Accepting Money For Du'ā

Q Is it permissible to accept money for making Du'ā? It has become customary in many places that at the time when Du'ā for the deceased or sick is said, a sum of money regarded as Hadyah (gift) is given to the Imām etc. Is this permissible? Can the Imām accept that money?

A It is not permissible to accept money for making Du'ā. Du'ā is an act of pure Ibādah (worship). It is not permissible to accept or charge money for Du'ā nor is it permissible to give the Imām etc. money for having made Du'ā. This customary practice is in the category of an arranged practice. It is not acceptable to perform acts of Ibādah for monetary gain. Such Du'ās accompanied by customary payment is devoid of Ikhlās (devotion) and is carried out for worldly motives, not for the sake of Allāh ﷻ.

Using the Words 'Qiblah or Ka'bah' for Spiritual Guides

Q Many disciples nowadays write the word Qiblah or Ka'bah with the names of their spiritual guide. Is this permissible?

A It is not permissible to write or utter such words of praise for any person, even though he may be a great spiritual guide. Allāh 🕮 informs us in the Holy Qur'ān disapproving the ways of the people of the Book who exaggerated in the matter of their religion. **"O People of the Book! Do not commit excesses in your religion and speak only the truth about Allāh. The Maseeh Eesā, the son of Maryam was but the Messenger of Allāh and His Word." (4:171)**

It is mentioned in the most authentic book of Ahādeeth, Saheeh al-Bukhāri, "Do not exaggerate in praising me as the Christians did regarding Sayyidunā Eesā 🕮. Listen carefully, I am the servant of Allāh 🕮, so proclaim that I am the servant and Messenger of Allāh 🕮. (Do not cross the limit of praises as the People of the Book did)."

If the Holy Prophet 🕮 did not tolerate such words of praise then how can it be acceptable for his followers. Hence the words Qiblah and Ka'bah should not be used in writing nor in calling the spiritual guides.

Performing Lengthy Salāh on the Night of Barā'at

Q On Laylatul Barā'at (15th night of Sha'bān) many people perform very lengthy Salāh which include specific amount of Surahs i.e. 25 times Sūrah Ikhlās in the 1st Rak'āt, 50 times in the 2nd Rak'āt etc. They greatly emphasise on performing these Salāh and quote the sayings of pious people. Should we perform these Salāh? Are there any Ahādeeth regarding these Salāh?

A There is no specific Salāh that is prescribed for the night of Barā'at. A person should perform Nafl as usual and because of the special virtue of the night of Barā'at every person should seek Allāh's 🕮 Mercy and Forgiveness.

1. It is reported from Sayyidunā Mu'āz Ibn Jabal 🕮 that the Holy Prophet 🕮 said, "On the 15th night of Sha'bān, Allāh 🕮 bestows His special attention on His entire creation. He then pardons His entire creation except an idolater and the one who harbours enmity." (Tabarāni has recorded this Hadeeth in Awsat, Ibn Hibbān in his Saheeh, Baihaqi, and Targheeb-wath-Tarheeb)

2. It is narrated from Sayyidunā Abdullāh Ibn Amr 🙵 that the Holy Prophet 🙵 said, "Allāh 🙼 looks with special attention towards His creation on the fifteenth night of Sha'bān and forgives all His servants except two categories of people; the person who harbours enmity and a murderer." Imām Ahmad reports this Hadeeth with a slightly weak chain of narrators.

(Targheeb-wath-Tarheeb)

3. It is related from Makhool 🙵 who narrates from Khatheer Ibn Murrah 🙵 that the Holy Prophet 🙵 said, "On the night of Sha'bān, Allāh 🙼 forgives all the inhabitants of the earth except an idolater and the one who harbours hatred for others." (Baihaqi)

Note: In the Islamic calendar, the night precedes the day. Hence the night between the fourteenth and fifteenth of Sha'bān is implied.

From these Ahādeeth we can realise the importance of this night but nowhere in the Ahādeeth can we find any mention of these Salāh. Shaykh Anwar Shāh Kashmiri 🙵 has written regarding this matter that the significance of the night of Barā'at is proven. There is however no proof for those weak and unacceptable narrations mentioned in certain books.

Shaykh Yūsuf Binnouri 🙵 writes in Ma'ārifus-Sunan that Shaykh Abū Tālib Makki 🙵 recorded these narrations in his book "Qootul-Quloob". Imām Ghazāli 🙵 following Shaykh Abū Tālib 🙵 did the same, and Shaykh Abdul Qādir Jilāni 🙵 has followed them in his book "Ghunyatut-Tālibeen". They mention a narration of Sayyidunā Ali 🙵 that discusses a Salāh of one hundred Rak'āts. However, Shaykh Ibnul-Jawzee 🙵 and others declared the narration to be Mowdhu (fabrication).

Imām Dhahabi, Ibnul-Arrāq, Imām Suyūti and Mulla Ali Qāri 🙵 and other scholars of Hadeeth (Muhaddithoon) have strongly refuted such Salāh.

Note: Imām Dhahabi 🙵 states regarding the book of "Ghunyatut-Tālibeen" that although it is the work of Shaykh Abdul Qādir Jilāni 🙵, many additions were made to his book after his death. The above book cannot be relied upon. As far as Ahādeeth are concerned, the opinion of the scholars of Hadeeth are always considered and not those of Wā'izeen (lecturers) and Sufis.

Furthermore, with all due respect towards the Mashāikh of Tasawwuf, the point mentioned is that the opinions of the scholars specialising in a particular field is always given preference over others, when that field is under discussion. Therefore, in the matter of the acceptance or rejection of narrations, the opinion of the Muhaddithoon will always take precedence.

Mulla Ali Qāri ﷺ has discussed the matter under a particular chapter regarding the prescribed Salāh of the night of Barā'at. After mentioning the Salāh, he declares them to be baseless and therefore concludes that these Salāh were first introduced in the fourth century in Baitul-Maqdis and therefore some Ahādeeth were fabricated in order to support these baseless methods.

Meelād-un-Nabi

Q What is the ruling regarding Meelādun Nabi?

A Shaykh Yūsuf Ludhyānwi ﷺ writes in his famous book "Differences in the Ummah and the Straight Path":

Meelādun Nabi is generally celebrated on the 12th of Rabee-ul Awwal. In present times it has been established as a hallmark of the people calling themselves Ahle-Sunnat. I wish to present a few important and noteworthy points regarding these celebrations.

1. The discussing of the various attributes of the Holy Prophet ﷺ is a virtuous and noble act. It constitutes a sign of Imān and a means of reviving and refreshing our Imān also.

His birth, youth, Prophethood, teachings, battles, sacrifices, Ibādah, character, piety, knowledge, happiness, anger, sorrow and the exemplary manner in which he conducted himself when encountered by different situations and circumstances all constitute a means of spiritual guidance. It is incumbent upon the Ummah to learn, teach, discuss and propagate all the actions of the Holy Prophet ﷺ and involvement in these constitutes praiseworthy Ibādah. Discussions of the wives, children, Sahābah ﷺ of the Holy Prophet ﷺ etc. even discussions concerning his clothing, horses, camels, infact anything remotely connected with this greatest of all Prophets are indeed acts of great merit.

2. The life of the Holy Prophet 🌸 can be divided into two stages. The first consisting of the period from birth to Prophethood and the second from Prophethood to demise. Various incidents concerning the first portion of his life have been recorded in the books of Ahādeeth and history. The second portion of his life which the Holy Qur'ān refers to as "a beautiful example" has been recorded to the minute detail in the books of Ahādeeth and Seerah. It has been recorded most perfectly and authentically down to the minute detail.

3. Our love and devotion to the Holy Prophet 🌸 can be illustrated in two ways. Firstly, to emulate every action of the Holy Prophet 🌸 to the extent that every follower of the Holy Prophet 🌸 becomes an exemplary specimen of the ways of the Holy Prophet 🌸. This is of vital importance. This emulation should at least be to such an extent that a person is easily recognised as a follower of the Holy Prophet 🌸.

The second manner is that wherever and whenever an opportunity arises one discusses and praises the beautiful lifestyle of the Holy Prophet 🌸, his actions, character, habits, etc. This in turn serves as a means of encouraging others to emulate his lifestyle.

The Sahābah 🌸, Tābi'een, A'immah (leaders) and Salaf-e-Sāliheen 🌸 (pious predecessors) adopted both these methods of propagating and emulating the lifestyle of the Holy Prophet 🌸. They endeavoured to bring into their lives every Sunnah of the Holy Prophet 🌸 and discussed the Sunnah of the Holy Prophet 🌸 in every gathering. It would be appropriate to cite a few examples of how the Sahābah's 🌸 practices conformed to the Sunnah of the Holy Prophet 🌸.

Prior to the death of Sayyidunā Umar 🌸, while he was in great pain due to the wounds on his body, a young man came to visit him. Upon looking at him, Sayyidunā Umar 🌸 reprimanded him saying, "Young man, your garment is below your ankles and this is contrary to the Sunnah of the Holy Prophet 🌸." Sayyidunā Abdullāh Ibn Umar 🌸 took so much interest and care in emulating the Sunnah of the Holy Prophet 🌸 that while proceeding for Hajj, he used to break his journey to rest wherever the Holy Prophet 🌸 rested.

Whichever tree the Holy Prophet 鑑 slept under he also slept under it. Wherever the Holy Prophet 鑑 relieved himself, Sayyidunā Abdullāh Ibn Umar 鑑 stopped and relieved himself at that place irrespective of having the need to relieve himself or not. Such noble people had true love for the Holy Prophet 鑑. Their love was not merely lip service but practical. They endeavoured to become living examples of the Holy Prophet 鑑 thus radiating and enlivening their surroundings.

The Sahābah 鑑 and the Tābi'een 鑑 travelled to many foreign places. Despite not knowing the languages of those places, their beautiful character and habits were so impressive that nations upon nations accepted Islām merely by observing the beautiful character of those great luminaries of Islām. This was the magnetism of the beautiful and noble life of the Holy Prophet 鑑, which every Muslim should adopt and follow.

4. The Salaf-e-Sāliheen 鑑 never arranged Meelād celebrations. It must be understood that the environment was filled with practical examples of the Seerah of the Holy prophet 鑑. It is obvious that the actions were at all times in accordance to the way of the Holy Prophet 鑑 and the subject matter of all their gatherings was the beautiful way of the Holy Prophet 鑑. There was no need to arrange gatherings under the banner of Meelād-un-Nabi. Sadly, as time passed by and people moved further away from the auspicious era of the Holy Prophet 鑑, we find hollow and false claims of love and emulation resounding all around us yet the true illustration of this love is not to be found.

Alhamdulillāh, this Ummah never fell prey to complete non-productivity. Even to this day, one will find people whose lives are in conformity to the Sunnah of the Holy Prophet 鑑. To these people every Sunnah of the Holy Prophet 鑑 is more valuable than this world and all its contents. However, one has to regretfully admit that such people are very few.

The majority of people are those of loud and hollow claims of following the way of the Holy Prophet 鑑. Sadly it is these same people who once or twice annually raise slogans of Meelād-un-Nabi and feel happy that they have fulfilled the rights of the Holy Prophet 鑑 and they feel that intercession of the Holy Prophet 鑑 would be made on their behalf.

Yet their lives do not even reflect an iota of the Seerah of the Holy Prophet ﷺ. They have diminished whatever remembrance there was of the Holy Prophet's ﷺ Sunnah from their lives and every moment of their lives is engulfed in trampling the Sunnah of the Holy Prophet ﷺ.

Their hearts would not even be affected if they were to have even an iota worth of knowledge, of the suffering and distress of the Holy Prophet ﷺ on knowing that his Sunnah is being destroyed.

They are only deceiving themselves by the conception that a few slogans of love and praise are all that the fulfilling of the rights of the Holy Prophet ﷺ entails.

5. During the first six centuries of this Ummah, the Muslims never arranged any Meelād celebrations.

The first Meelād was organised by Sultān Abu Saeed Muzaffar and Abul Khitāb Ibn Wāhia in the year 604 A.H. Special care was taken regarding the following things:
a) Specification of the 12th of Rabee-ul-Awwal.
b) The distribution of food with the intention of Isāle-Thawāb (sending reward) to the Holy Prophet ﷺ.

As a result of this new practice, the Ulamā were drawn into arguments and discussions concerning its permissibility and impermissibility.

Shaykh Fa'kahāni ﷺ and his colleagues refrained from these gatherings and ruled it an innovation, due to the condition attached to its organisation. Gradually, with the passage of time many baseless customs were introduced, with the result that today we see the great degeneration in these gatherings. Allāh ﷻ alone knows what more un-Islamic customs will be introduced. It is now necessary to examine these functions and celebrations.

6. A noteworthy point to consider is that this is such a practice that was not practiced during the time of the Sahābah ﷺ, Tābi'een and the Tabi' Tābi'een (successors) ﷺ. It only took root in Islām six centuries after the demise of the Holy Prophet ﷺ, yet it is now being labelled as a sign of Islām.

The people organising these gatherings are so-called Āshiq-e-Rasool (lovers of the Holy Prophet 🕌) and those who do not attend these gatherings are looked down upon.

What is the ruling of those who never attended these gatherings in the first six centuries of Islamic history? I wonder what their opinion is of these people. Have they ever thought that Islām was announced to have been complete on the occasion of "Hajjatul-Widā" on the plains of Arafah? Which Prophet has come thereafter to declare a so called "sign of Islām" which was not practiced during the first six centuries of Islamic history. Is Islām the home production of some layman such that whenever one pleases he may add or remove things from it?

7. It was customary in the pre-Islamic era to arrange annual ceremonies in remembrance of deceased relatives and leaders. Islām, on the contrary had terminated this practice due to the following two reasons:

Firstly: The things committed on these occasions do not have any true relationship with Islām. Islām is not in favour of external ornamentation and loud slogans.

Islām begins its invitation and nurturing through the reformation of the inner-self, namely; belief, good character and the doing of virtuous deeds. In Islām, outward decoration and ornamentation have no value when compared to true inner conviction and reality.

Secondly: Islām does not bear its leaves and fruits on special occasions only, but it is a sweet smelling long-lasting tree. The Holy Qur'ān very aptly describes this quality.

Islām is not bound to a few selected days or dates, however it encompasses a universal and infinite message. Furthermore, the other nations only have a handful of people that warrant these celebrations, whereas Islam has millions of such great people.

Islām boasts of the great personalities of the approximate 124,000 Prophets that were sent to this world in order to guide mankind. Then we have the great group of the Sahābah 🕌 whose number is not less than 124,000.

Thereafter we have the Ulamā, Imāms and Saints of every century. If Islām was to tolerate the permissibility of annual celebrations, not a moment would pass by without demanding a celebration. Thus this Ummah will not progress since all its precious time and energies would be wasted on annual celebrations of different personalities.

Since these celebrations are contrary to the spirit and message of Islām, the Holy Prophet 🌸, the Sahābah ⚜ and the people of the first six centuries never arranged such gatherings.

The customary Meelād began in the 7th century and people gradually added many customs to it, nobody had the audacity to name it 'Eid'.

This was due to the fact that the Holy Prophet 🌸 is reported to have said, "Do not make my grave an Eid." Detrimentally, this celebration has recently been given the honour of being referred to as 'Eid Meelād-un-Nabi.

Which Muslim is ignorant of the fact that the Holy Prophet 🌸 has reserved two Eids in Islām namely; Eidul-Fitr and Eidul-Adhā. If the birthday of the Holy Prophet 🌸 was worthy of being named Eid and if this was in conformity with the spirit of Islām, the Holy Prophet 🌸 would have declared this day as Eid himself.

Furthermore, if this was favourable to the Holy Prophet 🌸 or if not to him, then at least his Khulafā (successors) would have made this day, a day of Eid and celebrated his birthday. It is quite apparent that this was not done. One of two conclusions can be drawn from the above argument. Either we are wrong in naming this day Eid or (Allāh 🕌 forbid) it would appear that the Sahābah ⚜ were lacking in their love of the Holy Prophet 🌸 by failing to fulfil his right by not having a Meelād, and we who have come several centuries later, are true lovers of the Holy Prophet 🌸 and have instituted this necessary custom.

Furthermore, there are differences of opinion with regard to the exact date of the Holy Prophet's 🌸 birth. Some are of the opinion that it was on the 9th of Rabee-ul-Awwal while others feel that it occurred on the 8th of Rabee -ul Awwal.

The demise of the Holy Prophet 🌸 is unanimously accepted to have occurred on the 12th of Rabee-ul Awwal. Thus it would appear we have in fact chosen to celebrate a festival on a day when the Holy Prophet 🌸 departed from this earth. If someone were to ask us whether we are celebrating the birth or the death of the Holy Prophet 🌸, with regret it has to be admitted we would be unable to give a satisfactory reply. I regard the atrocity of naming this day as Eid to be a very serious matter. Infact I would classify it as 'Tahreef Fideen' (deliberate distortion in Islām).

Since the term Eid comes within the classification of specialised Islamic terminology, to deliberately change or distort Islamic terminologies is regarded as 'Tahreef Fiddeen'.

9. The manner in which this day is celebrated is most detestable and shameful. People reading erroneous praises, fabricated stories, which have absolutely no link with the books of Ahādeeth and Seerah, the breaking of the laws of Islām, etc have become the hallmark of these celebrations.

No care is given to the performance of Salāh, and Allāh 🕌 knows best what further un-Islamic activities takes place at such gatherings. At least some true respect and honour should be shown to the Holy Prophet 🌸. The most frightening part of this affair is that it is thought that the Holy Prophet 🌸 personally attends these gatherings.

Conclusion:
The gradual introduction of various customs and innovations into the celebrations of Eid Meelād-un-Nabi have no basis in Islām and are totally contrary to the spirit of Islām. It hurts one to think how the Holy Prophet 🌸 would react to such innovations when they are presented to him, and what would be the anger and distress of the Sahābah 🌸 if they were in our midst witnessing these shameless acts.

Birthday of the Holy Prophet 🌸

Q What should a Muslim do when it is the birthday of the Holy Prophet 🌸?

A There is no special function or Islamic custom to be observed on the birthday of the Holy Prophet ﷺ. Relatively what is demanded from the Holy Prophet ﷺ in order to fulfil his rights is to adhere to his Sunnah. Whoever claims to have love for the Holy Prophet ﷺ should remember him daily by practicing his teachings and by abundantly reciting Durood Shareef (salutations) upon him.

Decorating the Masjid

Q In our locality, the trustees and the committee members decorate the Masjid on the Holy Prophet's ﷺ birthday. Please comment.

A It is a Bid'ah (innovation) to decorate the Masjid with lights etc. on any occasion. It is not permissible to adopt this practice.

Allāh ﷻ Knows Best

16. CHAPTER ON

MONEY & FINANCE

Using Interest Money

Q Can interest money be used to pay interest which is charged by Building Societies or Mortgages? Also can it be used to pay for car, house insurances, council tax and road tax? Whatever the answer is, please could you explain why?

A Taking and giving interest is counted as one of the gravest and heinous sins.

Allāh ﷻ says, **"O you who believe! Fear Allāh and give up what remains (due to you) from Ribā (interest) (from now onward) if you are (really) believers. And if you do not do it, then be warned of war from Allāh and His Messenger." (2:278-279)**

The Holy Prophet ﷺ has cursed the person who gives and takes interest. It is stated in the Books of Ahādeeth, "The Holy Prophet ﷺ has cursed the person who takes interest and who gives interest and also cursed the ones who become witness over interest." (Mishkāt)

In one Hadeeth the Holy Prophet ﷺ states, "A person who involves himself in usury (interest) will be afflicted with 70 kinds of sins." Above all, the Holy Qur'ān has proclaimed the declaration of war against those who do not re-linquish taking interest.

From the aforementioned Quranic verse and Ahādeeth, it is apparent that interest is not permissible. Hence, getting loans and mortgages from financial institutes will be unlawful. The interest money which builds up in one's account cannot be used to pay mortgage, car or house insurances etc.

Interest money should be given to the most destitute person (without the intention of reward). The specification of 'without the intention of reward' is because one can only attain reward from Allāh ﷻ if charity is given from a pure (Halāl) income whereas interest is impure.

Interest Money in the Bank Account

Q What should I do with the interest money which builds up in my account, can I leave it in the bank?

A It is better to remove the interest money from the bank with the understanding that it is Harām, and it should not be mixed with other Halāl money. This interest money should then be spent amongst the poor without the intention of getting Thawāb (reward). It is important to know that this interest money cannot be used on oneself, i.e. for food, clothes, transport etc. nor can it be used for a Masjid or Madrasah (Islamic institute).

Working in a Financial Institution

Q Is working in a financial institution permissible? Or does it depend on what section you're working in?

A Generally, financial institutions run on the basis of interest, hence it would not be permissible. Allāh ﷻ has clearly prohibited interest in the Holy Qur'ān, **"Those who consume interest will not stand (on the Day of Resurrection) except like the standing of a person inflicted by Shaytān leading him to insanity. That is because they say, 'Trading is only like interest', whereas Allāh has permitted trading and forbidden interest. So whosoever receives an admonition from his Lord and stops consuming interest shall not be punished for the past; and his affairs is for Allāh (to judge); but whoever returns (to interest), such are the dwellers of the Fire - they will abide therein." (2:275)**

The above verse describes the condition of those indulging in interest. They shall rise on the Day of Judgement, totally bewildered and confused like that person whom Shaytān has inflicted with his touch.

Sayyidunā Abū Hurairah ؓ reports that the Holy Prophet ﷺ said, "On the night when I was taken to the Heavens (Mirāj), I passed by people whose bellies were swollen like houses. Their bellies were filled with serpents which could be seen from the outside. When I asked Sayyidunā Jibreel ؑ who these people were, he replied that they were those who consumed interest."

(Ahmad, Ibn Mājah)

One can well imagine the horror of a person confronted by a single serpent. How much worse would it be, if his belly was to be filled with them, moreover, if his belly was to be the size of a house? Such will be the state of those who consume interest.

The Holy Prophet ﷺ saw in a dream that a person was swimming in a river of blood and everytime he tried to come out, he was struck in the mouth with a rock flung by another person standing besides the river. The impact caused him to return to his original position each time. When the Holy Prophet ﷺ asked his two companions, Sayyidunā Jibreel عليه السلام and Sayyidunā Meekā'eel عليه السلام regarding that person, he was told that the person in the river was a person who dealt with interest. (Bukhāri)

This punishment is, most probably due to the fact that people who deal with interest oppress people and figuratively speaking suck their blood while resting in contentment. Due to the seriousness of the sin of interest, every person involved in the transaction is cursed.

Sayyidunā Jābir رضي الله عنه narrated that the Holy Prophet ﷺ cursed the consumer of interest, the giver, the recorder of the transaction, as well as the witnesses. He added that all share equally in the sin. (Muslim)

Sayyidunā Abdullāh Ibn Mas'ood رضي الله عنه reports that the Holy Prophet ﷺ said, "A single Dirham (currency of that time) that a person consumes knowing that it is interest is worse than committing adultery 36 times."

(Ahmad, Dār-Qutni)

The above mentioned Ahādeeth are clear and explicit in the prohibition of interest. Therefore one must avoid accepting a job at a bank that runs on the basis of interest transactions and dealings. It is prohibited to help and assist others in their interest based dealings. The Holy Qur'ān says, **"Do not help one another in sin and transgression."** (5:02)

One must decide between temporary worldly gains and the curse and anger of Allāh ﷻ and His beloved Messenger ﷺ.

If a person is already employed in a financial institution, then he is advised not to leave his job immediately, rather he should look for a job elsewhere. When he succeeds in obtaining one, he should immediately leave his employment. The important point here is that he should make full effort to find an alternative job.

Employment that has direct involvement with interest based transactions such as the work of a manager, cashier, clerk etc. will be Harām. However, if the employment in a financial institution is such that it does not have a direct involvement whatsoever with interest based transactions, such as a job of being a guard, cleaner etc. then this kind of job is permissible. Even though it is better to avoid this as well.

As for the income from such jobs, it has to be borne in mind that the money stored in a financial institution such as a bank is not 100% interest money.

The cash stored in the bank and from which the wages are given consists of the depositors, depositing their money in the accounts, capital put in by the owners of the bank, and also interest money. Infact, the portion of interest money is less in comparison to the other two types of income.

Therefore, the wages received from the bank is a mixture of unlawful and lawful wealth of which the majority is lawful. As such, it is permissible to accept this money as income, provided the actual job is permissible.

Allāh ﷻ Knows Best

17. Chapter on
Miscellaneous

At the Times of Difficulties

Q I am at the moment facing many problems and difficulties. Is there any supplication I can recite in order to repel such difficulties?

A The following verse from the Holy Qur'ān should be recited:

الٓمّ ۝ ٱللَّهُ لَآ إِلَٰهَ إِلَّا هُوَ ٱلْحَىُّ ٱلْقَيُّومُ ۝

"Alif Lām Meem. There is none worthy of worship but He. The Ever Living, the One Who sustains and protects all that exists." (3:1-2)

According to a Hadeeth, the Ismul-Azam (the Greatest Name) is contained in this verse. It is most effective if this verse is read constantly at the time of difficulties.

One can also recite the following verse of the Holy Qurān:

لَّآ إِلَٰهَ إِلَّآ أَنتَ سُبْحَٰنَكَ إِنِّى كُنتُ مِنَ ٱلظَّٰلِمِينَ ۝

"There is no God but You. You are Pure (and) surely, I am from amongst the transgressors." (21:87)

Sayyidunā Yūnus رضى الله عنه was saved from the stomach of the fish due to this supplication, and in the same way every Muslim who recites this verse abundantly will be saved from all difficulties.

Durood Shareef is a good spiritual remedy for all sorts of calamities. Hence, recite Durood Shareef abundantly.

Zam Zam Water is a Cure for all Illnesses

Q Zam Zam water is said to be a cure for all ailments. Is this true?

A It is proven from authentic Ahādeeth that there is remedy and cure in the blessed water of Zam Zam. This is also proven from many incidents in which Allāh ﷻ has cured and healed people of illnesses and diseases, sometimes in cases where medicine had failed to do so and the medical doctors had despaired of the patient's recovery.

It is related by Ibn Mājah that the Holy Prophet 器 has said, "The water of Zam Zam is for the purpose for which it is drunk. So, whoever drinks it for the purpose of healing himself from any illness, Allāh 器 willing, he will be healed from that illness. Sayyidunā Abdullāh Ibn Abbās ﷺ narrates that the Holy Prophet 器 said, "The best water on the surface of earth is the water of Zam Zam. In it is complete nourishment and cure from illness." (Tabarāni)

Sayyidunā Abu Dharr ﷺ lived on Zam Zam water for an entire month, during which nothing entered his stomach except Zam Zam water, but he did not feel any hunger. The incident is mentioned in Saheeh al-Muslim when Sayyidunā Abu Dharr ﷺ became a Muslim, he said, "O Messenger of Allāh 器, I have been here for 30 days." The Holy Prophet 器 asked, "Who fed you?" Abū Darr ﷺ replied, "I had no food apart from Zam Zam water, but I gained so much weight that I could feel the folds of fat on my stomach, and I did not feel hungry at all." The Holy Prophet 器 said, "It is blessed and it provides complete nourishment."

From this Hadeeth we can understand that the blessed water of Zam Zam is a remarkable substitute for food and it removes not only thirst but hunger from an afflicted person. Hence it is reported by Sayyidunā Abdullāh Ibn Abbās ﷺ concerning Zam Zam, "We used to call it Ash-Shabbā'ah (that which satisfies), the best help in providing for ones children."

There are so many other virtues regarding the blessed water of Zam Zam. One fact which is sufficient to establish its supremacy and virtue is that when Sayyidunā Jibreel 器 split the noble chest of the Holy Prophet 器, he washed his heart with Zam Zam water. If there had been any better water he would have washed the most exalted Prophet 器 with it.

Age of the People in Jannah

Q What will the age be of the people who will enter Jannah?

A Age of the people in Jannah will be thirty-three years old. Sayyidunā Miqdād ﷺ narrates that the Holy Prophet 器 said, "Every person who dies as a result of miscarriage or of old age or middle age will be resurrected at the age of thirty-three."

If he/she is from the people of Jannah, then he/she will have the form of Sayyidunā Ādam ﷺ, the appearance of Sayyidunā Yūsuf ﷺ and the heart of Sayyidunā Ayyub ﷺ.

The people of Jannah will never grow old and will remain permanently at the age of thirty-three. The wisdom behind this age is that a person is at the peak of his physical strength and his body parts are fully developed. Therefore he/she can experience maximum pleasure from the bounties of Jannah.

The Virtues of Daughters

Q My wife till now has only given birth to daughters. We are really yearning to have a male child. Furthermore, my wife always remains in a state of sadness and grief for this reason. What do you advise?

A Allāh ﷻ states in the Holy Qur'ān, **"To Allāh belongs the Kingdom of the heavens and the earth, He creates what He wills, He bestows females to whom He wills, and bestows males to whom He wills. Or He gives them males and females, and He makes barren whom He wills. Indeed, He is the All-Knower, All-Powerful." (42:49-50)**

From these verses we clearly understand that everything is in the Hands of Allāh ﷻ. It is He who bestows sons and daughters to whom He wishes through His infinite Wisdom and Knowledge.

It is very unfortunate that many parents express extreme joy and happiness upon the birth of a male child whilst they feel disheartened and at times frustrated upon the birth of a female child. We should always remember that children are a blessing from Allāh ﷻ, whether the child is a girl or a boy. Parents should express their gratitude to Allāh ﷻ for blessing them with a child. There are many couples who are even deprived of children let alone merely female.

We should ponder over the following Ahādeeth and realise the virtues of daughters. Sayyidunā Anas ﷺ narrates that the Holy Prophet ﷺ said, "Whoever maintains two girls until they attain maturity, he and I will come on the Day of Judgement like this" (and he joined his two fingers). (Muslim)

Sayyidah Ā'ishah 🌸 narrates, "A woman came to me with her two daughters. She asked me for charity, but she found nothing in my house except one date, so I gave it to her. She accepted it and then divided it between her two daughters, but she did not take a share of the date herself. She then got up and went out with her two daughters. Subsequently, the Holy Prophet 🌸 visited me and I narrated this incident to him. Thereupon the Holy Prophet 🌸 said, 'He who is engaged in the responsibility of bringing up daughters and treats them with kindness, they will be a protection for him against the Fire of Hell." (Bukhāri, Muslim)

In a Hadeeth narrated by Imām Tabarāni 🌸 in his book Mu'jam, relates that the Holy Prophet 🌸 said, "When a female child is born, Allāh 🌸 sends His angels to that house. They come to the residents of that house and pray that peace be upon them. The angels then cover the newly born girl in the shadow of their wings and caressing the head of the baby with their hands say that this is a weak and frail child. Whoever will bear the responsibility of her upbringing will go on attaining the blessings of Allāh 🌸 as long as that individual remains alive." (Tabarāni)

Hoors of Jannah

Q If men will receive Hoors, what will women receive?

A Mufti Mahmood Hasan Gangohi 🌸 writes in his Fatāwa book (Fatāwa Mahmoodiya) that the wives of the believers will stay with their own husbands. Women who never married in this world will be given a choice to get married with any (unmarried) man they wish. If they do not like any of them, a special man will be created for them, (similar to the Hoors) and Allāh 🌸 will join both of them in marriage. Imām Āloosi 🌸 also mentions in his Tafseer that a person's wife in this world will remain his wife in the Hereafter. Furthermore, according to a narration, it is mentioned that the women of this world (the pious women) will be more beautiful than the Hoors in Jannah. Thus, the wives will become the queens of the Hoors.

Allāh 🌸 Knows Best

APPENDIX

Eating Halāl

&

Salām
Islamic Greeting

THE TWO TOPICS ARE TRANSCRIPTS OF DISCOURSES
DELIVERED BY SHAYKH MUFTI SAIFUL ISLĀM

Eating Halāl

"O you who believe! Eat from the pure things which We have provided for you." (2:172)

Islām - A Complete Religion

We must realise that Islām is a complete religion and a complete way of life. It governs us, teaches us and directs us to achieve success in this world and in the Hereafter. Islām has the solution to all our modern day problems, difficulties, hardships and Masā'il (juristic issues). There exists no aspect of life that is not included in its teachings and moral guidelines.

Unfortunately, many of us today do not consider Islām in the matters of marriage, social, economic and political lives. We conduct business as we please, buying and selling any commodity as we wish. Many of us seek employment at any institution without paying the slightest heed to whether the employment is Halāl or Harām. Allāh ﷻ states in Sūrah Al-Baqarah, **"O you who believe, enter into Islām completely and do not follow the footsteps of Shaytān, for verily he is your clear enemy." (2:208)**

This particular verse was revealed regarding certain Companions ؓ who had reverted from Judaism to Islām but wished to uphold some of their Judaic traditions such as to esteem Saturday and abstain from consuming camel's meat. They also informed the Holy Prophet ﷺ that since the Tawrah was the book of Allāh ﷻ, they recited it in their Tahajjud Salāh. Allāh ﷻ revealed the above verse on this occasion, instructing them that after the advent of Islām no other religion should be adhered to. (Durrul Manthoor and Baydāwi)

Islām - A Religion for All

The aforementioned verse also instructs every Muslim to embrace all the commandments of Islām and practice them accordingly irrespective of their status. This is binding upon the ruler and the subject, the big and the small, the employer and employee, the businessman and the farmer alike. Allāh ﷻ our Creator, our Lord, our Master loves us immensely and is very Compassionate towards us.

Allāh ﷻ states in the Holy Qur'ān, **"It is He Who created for you all that is on the earth." (2:29)**

No doubt that everything on the earth is created for our advantage but He also states in other verses, **"O Mankind; eat from that which is lawful (Halāl) and good on earth and follow not the footsteps of Shaytān. Verily, he is your clear enemy." (2:168)**

"O you who believe, make not Harām (unlawful) the pure (all that is good regards to food, deeds, beliefs, persons etc.) which Allāh has made lawful (Halāl) for you and transgress not, verily Allāh does not like the transgressors. Eat from the lawful (Halāl) and pure sustenance which Allāh has provided for you, and fear Allāh in whom you believe." (5:87-88)

Therefore we need to be careful about what we consume, identifying whether it is Halāl or Harām.

Abstaining from Harām

When Allāh ﷻ announced the completion of His Deen on the occasion of Hajjatul-Widā (farewell Hajj), in addition, He also mentioned some unlawful things for protecting our bodily system.

Allāh ﷻ states in the Holy Qur'ān, **"The things which are forbidden for you are: Maytah (dead animal), blood, flesh of swine (pork) and that on which Allāh's Name has not been mentioned while slaughtering (or what has been slaughtered other than the name of Allāh). And (also prohibited are those animals that are) strangled to death, violently beaten, fallen (from high places), or gored to death and what has been partly eaten by a predator unless you are able to slaughter it (before its death). And that (animal) which has been slaughtered at the altars (stone shrines) and (also forbidden) is to use arrows seeking decision. (All) these are acts of sin. This day those who have disbelieved have relinquished all hope of your religion (Islām) so fear them not, but fear Me. This day I have perfected your religion for you, and completed My favour upon you and have chosen for you Islām as your religion." (5:3)**

Allāh ﷻ also states, **"This day, all kinds of pure things have become lawful for you." (5:5)**

The aforementioned verses express the importance of consuming Halāl and abstaining from Harām to this extent that Allāh ﷻ reiterates the declaration of certain categories of meat to be prohibited along with the mentioning of perfection of our beautiful religion, Islām.

Command upon the Prophets ﷺ to Consume Halāl

Similarly Allāh ﷻ states in another verse, **"O Messengers, eat of the Tayyibāt (all kinds of Halāl foods), and do righteous deeds. Verily, I am aware of what you do." (23:51)**

The most beloved people to Allāh ﷻ are His noble Messengers. If Allāh ﷻ has instructed them to eat pure and Halāl food and to do righteous deeds, then how important is it for the Believers? In this verse, there is a unique connection between the consumption of Halāl food and the performance of righteous deeds. Allāh ﷻ first commences with the command of consuming Halāl food and thereafter the performing of righteous deeds.

The more pure the food is, the better the good deed will be. Allāh ﷻ will enable a person to carry out good deeds due to consuming Halāl and pure food. Halal food plays a great influence in our worship too. If food, clothes and other belongings are not lawful then our worship is affected as well.

Why Our Du'ās are Not Accepted?

Sayyidunā Abū Hurairah ؓ narrates that the Holy Prophet ﷺ said, "Allāh ﷻ is Pure and accepts only which is pure and Allāh ﷻ has commanded the faithful to do that which He has commanded the Messengers. Allāh ﷻ states, "O Messengers! Eat from the pure things and do righteous deeds." He also states, "O you who believe! Eat from the pure things which We have provided you."

Then the Holy Prophet 鑑 mentioned a man, having travelled for a long distance, dishevelled hair and covered in dust who raises his hands towards the sky exclaiming, "O My Lord, O My Lord!" Whilst his food is Harām, his drink is Harām and his clothing is Harām, so how could he expect his Du'ā to be answered?" (Muslim)

This Hadeeth clearly illustrates the importance of eating Halāl, earning Halāl livelihood and refraining from all types of Harām and doubtful sources. Consuming and earning Halāl is one of the vital factors for our supplications to be accepted by Allāh 鑑.

Halāl and Harām are Clear

Our religion Islām has made matters very clear. It is narrated by Sayyidunā Nu'mān Ibn Basheer 鑑 that the Holy Prophet 鑑 said, "Halāl is clear and Harām is clear and between them are unclear (doubtful) matters. So whosoever forsakes those doubtful matters lest he may commit a sin, will definitely avoid what is clearly unlawful, and whosoever indulges in these doubtful things openly is likely to commit that which is clearly unlawful. Sins are Allāh's 鑑 Himā (i.e. private pasture) and whoever grazes (his sheep) near it, is likely to trespass over it." (Bukhāri)

Abstaining from Doubtful Matters

Imām Tirmizi 鑑 has recorded a Hadeeth regarding doubtful matters that is worth implementing into our everyday life pertaining to income, food, clothing and all other matters. He narrates on the authority of Sayyidunā Hasan Ibn Ali 鑑 that the Holy Prophet 鑑 said, "Leave that which puts you in doubt and do that in which you have no doubt."

If we apply this golden principle into our daily lives then how easy will everything become. Alhamdulillāh, there are many types of food available which are Halāl and not doubtful. It only requires us to restrain our Nafs and desires from transgressing towards doubtful and Harām foods.

If we for a moment observe the lives of the Holy Prophet 鑑 and his noble Sahābah 鑑, we will acknowledge how they abstained from Harām and how precautious they were in doubtful substances.

They are exemplary role models for our Muslims today especially concerning doubtful issues. Their habits and traits as a whole are worth following, as they were the people specially chosen by Allāh 繋 to be the Companions of His beloved Prophet 繋. The Holy Prophet 繋 said, "I have been sent in the best period of human history." The time of the Holy Prophet 繋 was itself a blessed period, and those that were honoured with his companionship were infact the cream of that age.

The Holy Prophet's 繋 Sleepless Night

It is mentioned in the books of Ahādeeth that once the Holy Prophet 繋 spent a sleepless night. He would turn from side to side and could not sleep. His noble wife asked him, "O Prophet of Allāh 繋! Why can't you sleep?" He replied, "A date was lying about, I took it and ate it, lest it should be wasted, now I am troubled lest it might be from Sadaqah."

Sadaqah whether monetary or food was not permissible for the Holy Prophet 繋 and his noble family. Most probably, the date belonged to the Prophet 繋 himself, but because people sent him their Sadaqah (for distribution), he could not sleep with the apprehension that it might be of Sadaqah. It was due to the fear of Allāh 繋 that he was sleepless during the night. It is ironic for those who assert to be the followers of the Holy Prophet 繋 yet indulge in Harām affairs such as unlawful business, usury, corruption, theft etc?

The Holy Prophet 繋 Accepts a Woman's Invitation

On another occasion, the Holy Prophet 繋 was returning from a funeral when a woman approached him and requested him to partake in some food in her house. He went in with some of his noble Sahābah 繋. When the food was served, the Holy Prophet 繋 took a morsel and began to chew it but it would simply not go down his throat. He remarked, "It seems that the animal has been slaughtered without the permission of its owner." The woman replied, "O Messenger of Allāh 繋, I had requested a man to purchase a goat for me from the market, but he could not obtain one. My neighbour had purchased a goat. Therefore, I sent the man there with some money to buy it from them. My neighbour's husband was out so his wife handed over the goat to him."

The Holy Prophet ﷺ directed her to go and serve the meal to the captives. It is reported from certain biographers regarding the pious servants of Allāh ﷻ that food obtained from doubtful sources would simply not go down their throats. Therefore, this is not a surprising fact regarding the Holy Prophet ﷺ who attained the highest degree of piety.

Sayyidunā Abū Bakr ؓ and a Soothsayer's Food

It is reported that Sayyidunā Abū Bakr ؓ once had a slave who used to give him a portion of his daily income as the master's share. Once he brought him some food and Sayyidunā Abū Bakr ؓ took a morsel out of it. The slave remarked, "You always primarily enquire of the source of what I bring to you, but today you have not done so." He replied, "I was feeling so hungry that I failed to do that. Tell me now where did you purchase this food?"

The slave replied, "Before I had embraced Islām, I practised soothsaying. During those days, I came across some people for whom I practised some of my charms. They promised to pay me later on. I happened to pass by those same people today and while they were engaged in a marriage ceremony, they gave me this food." Sayyidunā Abū Bakr ؓ exclaimed, "Ah! You would have surely destroyed me."

Then he tried to vomit the morsel he had swallowed, but he could not do so as his stomach had been quite empty. Someone suggested that he drinks water to his fill then try to vomit. He sent for a big glass of water and kept on drinking and vomiting until the morsel came out. Somebody remarked, "May Allāh ﷻ have mercy upon you, you put yourself through so much trouble for one morsel."

To this, he replied, "I would have thrust it out even if I had to end my life, for I have heard the Holy Prophet ﷺ saying, "The flesh nourished by Harām food is destined for the Fire of Hell". I therefore made haste to vomit this morsel, lest any portion of my body would become nourished by it."

Many stories of this nature have been reported about Sayyidunā Abū Bakr ؓ. Out of caution, he never consumed anything unless he was certain of its source. Even the slightest doubt of it not being Halāl would cause him to vomit what he had taken in.

Sayyidunā Umar ⟿ Vomits Out the Milk of Sadaqah

An incident occurred with Sayyidunā Umar ⟿ that one person brought him some milk. When he took it, he noted its unusual taste and asked the person how it had come into his possession. He replied, "The camels given in Sadaqah were grazing in the desert and the attendants gave me this milk out of what they got from them." When Sayyidunā Umar ⟿ heard this, he put his hand inside his mouth and vomited what he had taken.

Such God-fearing people not only abstained from Harām food, but were also most anxious to avoid any doubtful morsel finding its way inside them. They could not possibly consume anything that was Harām, which is so normal these days.

Imām Abū Haneefah's ⟿ Piety

Abdullāh Ibn Mubārak ⟿ relates, "On one occasion a few stolen goats were found amongst the goats of Kūfa. On hearing this, Imām Abū Haneefah ⟿ enquired about the maximum age of a goat. When informed that goats normally live for up to seven years, he abstained from eating goat meat for seven years."

In one of his biographies, it is mentioned about Imām Sāhib ⟿ witnessing a soldier who after consuming a piece of meat disposed the remainder in a river in Kūfa.

Imām Sāhib ⟿ made enquiries about how long a fish lives. The people informed him of a certain period, and thus he abstained from eating fish for that entire period.

Just ponder over the incidents of our pious predecessors. How much sacrifices they made to safeguard themselves from consuming Harām or even doubtful nourishment. After all, you are what you eat. Hence, such people became the guiding and illuminating stars in this world and will be in the Hereafter.

An Incident of Imām Shāfi'ee 🕮 and Imām Ahmad Ibn Hanbal 🕮

Once Imām Ahmad Ibn Hanbal 🕮 became the guest of Imām Shāfiee 🕮. Although Imām Ahmad 🕮 was a student of Imām Shāfi'ee 🕮, the latter use to honour and respect the former immensely. Thus, Imām Shāfi'ee 🕮 ordered his daughter to prepare the finest food and show great hospitality towards the great Imām. She complied with her father's wishes but in the morning when the great Imām departed from their house, the daughter complained to her father.

She stated, "You mentioned that he was a great Imām and saint, however I found three things contrary to his piety. Firstly, he ate a lot of food whereas pious people eat less food. Secondly, he did not perform Tahajjud Salāh and thirdly, and the most serious of all, is that he performed Fajr Salāh without Wudhu."

Imām Shāfi'ee 🕮 initially reprimanded her for making such remarks but he himself in private related the incident to Imām Ahmad Ibn Hanbal 🕮.

Imām Ahmad 🕮 replied:

"Firstly, the reason I ate plentiful was that the food was purely hundred percent Halāl as I observed the Barakah, Noor and blessings on the Dastarkhān (table cloth) which I did not observe anywhere else. Hence the more I ate, the more Barakah and blessings I acquired.

Secondly, I stayed awake throughout the night deriving and deducing Masā'il from the Holy Qur'ān and Ahādeeth. I managed to derive seventeen Masā'il for the Muslim Ummah. Despite Tahajjud being an act of Ibādah, its benefits are restricted only to myself whereas the deriving of Masā'il is not only beneficial and rewardable for me but for the Muslim Ummah also. So the rewards are greater for this action, thus I did not perform Tahajjud Salāh.

Thirdly, I did not perform Fajr Salāh without Wudhu because I remained awake throughout the entire night deriving Masā'il (and nothing that breaches Wudhu took place), the Wudhu remained intact so therefore I performed Fajr Salāh with the Wudhu of Ishā Salāh." Subhānallah!

Consuming Halāl enables a person to perform virtuous and righteous deeds as well. The more pure the food is, the better and greater the Ibādah will be and therefore the closer he will be to Allāh 🕮.

Halāl Stickers

Therefore, my dear brothers and sisters, if this is the state of such pious servants of Allāh 🕮 then what level have we plunged to? We have not bothered to put any emphasis on this very important matter. How confident are we of what we are eating is Halāl if we do not express any concern about it. Especially with recent reports that have been published exposing some products to be labelled as Halāl whilst containing traces of pork? Considering this, will the Halāl sticker on the product or on the shop window be sufficient to justify it being Halāl?

Prophecy of the Holy Prophet 🕮

The Holy Prophet 🕮 had prophesised regarding this inevitable dilemma 1400 years ago. The Hadeeth is found in Saheeh Al-Bukhāri narrated by Sayyidunā Abū Hurairah 🕮 that the Holy Prophet 🕮 said, "A time will come upon the people when one will not care how one gains (ones money, food, clothing etc.) either through Halāl or Harām source."

In another Hadeeth narrated by Imām Ahmad 🕮 in his Musnad on the authority of Sayyidunā Sād Ibn Abi Waqqās 🕮 that the Holy Prophet 🕮 said, "The Day of Judgement will not come until there will be such a people who will eat with their tongues just as cows eat with their tongues."

Unfortunately, we are witnessing this within our Muslim community, consuming anything and everything without the slightest fear of its source. Remember my brothers and sisters, it is our duty and obligation to carry out a thorough investigation to the best of our ability of the food that we consume.

The Hadeeth of Baihaqi clearly states, "That individual will not enter Paradise who has been nourished with Harām."

We have to make this matter very clear even with regards to Halāl livelihood as it is mentioned in the Hadeeth of Mishkāt, "Earning a Halāl livelihood is an obligation after the other obligations."

As Salāh, Fasting, Hajj and Zakāt are obligatory upon ourselves, similarly, earning Halāl income is also obligatory upon us.

Remember, we will be questioned on the Day of Judgement about the food that we consumed, whether it was Halāl or Harām, and whether we fed our families Halāl or not?

Imām Bukhāri ﷺ and Imām Muslim ﷺ have narrated a Hadeeth, "Be aware! Everyone of you is a shepherd and everyone of you will be questioned about his herd."

Therefore, each one of us is a custodian and each one of us will be questioned about our subordinates. Let us prepare ourselves before it is too late. Let us awaken from the slumber of laziness, neglect and complacency and acknowledge the reality.

May Allāh ﷻ give us all the ability to consume Halāl food, earn a Halāl livelihood and may He through His infinite grace save us from all types of Harām food, Harām livelihood and doubtful things. Āmeen.

Salām
Islamic Greeting

"When you are greeted with a greeting, then reply with a better greeting or return the same (greeting). Verily Allāh takes account of everything." (4:86)

The Holy Prophet ﷺ - A Perfect Role Model

Islamic lifestyle has no parallel. Islām provides moral guidelines to every aspect of human life and gives the solution to our daily problematic issues. The Holy Prophet ﷺ is an exemplary role model for the whole of mankind. So the question arises, why is there any need for Muslims to emulate the conduct of others?

Amongst the Islamic teachings is the inculcating of humility, sympathy and unity in order to attain stability in our lives. Consider for example, the Islamic conduct pertaining to eating and drinking. The Holy Prophet ﷺ demonstrated this conduct verbally as well as practically.

He said, "I eat as a slave eats." It was the noble character of our beloved Prophet ﷺ to eat whilst sitting in a humble position with his body inclined towards the food. He would eat quickly with appreciation.

In contrast, we eat with great pride and with style. There is no sign of humility in us when we eat. Such arrogant conduct is the result of the reality of life being hidden from us. Once the reality becomes revealed to a person, he will realise that whatever he is eating is from the Court of the King of kings (Allāh ﷻ) and that He is observing every action that we do.

Thus automatically, the humble manner of the Holy Prophet ﷺ will be adopted. When the greatness of a Supreme Being is rooted in the heart then all stages will be traversed with ease.

The fact is that we lack the ability to realise that Allāh ﷻ is watching us. Now, when Islām possesses its code of conduct in a state of perfection, then what need do Muslims have to emulate others?

Honour, self-respect and our claim of the perfection of our Deen demands that we strictly adhere to its teachings entirely and to the moral code of conduct ordained by Allāh ﷻ and the Holy Prophet ﷺ.

Muāsharāt - An Essential Part of Deen

We must endeavour to adopt the beautiful teachings of Islām in every aspect of our life. Reformation of Muāsharāt (social conduct) is imperative since it is an essential branch of Deen. Just as Salāh and Sawm are compulsory, so too is Muāsharāt. Nowadays people not only consider Muāsharāt as insignificant but also no longer view it as an integral aspect of Deen.

Infact, all the books of Ahādeeth consist of chapters pertaining to Muāsharāt. The scholars of the past have elaborated on this spectrum of life. But unfortunately, no one is prepared to pay any heed to this vital branch of Islām.

The Ādāb (etiquettes) of Muāsharāt are continuously diminishing by the day even though they are normal things. Our beautiful Islamic teachings are daily being disregarded by the Muslims themselves. This surely is an indication that the Day of Qiyāmah is very close.

Five Signs before the Day of Judgement

Sayyidunā Abdullāh Ibn Mas'ood ﷺ relates that our beloved Prophet ﷺ said, "Before the Day of Qiyāmah, from amongst the many signs to come will be:

1. The offering of Salām will be confined to acquaintances.
2. Businesses will expand to the extent that the wives will begin to assist their husbands to conduct trade.
3. Family relations will be severed.
4. Those giving false testimony will become heroes, and true testimony will be suppressed.
5. The competent and the incompetent will begin to write books." (Ahmad)

Sadly, the aforementioned signs are rampant amongst the Muslims today. I would like to merely touch on the first sign mentioned in this Hadeeth of Musnad Ahmad.

Islamic Greeting

The Hadeeth states that offering Salam will be confined to acquaintances only. This is precisely what is happening in our society today. We must adopt the correct teachings and methods concerning this matter.

We know that every civilised community on earth has a particular mode of greeting which is expressed when members of the community meet. These words of salutation are to express friendship and courtesy. None of these phrases compare with the greeting of Islam, which is not only a greeting, but also a Du'ā (supplication).

Before the advent of Islam, the Arabs greeted one another with such phrases as حيّاك الله (may Allah ﷻ grant you life) or أنعم صباحاً (may you be blessed this morning).

In today's society, "hello", "good morning", "good afternoon" and "good-bye" etc. are used to exchange greetings.

History of Salam

Allah ﷻ replaced all modern methods of greeting with the best greeting which was used by all the noble Prophets عليهم السلام. He has commanded the progeny of Sayyidunā Ādam عليه السلام to greet each other with the salutation of Salam (peace) which is infact a Du'ā (supplication).

Sayyidunā Abū Hurairah ؓ relates that the Holy Prophet ﷺ said, "Allah ﷻ created Ādam عليه السلام and his height was sixty arms length. Allah ﷻ said to him, 'Go and offer Salam (salutations of peace) to them (a group of angels, who were seated) and listen to their reply for that will be your greeting and the greeting of your progeny.' So he said to them 'As-Salāmu-Alaikum (peace be upon you).' They replied, 'Wa-Alaikumus-Salām Wa Rahmatullāh (may peace and mercy of Allah ﷻ be upon you).' They added, 'Wa Rahmatullāh' (and the mercy of Allah ﷻ).

Whosoever will enter Jannah (Paradise) will be according to his (Ādam ﷺ) height and He (Allāh ﷻ) had reduced the height of His creation up to this time (the period of the beloved Prophet ﷺ). (Bukhāri, Muslim)

As-Salām is an Attribute of Allāh ﷻ

According to one Hadeeth, Sayyidunā Abdullāh Ibn Mas'ood ﷺ relates that the Holy Prophet ﷺ said, "Salām is from the attributes of Allāh ﷻ which He has placed on earth. Therefore, make Salām (greeting) common amongst you."(Adabul-Mufrad)

Reality of the Islamic Greeting

The Islamic greeting (Salām) is an inclusive term and also a Du'ā which encompasses all that which brings about peace and good fortune to a Muslim's life. Whilst a Muslim is wishing his fellow Muslim brother peace, he is simultaneously praying for his protection from all misfortunes, calamities etc.

Therefore, Islām has modified the pre-Islamic and modern methods of greeting to As-Salāmu-Alaikum, which means (may peace be upon you i.e. may you be free from all difficulty, calamity and anxiety).

The Islamic greeting not only illustrates an example of friendship and respect but also fulfils the rights of a Muslim in the form of a Du'ā. When greeting a Muslim we are beseeching Allāh ﷻ to save that person from all calamites and worries.

It is not only a Du'ā i.e. 'may you live long' but 'may you also have a prosperous and protected life'. It also reminds the Muslims to whom it is expressed, that both of us are in need of Allāh ﷻ. We cannot benefit nor harm one another without Allāh's ﷻ will.

The greeting of Salām is regarded as an act of Ibādah (act of worship) because it is said in compliance with the teachings of our beloved Prophet ﷺ. By correctly understanding the reality of the Islamic greeting and making it a universal mode of greeting, it can be the cause of resolving many of the problems facing Muslims.

That is why our beloved Prophet 🕮 has strongly exhorted us to make the Salām frequent amongst ourselves.

Virtues of Salām

Allāh 🕮 has instructed us to greet our Muslim brothers and sisters. Allāh 🕮 states in the Holy Qur'ān, **"When you are greeted with a greeting, then reply with a better greeting or return the same greeting. Verily Allāh takes account of everything." (4:86)**

This verse instructs us to greet our fellow Muslims with Salām. It is Sunnah to offer Salām but to reply to Salām is Wājib (compulsory).

Sayyidunā Imrān Ibn Husain 🕮 relates, "A man came to the Holy Prophet 🕮 and said, 'As-Salāmu Alaikum,' the Holy Prophet 🕮 replied to him and the man sat down. The Holy Prophet 🕮 then said, "Ten," (meaning for him are ten rewards).

"Thereafter another man came and said, 'As-Salāmu Alaikum wa Rahmatul-lāh'. The Holy Prophet 🕮 replied to him and the man sat down. The Holy Prophet 🕮 said, "Twenty," (his reward will be twenty).

"Thereafter, another man came and said, 'As-Salāmu Alaikum wa Rahmatul-lāhi wa Barakātuh'. The Holy Prophet 🕮 responded to the man and he sat down. The Holy Prophet 🕮 said, "Thirty," (his reward will be thirty).
(Tirmizi, Abū Dāwood)

In another similar Hadeeth, Sayyidunā Ali 🕮 relates that the Holy Prophet 🕮 added, "Thirty for you, O' Ali, you and I are equal in Salām. Whosoever passes by a gathering and he greets them with Salām, for him is recorded ten rewards and ten of his sins are forgiven, and he will be raised ten stages in rank."(Ibnus Sunni)

Just ponder over the tremendous rewards for offering Salām and replying to Salām. Salām is the best greeting for wishing peace and tranquillity. We should offer Salām to all Muslims, irrespective of whether they are acquaintances or strangers.

Best Act in Islām

Sayyidunā Abdullāh Ibn Amr Ibn Ās ؓ relates that a man asked the Holy Prophet ﷺ, "What act is the best in Islām?" He replied, "To feed people, (for gaining reward) and to greet people with Salām, those who you know and those who you don't know." (Bukhāri, Muslim)

As I have quoted the Hadeeth of Sayyidunā Abdullāh Ibn Mas'ood ؓ earlier that from amongst the signs of Qiyāmah, is a person who will only offer Salām to his acquainted ones, not because of Muslim brotherhood.

(Musnad Ahmad)

Sayyidunā Abū Hurairah ؓ reports that the Holy Prophet ﷺ said, "You will not enter Paradise until you become true believers, and you will not become true believers until you love one another. Should I not inform you that which will instil love in one another? To spread Salām amongst you."

(Muslim)

In a Hadeeth narrated by Sayyidunā Abdullāh Ibn Salām ؓ it is mentioned that the Holy Prophet ﷺ said, "O people! Make Salām common amongst you, provide (people) with food, perform Salāh (Tahajjud) while people are asleep (in return) you will enter Jannah with peace." (Tirmizi)

Our Condition Today

Today Salām is neglected from our lives. We now live in a time where blood relatives cannot stand the sight of one another. To the extent Muslims have severed relationships with close and beloved ones. It is unfortunate to see how many Muslim parents and their grown up sons and daughters have severed their ties with each other, not even willing to offer Salām to each other. It is the pride and arrogance in our hearts which has distanced ourselves away from each other – diverting us further away from the true path and understanding of Islām. If one initiates the Salām, the Hadeeth gives glad tidings that such a person is immune from pride and he is closer to Allāh ﷻ.

Sayyidunā Abdullāh Ibn Mas'ood ؓ relates that the Holy Prophet ﷺ said, "The one who initiates Salām first is free from pride." (Baihaqi, Mishkāt)

In another Hadeeth, Sayyidunā Abū Umāmah ﷺ relates that the Holy Prophet ﷺ said, "Indeed the closest person to Allāh ﷻ is the one who initiates the Salām."

In today's society, either we entirely neglect to offer Salām, or wait in anticipation for others to initiate the Salām, even then we do not reply to the Salām, which is Wājib (compulsory).

The Practice of the Noble Companions

The noble Companions of the Holy Prophet ﷺ acting upon this Hadeeth would go out specifically to say Salām to others. One such Companion was Sayyidunā Abdullāh Ibn Umar ﷺ. He would go out to the market place solely for offering Salām to the people.

Sayyidunā Tufail ﷺ relates, I once came to Sayyidunā Abdullāh Ibn Umar ﷺ who made me follow him to the market, I asked him, "What do you intend to do in the market place? You do not stop to buy nor enquire about the quality or origin of the merchandise. You don't enquire about the prices nor join those sitting in the market?"

He remarked, "Come here and let us talk." Sayyidunā Abdullāh Ibn Umar ﷺ said, "We go there so that we give Salām to whoever we meet."

(Muwatta Imām Mālik, Baihaqi)

It is mentioned in another Hadeeth related by Tabarāni that whosoever greets twenty Muslim men (or women) collectively or individually in a day and suddenly passes away on that same day, Jannah will become compulsory upon him, and if it be during the night then likewise.

Moreover, it is narrated in another Hadeeth, "Whoever offers Salām to ten Muslims, it would be as if he had freed a slave and if he passed away on that day, Jannah will become necessary for him."

(Awjazul Masālik - Shaykh Muhammad Zakariyā ﷺ)

Frequent Salām

Our beloved Prophet 卷 emphasised the offering of Salām to such an extent that Sayyidunā Abū Hurairah 卷 relates that the Holy Prophet 卷 said, "Whoever meets his brother he should offer Salām. If they are separated by a tree, wall or a stone then they should greet one another upon meeting (again)." (Abū Dāwood)

Salām also fulfils the right of a Muslim. Sayyidunā Abū Hurairah 卷 relates that the Holy Prophet 卷 said, "The rights of a Muslim over another are five." They asked, "What are they?" He replied, "When he meets him he greets him (with Salām), when he invites him he accepts it, when he advises him he accepts the advice, when he sneezes and says 'Alhamdulillāh', he should respond by saying 'Yarhamukallāh', when he is ill he visits him and when he dies he accompanies his Janāzah." (Bukhāri, Muslim)

Let us practise this beautiful Sunnah of the Holy Prophet 卷 with a pleasant countenance. It may seem insignificant in our eyes but in the eyes of Allāh 卷, it is virtuous, deserving tremendous reward in return. Our beloved Prophet 卷 said, "Do not belittle any good deed, though it may be meeting your Muslim brother with a countenance of affection and happiness."

(Muslim)

Act of Charity

Sayyidunā Hasan 卷 relates that the Holy Prophet 卷 said, "It is an act of charity that you greet people while you show affection and happiness."

(Ibn Abi Dunyā)

Nowadays, we assume Sadaqah to be merely giving money to charities whereas our beloved Prophet 卷 is offering us a prescription where we can achieve the reward of charity all the time.

We encounter all kinds of people on a daily basis from our close family members and acquaintances to unfamiliar people on the street. Let us inculcate this noble habit of smiling when we meet our Muslim brothers and sisters.

It is recorded in a Hadeeth in Tirmizi by Sayyidunā Abū Zarr ﷺ, that the Holy Prophet ﷺ said, "For you to smile when meeting a Muslim brother is a (reward of) Sadaqah (charity) and for you to enjoin him to do good and prevent him from doing evil is (also) Sadaqah. When you guide a man who is astray is a Sadaqah, to remove any obstacle, thorn and bone from the road is a Sadaqah for you and to fill water into your Muslim brother's container from your container is also a Sadaqah for you."

It is reported that on one occasion when Sayyidunā Yahyā ﷺ met Sayyidunā Eesā ﷺ he initiated the Salam, he was also replied with Salam. Whenever he met him, he was happy and smiling whilst Sayyidunā Eesā ﷺ was sorrowful as if he resembled a crying person. Sayyidunā Eesā ﷺ said to him, "You smile like a happy person as if you are secure and protected." Sayyidunā Yahyā ﷺ said, "You show much sorrow like a crying person as if you have despaired." Instantly, Allāh ﷻ revealed to Sayyidunā Eesā ﷺ, "The one who smiles is the most dearest to me." (Tirmizi)

Salām to Children

Our beloved Prophet ﷺ demonstrated a perfect example of commencing the Salām to the extent that he would also offer Salām to children.

Sayyidunā Anas Ibn Mālik ﷺ once passed by some children and offered Salām to them and said, "The Holy Prophet ﷺ used to do this to them"

(Ahmad, Nasai)

In a Hadeeth of Abū Dāwood it is mentioned that the Holy Prophet ﷺ used to offer Salām to children who were playing when he passed them.

Moreover, when we converse over the telephone the same rule is also applicable. To initiate the Salām will be an act of Sunnah and if the caller greets the one answering the telephone it will become Wājib for him to reply to the Salām. Even when entering ones home Salām should be offered. Allāh ﷻ says in the Holy Qur'ān, **"When you enter homes, salute your people with the greeting of peace, a greeting from Allāh (which is) full of blessing and purity." (24:61)**

Sayyidunā Anas ﷺ relates that the Holy Prophet ﷺ said to him, "O' my son! When you enter your home greet with the salutation of peace. It would be a blessing for you and the members of your family." (Tirmizi)

There are many blessings that descend from Allāh ﷻ when offering Salām to our family members. What better reward can there be for this noble act.

Sayyidunā Abū Umāmah ﷺ says that the Holy Prophet ﷺ said, "Three types of people are in Allāh's ﷻ protection. If they live, Allāh ﷻ will be sufficient for them and if they die they will be admitted into Jannah: (1) Whosoever enters his home saying Salām, he is protected by Allāh ﷻ, (2) Whoever goes to the Masjid is in Allāh's ﷻ protection, (3) Whoever goes in the way of Allāh ﷻ is in Allāh's ﷻ protection." (Ibn Hibbān)

Salām when Entering the Home

The procedure of entering the home is that first the Du'ā of entering the home should be recited which is:

اللّٰهُمَّ إِنِّى أَسْأَلُكَ خَيْرَ الْمَوْلَجِ وَ خَيْرَ الْمَخْرَجِ بِسْمِ اللّٰهِ وَلَجْنَا وِبِسْمِ اللّٰهِ خَرَجْنَا وَ عَلَى اللّٰهِ رَبِّنَا تَوَكَّلْنَا

(Translation): "O Allāh ﷻ I seek from You the best of returning and the best of emerging. We enter with Allāh's ﷻ Name and leave with Allāh's ﷻ Name and upon Allāh ﷻ our Sustainer do we depend."(Abū Dāwood)

Thereafter, As-Salāmu Alaikum should be said audibly. Let us implement this into our daily lives so that we can attain the blessings and protection from Allāh ﷻ. Unfortunately, today we are so heedless that we fail to offer Salām to our families and vice versa. This sometimes becomes a root problem in the breakages of family ties.

In our daily lives, the father or husband will return home with a grumpy face or very exhausted without a smile or Salām. Rather the first demand the husband makes upon entering the home is, "Get my food on the table". The wife will respond with resentment and use harsh words such as, "I am not your slave" or "who do you think I am?" This will inevitably result in arguments, physical or verbal abuse or even divorce.

Ādāb of Salām

The Holy Prophet ﷺ would occasionally refuse entry to the one who failed to offer Salām. Sayyidunā Kildā ؓ reports that once Sayyidunā Safwān Ibn Umayyah ؓ sent him with milk and a lamb and some cucumbers for the Holy Prophet ﷺ whilst the Holy Prophet ﷺ was at the top of the valley. He says, "When I entered, I did not offer Salām." Thereupon, the Holy Prophet ﷺ said, "Go out, come back, and say As-Salāmu Alaikum, may I enter?"

It is reported in a Hadeeth that if Salām upon entering one's residence is neglected, then Shaytān becomes dominant in that home.

Sayyidunā Jābir ؓ relates that the Holy Prophet ﷺ said, "When a person remembers Allāh ﷻ when he enters his home and when he eats, Shaytān says to his party, 'There is no accommodation for the night and neither any supper for you here.' However, if he enters without remembering Allāh ﷻ, then Shaytān says to his group, 'You have secured your night accommodation and if he fails to mention Allāh's ﷻ Name when he begins his meal, then Shaytān says, 'You have secured your night accommodation and supper." (Muslim)

It is common nowadays for people to increasingly complain about the effect of Jinns, black magic etc whereas we have failed to understand why this is on the increase at an alarming rate. If we adhere to the teachings of our beloved Prophet ﷺ then there will be peace and tranquillity in our homes.

Perfect Role Model

Let us adopt the Sunnah of our beloved Prophet ﷺ in every aspect of our lives. We will then realise and witness its fruits in this life and the Hereafter.

Our beloved Prophet ﷺ was an exemplary role model in every aspect of life. If you wish to become a good father, then observe the example of the noble father of Sayyidah Fātimah ؓ. If you want to become a good husband then observe the example of the noble husband of Sayyidah Ā'ishah ؓ and Sayyidah Khadījah ؓ.

If you want to become a good ruler then see the exemplary practice of the Holy Prophet 🌸 as a ruler in Madeenah. Similarly, for you to become an excellent worker or trader then refer to the excellent example of the Holy Prophet 🌸 as a shepherd in the hills of Makkah and his trading in Syria. The Holy Prophet 🌸 was a trader, a reformer, a politician, an economist and so on. In every sphere of life we have a role model in the form of the Holy Prophet 🌸.

Should I Forsake the Sunnah for the Sake of these Fools?

A prime example of love and devotion for the Sunnah of the Holy Prophet 🌸 is the incident of Sayyidunā Huzaifah Ibn Yamān 🌸 in the presence of the king of Persia (modern day Iran). Sayyidunā Huzaifah Ibn Yamān 🌸 was once beckoned by Kisrā, the king of Persia, to his court for negotiations. When he reached there, the king presented food to him to illustrate his hospitality. Whilst Sayyidunā Huzaifah 🌸 was eating, he accidently dropped a morsel on the ground. In this regard, the Holy Prophet 🌸 said, "If a morsel of food drops from one of you then pick it up, remove the dirt and eat it. Do not leave it for the Shaytān."

Sayyidunā Huzaifah 🌸 remembering this Hadeeth went to pick up the morsel. However, a man sitting next to him attempted to prevent him by saying, "This is a court of one of the world's super powers. If you pick up the morsel and eat it you will lose all your credibility in their eyes. Therefore, do not pick up the morsel, as it is not an appropriate time." Sayyidunā Huzaifah 🌸 responded, "Should I forsake the Sunnah of the Holy Prophet 🌸 for the sake of these fools?"

Whether they like it or not, even if they ridicule me I am not prepared to abandon the Sunnah of the Holy Prophet 🌸. The question to consider here is did they (the Sahabah 🌸) earn respect on account of their deeds, or today are we earning respect or not?

They earned respect that on one hand, they picked up a morsel from the ground to consume it merely to follow the Sunnah and on the other hand, they crushed the symbols of pride to dust with great force as the Holy Prophet 🌸 prophesised.

"Once the Kisrā (the title given to the king of Persia) is perished, there will never be another Kisrā ever again."

As a result, the noble Companions attained success in both worlds and conquered the Persian Empire by following the Sunnah of the Holy Prophet ﷺ.

May Allāh ﷻ grant us all the ability to follow the Sunnah of the Holy Prophet ﷺ in the correct manner. Āmeen!